PROTECTING CIVILIANS IN WAR

Protecting Civilians in War

The ICRC, UNHCR, and their Limitations in Internal Armed Conflicts

MIRIAM BRADLEY

OXFORD
UNIVERSITY PRESS

OXFORD
UNIVERSITY PRESS

Great Clarendon Street, Oxford, OX2 6DP,
United Kingdom

Oxford University Press is a department of the University of Oxford.
It furthers the University's objective of excellence in research, scholarship,
and education by publishing worldwide. Oxford is a registered trade mark of
Oxford University Press in the UK and in certain other countries

First Edition published in 2016
Impression: 2

Published in the United States of America by Oxford University Press
198 Madison Avenue, New York, NY 10016, United States of America

British Library Cataloguing in Publication Data
Data available

Library of Congress Control Number: 2015952192

ISBN 978–0–19–871638–9

Printed in Great Britain by
Clays Ltd, St Ives plc

Acknowledgements

This book builds on doctoral research completed at Oxford University in 2012, and along the way, the project has benefited from practical, intellectual, and personal inputs from many individuals and institutions. For my doctorate, I received sponsorship from Joseph Sassoon and additional funding from the Department of Politics and International Relations and from St Antony's College, Oxford. My doctoral fieldwork in Colombia was also supported by a scholarship from Santander bank. Lots of people contributed to making my doctoral studies happy and productive, but Louise Fawcett, Joseph Sassoon, and Dave Zarnett deserve special mention for their support and encouragement throughout.

I was fortunate to go on to a postdoctoral fellowship in the Programme for the Study of International Governance at the Graduate Institute of International and Development Studies in Geneva. I am grateful to Tom Biersteker for giving me complete flexibility during the fellowship, which enabled me to focus on the book and to undertake additional field research in the Democratic Republic of Congo and Myanmar. Andreas Indregard and Susanne Kempel were excellent hosts in Yangon, sharing their wonderful home as well as their expertise and insights.

Several people took time to read and comment on draft sections of my thesis or of the book manuscript. I am especially grateful for input from Guy Goodwin-Gill, Andy Hurrell, Neil MacFarlane, Eduardo Posada-Carbó, Dave Zarnett, and Roger Zetter.

David Forsythe, Stephen Hopgood, Adam Roberts, and Hugo Slim all read my doctoral thesis in its entirety, and provided excellent feedback and suggestions, without which this book would probably not exist, and would certainly be a far poorer offering.

Finally, this book would have been impossible without the input of the many current and former ICRC and UNHCR staff I spoke to at headquarters in Geneva, and in Colombia, the Democratic Republic of Congo, and Myanmar. They gave generously of their time and reflections, and my biggest thanks go to them. I know some of them will disagree with some of the arguments I make, and some of the conclusions I draw, but I hope I have represented their experiences accurately and fairly. For all my criticisms of the organizations they work for, these individuals were—without exception—deeply committed to the civilians they sought to protect.

Contents

Tables

Introduction

States are supposed to ensure the physical security of their citizens, but in the context of civil war they are very often either unwilling or unable to do so. Indeed, in many such cases, the state itself perpetrates violence against its own people. In recognition of the inability or unwillingness of some states to protect their citizens, a norm of 'conditional sovereignty' or 'sovereignty as responsibility' has emerged. Since the end of the Cold War in particular, a reconceptualization of ideas about security and state sovereignty has paved the way for increasing international involvement in issues that had previously been considered domestic affairs. Thus, the concept of human security, introduced by the UN Development Programme in its 1994 Human Development Report, emphasizes individual, rather than state, security (UNDP 1994). In the same decade, the notion of 'sovereignty as responsibility', according to which sovereignty entails state responsibility for the protection of its people, was promoted (Cohen and Deng 1998; Deng et al. 1996). The idea is that where a state fails in this responsibility, it loses its right to freedom from outside intervention in its affairs.

Despite widespread support for the idea of sovereignty as responsibility in the abstract, the content and meaning of the norm in practice is contested and unclear. If there is general agreement that 'something must be done' when a state is 'unwilling or unable' to protect its people, it is much less clear what threshold of ill-will or inability must be reached to kick the amorphous international community into action, and what it is that should be done if and when that threshold is reached (or how to generate the political will to do it). Indeed the notion of sovereignty as responsibility was the intellectual antecedent to both the agenda for the protection of internally displaced persons (IDPs) and the so-called responsibility to protect doctrine, each of which calls for a different kind of international response. While the former emphasizes a response from international non-governmental organizations (INGOs) and civilian UN agencies, the latter focuses mainly on military intervention.

Although much of the debate focuses on the conditions under which there exists a right or duty to intervene militarily when a state fails to protect its people, by far the most common international response is a civilian, humanitarian one. The UN had sixteen peacekeeping operations ongoing in 2013, while the Office for the Coordination of Humanitarian Affairs was working in over forty countries, and the World Food Programme (WFP) provided food assistance in seventy-five different field operations. The budget for UN Peacekeeping operations for the fiscal year 1 July 2013 to 30 June 2014 was about USD 7.83 billion, compared with global funding for international humanitarian action in excess of USD 14 billion in 2013. While much of that is spent on the more traditional humanitarian activities concerned with the provision of food aid, blankets, and shelter, in recent years a significant proportion has been devoted to efforts to protect people affected by armed conflict and other kinds of emergency. Indeed, protection is the area around which there has been simultaneously most growth and most confusion in humanitarian organizations.

This book sets out to reduce that confusion. Specifically, it analyses how the International Committee of the Red Cross (ICRC) and the Office of the United Nations High Commissioner for Refugees (UNHCR) understand protection, and how they put that understanding into practice in Colombia, the Democratic Republic of Congo (DRC), and Myanmar. These are arguably the two most important humanitarian agencies for protection, and both have protection at the heart of their mandates. This book explains why they go about protection the way they do, and highlights the ways in which their resulting approaches to protection are inherently limited.

BACKGROUND

The complex emergencies of the 1990s prompted greater recognition that providing material assistance to conflict victims is insufficient in the context of armed conflict, and too often results in the 'well-fed dead'. This phrase gained common currency among aid workers and commentators in respect of Bosnia in the early 1990s, and points to the apparent futility of providing material aid to those facing violent attack. A *New York Times* article summed up the underlying sentiment: 'The people of Bosnia remain unprotected. What good will it do for them to have food in their stomachs when their throats are slit?' (*New York Times* 1992: 296). The article argues for more concerted political and military action to protect the Bosnian population. However, in Rwanda in 1994, such action once again failed to materialize and, following the genocide and the subsequent militarization of the refugee camps in neighbouring countries, further soul-searching took place among humanitarians and the wider international community (DANIDA 1996; Terry 2002).

Some important conclusions emerged from the Bosnian, Rwandan, and numerous other experiences in the 1990s. While it was clear that humanitarian action should not be a substitute for political action, it was equally clear that in many cases governments used humanitarian assistance to disguise political inaction, and hence to avoid more difficult interventions (DANIDA 1996: 46; Paul 1999: 1). Moreover, humanitarian action itself did not for the most part have the protection of civilians from violence at its heart (Paul 1999: 1). Since then, greater emphasis has been placed on the protection of civilians, and a good deal of policy literature has focused on what humanitarians do and can do to protect civilians (Ferris 2011; InterAction 2004, 2006; O'Callaghan and Pantuliano 2007; Pantuliano and O'Callaghan 2006; Slim and Bonwick 2005). However, there is a consensus among humanitarians that outcomes are falling short of intentions, and that the increased emphasis on protection by humanitarian actors has failed to yield a corresponding improvement in the security of the civilian population. Thus in 2009, Marc DuBois, then Executive Director of the UK branch of Médecins Sans Frontières (MSF), reported that his 'last visit to Darfur revealed no shortage of the "well-fed raped" or the "well-fed harassed and intimidated"' (DuBois 2009: 2).

Protection is a contested concept, one which is (implicitly or explicitly) understood differently by different actors and in different contexts. As the examples above make clear, there is a common understanding that protection is about violence. However, in defining the concept in detail, and in putting the idea into practice, numerous variations arise, and the focus on violence and insecurity is all too often lost in the process. In the context of protecting civilians in the midst of armed conflict, protection may encompass legal, political, humanitarian, and rights-based approaches, all of which may overlap with one another. This poses a problem for conceptual clarity, and can cause operational confusion as protection may refer both to the provision of physical security and to the establishment and maintenance of a special legal status for particular categories of protected persons (O'Callaghan and Pantuliano 2007: 5; Roberts 1996: 9). In order to transcend confusion around protection understood as simultaneously a need, an objective, a legal right, and a humanitarian activity, this book takes care to distinguish clearly between the means (activities) and the ends (objectives) of protection. It also conceptualizes protection narrowly, with a focus on the physical safety and security of civilians, on the basis that protection is fundamentally about violence, and the objectives of any protection activity must be about protecting people from violence.

Existing explanations for shortcomings in humanitarian protection tend to blame factors that are deemed to be beyond the control of humanitarian agencies themselves, and follow one of two contrasting logics. On the one hand, it is argued that it is impossible for humanitarian organizations to protect civilians in armed conflict when faced with armed parties who deliberately target civilians. Agencies such as the ICRC and UNHCR lack coercive power to change the behaviour of armed parties to a conflict, and these kinds of explanations thus place blame for shortcomings in protection outcomes on exogenous factors rather than on the humanitarian agency itself or the activities it undertakes. These explanations are right to point to the behaviour of armed parties as the primary protection problem. Indeed it is a central contention of this book that the actions of combatants are absolutely key to determining the level of security or insecurity experienced by civilians in contexts of armed conflict. However, a lack of coercive power on the part of humanitarian agencies does not mean that they have no influence on the behaviour of armed actors. Therefore, it is not accurate to portray the behaviour of armed parties as entirely exogenous to the protection efforts of humanitarian agencies. Moreover, the ICRC and UNHCR purport to play a role in protecting civilians, so if protecting civilians requires changes in the behaviour of armed actors, we need to examine the efforts of the ICRC and UNHCR to induce such behaviour change. It is one thing—and absolutely correct—to blame those who perpetrate violence for the resulting civilian insecurity, but it is quite another to blame them for the failures or shortcomings of international humanitarian agencies.

On the other hand, shortcomings in humanitarian agency efforts to protect civilians are explained through an almost opposite logic which suggests that various obstacles to their work prevent them from being more effective. These obstacles take different forms, and again place the blame on factors and actors external to the humanitarian agencies themselves. For example, references to lack of access imply that if only agencies could gain access to insecure civilians, then they would be able to protect them. In addition, insufficient (or misplaced) international political and financial commitment is identified as a reason why humanitarian agencies cannot undertake sufficient protection work. Similarly, the nature of accountability in humanitarian programming is cited as an explanation for international humanitarian agencies focusing on the kinds of activities prioritized by those who pay for humanitarian action (mainly donor states) rather than by those who are intended to benefit from it (Knox-Clarke and Mitchell 2011: 4; Loescher 2001: 350; Loescher, Betts, and Milner 2008: 2). The underlying rationale to such explanations is that if only humanitarian agencies were able to get on with their jobs free from externally imposed obstacles and influence, they would be able to protect people. In other words, they equate protection activities with protection outcomes.

Undoubtedly, the ICRC and UNHCR (and other international humanitarian agencies) do face a number of externally imposed obstacles and restrictions that shape their respective approaches to protection, and necessarily limit the scope of those approaches. However, the exogeneity of all of these factors can be exaggerated. Moreover, the external constraints do not tell the whole story. Therefore, the focus of this book is on the organizations themselves, and their understandings of protection. This is not in any way to deny the importance of other actors in determining the level of civilian security or insecurity, but by focusing on the ways in which the ICRC and UNHCR conceptualize and practise protection, the analysis in this book adds another layer to our understanding of why protection outcomes are so often so disappointing. There are two important reasons for offering such a critique of humanitarian approaches to protection. First, identifying the limitations of these approaches can help to readjust inflated expectations in the public rhetoric of some humanitarian organizations and the international community more broadly (DuBois 2009; Rieff 2002). Inflated expectations are dangerous because they risk undermining civilians' own protection strategies and serving as a justification for political inaction and restrictive asylum policies. Second, explaining not only the ways in which these approaches are limited in scope, but also the reasons for those limitations, can contribute to improved policy responses.

In explaining and critiquing the protection work of the ICRC and UNHCR, this book presents two linked sets of arguments. First, institutional factors—notably organizational history, structure, and culture—explain much of why ICRC and UNHCR conceptualizations of protection look as they do. Second, the ICRC and UNHCR approaches to protection are state-centric, legalistic, and bureaucratic, and as a consequence are limited in scope. UNHCR views states as part of the problem and almost all of the solution, working mainly at least one step removed from the violence that is the main protection problem, and paying insufficient attention to both state and non-state armed actors. The ICRC views both states and armed non-state actors as parts of the solution at the field level, but its protection approach is heavily dependent on a state-centric international legal framework, which is not sufficiently adapted to the realities of contemporary armed conflict and violence.

THE ICRC AND UNHCR

In 1859, Henri Dunant witnessed soldiers of both sides in the Battle of Solferino dying on the battlefield without medical care or assistance, and responded by sending for medical supplies and recruiting local women to tend the wounded (Dunant 1959). This notion of providing humanitarian assistance to the victims of war was later institutionalized by Dunant and four fellow Genevans with the establishment of the ICRC in 1863, and the negotiation of the Geneva Convention for the Amelioration of the Condition of the Wounded in Armies in the Field in 1864 (Boissier 1985 (1963): 49, 117). Originally, then, the object of protection for the ICRC was not civilians but wounded soldiers, and the primary means was medical assistance. However, over time the mandate of the ICRC has expanded to include other categories of person, and other means of protection.

The mandate of UNHCR has similarly expanded. UNHCR was set up by states in 1951, not to protect civilians in the midst of armed conflict, but rather to provide or to negotiate international protection and solutions for refugees, specifically for Europeans displaced by World War II. Over time, the role of UNHCR with respect to refugees changed and expanded, and this institutional history has played an important part in shaping the UNHCR understanding of protection in internal conflicts, protection that is mainly directed at IDPs. The object of protection for UNHCR has expanded beyond those who have fled persecution across an international border to include, for example, those fleeing generalized violence, and those displaced within their country of origin (Betts 2012; Loescher 2001; Loescher et al. 2008). Thus, UNHCR now addresses a number of issues that were not envisaged in 1951, such as protracted refugee situations, and climate change-induced displacement (Hall 2010; Milner and Loescher 2011; Slaughter and Crisp 2009).

This book focuses on the ICRC and UNHCR because they are the most significant humanitarian protection agencies in terms of the scale of their own protection operations, as well as their wider influence on other protection actors. According to the Financial Tracking Service (FTS) of ReliefWeb, the ICRC, UNHCR, and UNICEF each received in the region of USD 60 million for protection/human rights/rule of law activities in 2012, around double the amount received by the next biggest recipient of funding for such activities—the International Organization for Migration (IOM), with under USD 30 million. This is not a perfect measure[1] of expenditure on protection activities, but it does give a strong indication that the ICRC and UNHCR are two of the three biggest protection spenders. Both the ICRC and UNHCR also wield influence on other humanitarian agencies through various mechanisms. The ICRC is widely seen as a moral authority on protection, and during the second half of the 1990s led a series of annual workshops on protection involving professionals from the fields of human rights and refugee law, humanitarian law, field work, and academia (Giossi Caverzasio 2001); a second series took place in 2009 (ICRC 2009). UNHCR is influential as the lead agency for the Global Protection Cluster under the 'cluster approach'[2] of the UN

[1] Data for the FTS is provided by donors or recipient organizations, and consequently the figures do not include any funding which both the donor and the recipient choose not to report; thus donations within the Middle East, for example, may be underreported (Harmer and Cotterrell 2005). There may also be some double counting. Furthermore, the categorization of funding as for 'protection/human rights/rule of law' may be defined differently by different data providers and may include activities other than those whose sole (or even primary) purpose is civilian protection.

[2] The UN cluster approach refers to a coordination structure involving both UN and non-UN humanitarian organizations at both the global level and country level. Each cluster focuses on a

humanitarian reform initiative, a role which includes responsibility for 'leading the development of standards and policies for IDP protection, helping to build capacities among participating agencies, and coordinating operational support for new and ongoing emergencies' (UNHCR 2007c, para. 32). In this capacity, for example, UNHCR has developed protection handbooks for use by other humanitarian actors as well as UNHCR itself (Crisp, Kiragu, and Tennant 2007; Global Protection Cluster Working Group 2010).

COLOMBIA, THE DRC, AND MYANMAR

This book analyses both how protection is understood by the ICRC and UNHCR at the global policy/headquarters level, and how those understandings are put into practice in Colombia, the DRC, and Myanmar. Analysing the protection work of the ICRC and UNHCR in concrete field operations serves two main purposes. First, it offers illustrations of how their policies at the global level are translated into practice at the local level, thus providing a fuller picture of their protection approaches, particularly in terms of the activities undertaken. Second, their experiences at the level of implementation offer insights into the extent to which the approaches are adapted to the contexts for which they are intended, and into the effectiveness of those approaches in practice. We are thus able to draw lessons from the experience of implementation with respect to the appropriateness and adequacy of the policy approaches themselves.

These three country contexts were selected for a number of reasons. Most importantly, both the ICRC and UNHCR have sizeable operations in all three of these countries. This means not only that each one is of significant policy importance for these two organizations, but also that, in conducting the research for this book, it was possible to talk to several staff members in each context. This facilitated a much broader picture of the protection work of the ICRC and UNHCR, and of the perspectives of different staff members,

particular aspect of emergency response: food security; camp coordination/management; early recovery; education; emergency shelter; emergency telecommunications; health; logistics; nutrition; protection; and water, sanitation, and hygiene. At the global level, the approach aims to strengthen preparedness and technical capacity. At the country level, the aim is to improve predictability, accountability, and partnership to improve prioritization of resources and coverage of response. Each cluster has a clearly defined lead agency, and a provider of last resort. For conflict-induced IDPs, UNHCR is the Global Cluster Lead for the three clusters of protection, emergency shelter, and camp coordination and camp management. In situations where internal displacement is exclusively due to natural or man-made disasters, UNHCR has joint responsibility at the field level with UNICEF and the OHCHR. The ICRC does not participate in the cluster approach, though it acts as an observer at many of the global-level cluster meetings.

than would have been possible in countries with smaller and more limited operations. For different reasons, each of these country contexts is also of significant international policy importance more generally, and each is subject to a different kind and level of international involvement. Colombia is a major recipient of US military aid, the DRC is host to the largest ever UN peacekeeping mission (MONUSCO), and after many years as a 'pariah state', and following recent moves towards democracy, Myanmar is subject to a massive increase in interest and engagement from Western governments and international agencies.

While there is no such thing as a typical conflict, these three countries conform to certain trends in contemporary conflict in that they are characterized by internal armed conflict with significant international dimensions, and multiple armed non-state actors with a mixture of economic and political motives. Ethnic dimensions are significant in Myanmar and to some extent in the DRC, Colombia is characterized by both traditional armed conflict and high levels of urban violence, and Myanmar combines traditional armed conflict in several areas with severe communal violence in Rakhine state. Thus, although these three country contexts cannot be said to offer a representative sample, they do offer variation along a number of dimensions which helps us to understand how different conflict characteristics affect the ways that the ICRC and UNHCR translate their protection approaches from policy into practice.

The rest of this section provides a brief outline of the salient characteristics of each country context. This is not intended to be a comprehensive analysis, and does not examine the causes or motivations behind the different conflicts, the complexity of which renders succinct explanation impossible. The aim is only to provide sufficient outline of the conflict parameters and participants to frame the analysis of ICRC and UNHCR protection work in subsequent chapters.

Colombia

The Colombian conflict dates back to the 1960s and involves a number of different armed groups.[3] The long-standing groups still in operation are the military forces of the state (army, navy, air force, and police), and two main left-wing guerrilla groups: the Revolutionary Armed Forces of Colombia and the National Liberation Army (known by their Spanish initials FARC

[3] For more detail on the political and conflict context of Colombia, see Bergquist et al. (2001), Brittain (2010), Dudley (2004), Hristov (2009), IISS (2011), Posada Carbó (2011), Richani (2002), Safford and Palacios (2002).

and ELN respectively). During the 1980s, paramilitary 'self-defence' groups were created by wealthy landowners to protect themselves and their economic interests from guerrilla violence. In 1997, these paramilitary groups formed a national umbrella organization known as the United Self-Defence Forces of Colombia (AUC). From 2003 to 2006, the AUC underwent a demobilization process during which more than 30,000 paramilitary combatants formally demobilized (Oficina Alto Comisionado para la Paz 2006: 8). However, some never demobilized, and others rearmed after demobilizing. Thus, a number of so-called new groups (also known as emerging groups or neo-paramilitaries) emerged, using the same structures, controlling the same zones, and incorporating many of the same individuals as the former AUC blocs (Denissen 2010; International Crisis Group 2007, 2012; Porch and Rasmussen 2008; US State Department 2009, 2010). Formal peace talks between the government and the FARC began in October 2012, and were ongoing at the time of writing (2015). However, field research in Colombia was undertaken for this book between July and September 2010, when no such peace process was in place.

The FARC and ELN have posed threats to civilians primarily through kidnapping, extortion, bombs, landmines, and the recruitment (with varying degrees of coercion) of civilians (particularly teenagers) into their forces. Kidnapping for ransom was once a major source of income for the FARC, and to a lesser degree for the ELN, which also relied heavily on extortion of oil companies. However, both groups came to derive most of their income from involvement in the production of illegal narcotics, and rates of kidnapping declined in the first decade of the twenty-first century (Hanson 2009). Guerrilla bombings in large urban areas and in rural areas have been a significant cause of civilian injuries, and also of some deaths (Restrepo and Spagat 2004). For the period 1999 to 2008, Colombia was the country with the third-highest number of reported casualties from landmines, after Afghanistan and Cambodia, and in 2012 Colombia had the second-highest number after Afghanistan. However, the number of casualties in Colombia has been decreasing since a peak of around 1,200 in 2005 and 2006, and an unusually high percentage of these have been military casualties (International Campaign to Ban Landmines 2009: 38, 296; 2013: 41). Nevertheless, it is possible that military casualties are over-reported and civilian casualties under-reported. The guerrilla groups have used mines for two main purposes: to protect coca fields from manual eradication; and to protect the paths to guerrilla camps. The impact on civilians of the mines has been largely incidental and not something that was valued by the guerrillas—indeed, if the area was one of civilian support for the guerrillas, civilian casualties from the mines were likely to be detrimental to the guerrillas by diminishing support for them. In many cases, the guerrilla group would inform the civilian population which areas to avoid because civilian landmine casualties represented a double blow to the armed group: not only did they impact negatively on civilian support, but they wasted a landmine.[4]

While massacres have also been committed by Colombian guerrilla groups, they have more commonly been perpetrated by the former paramilitary organizations and the neo-paramilitary groups (Restrepo and Spagat 2004; Verdad Abierta 2010). Likewise, assassination, or the threat of assassination, has been used primarily by the former AUC paramilitary groups and the neo-paramilitaries to punish or prevent particular civilian actions or behaviour (Verdad Abierta 2011). In particular, individuals were targeted if they collaborated (or were thought to collaborate) with the guerrillas, if they were trade unionists or leaders of displaced or indigenous communities, or if they were involved in land or human rights activism (Somos Defensores 2011, n.d.; Verdad Abierta 2011). Whereas the guerrilla groups have generally carried out assassinations quite openly, a number of disappearances have been attributed to the paramilitaries. According to the Office of the Human Rights Ombudsman of Colombia, the official number of disappeared in Colombia is over 60,000, and the true number may well be higher than the official number (Defensoría del Pueblo 2011). Sexual violence against civilians has been perpetrated by paramilitaries more than any other party to the conflict. Of a sample of testimonies of incidents of sexual violence connected to the armed conflict collected by the Constitutional Court, 58 per cent were attributed to paramilitaries, 23 per cent to government forces, and 8 per cent to guerrillas (Oxfam 2009: 14).

Links between the national military and the former AUC paramilitary organizations have been well documented, and confirmed by the Supreme Court. These links permeated all levels of the public forces and went beyond the military to politicians at both local and national levels (Hanson 2008). Incidents of collaboration between some members of the government security forces and the emerging armed groups have also been documented (US State Department 2009, 2010). Through acts of both omission and commission, the army in particular has facilitated atrocities perpetrated by the former paramilitary blocs against the civilian population and as such the public forces have posed a significant (albeit sometimes indirect) threat to civilians. The public forces have also posed a direct threat to civilians, in particular through extrajudicial killings. For example, in the early years of the Uribe administration, the 'falsos positivos' scandal emerged. 'Falsos positivos' refer to incidents in which the Colombian security forces (often in collaboration with paramilitaries) murdered civilians and then dressed them in guerrilla uniforms to pass them off as guerrillas killed in combat, in an effort to meet targets for

[4] In some areas if a *campesino* was killed or injured by a FARC landmine planted in an area where civilians were advised not to go, the FARC charged the family 400,000 pesos (approximately USD 220) for the cost of replacing the landmine.

combating the guerrillas, and to get rid of suspected guerrilla sympathizers against whom they lacked sufficient evidence to arrest and prosecute (US State Department 2009, 2010).

Individuals in Colombia may face threats because they have been involved (or are thought to be involved) in activism on issues which are sensitive for armed actors, including the public forces. For example, leaders of indigenous organizations and those who speak out on land issues are often targeted. Land is a central issue in the Colombian conflict (Richani 2002; Thomson 2011). People have been displaced as a deliberate strategy to clear the land either to give a particular armed group control over the territory and strengthen their position in the conflict, or to facilitate coca cultivation, megaprojects, mineral extraction on the land, or the transportation of goods and weapons across the land. Activism on land issues is dangerous, as those with vested interests threaten individuals engaged in land activism, and individuals and communities who have been displaced and seek to return to reclaim their lands (Human Rights Watch 2013).

The threat of recruitment into the guerrilla forces, accompanied by varying levels of force, has been a common cause of displacement in Colombia. Indigenous and Afro-Colombians were often forcibly recruited into non-state armed groups because they know the geography of the zones, and this knowledge makes them particularly useful to all of the armed groups. In many cases, families displaced to avoid recruitment, especially if they had teenage children. Displacement from the threat of forced recruitment could be an effective protection strategy, because groups were unlikely to pursue a family who left to avoid recruitment. A family in a guerrilla-controlled area also normally had to leave if the son joined the army or police (although sometimes the guerrillas just forbade family contact with the son).

The fumigation of illicit crops is an activity carried out by, or in conjunction with, the public forces. It is a direct cause of health problems associated with the chemicals used, and of loss of livelihoods, as licit crops are destroyed together with the illicit (Livingstone 2003: 136–42). Fumigation is frequently also a cause of displacement, as those affected flee the associated violence or seek alternative livelihoods elsewhere. The stated objective of fumigation is the elimination of coca cultivation, the 'war on drugs' being one of the major justifications for US financial, political, and military support to Colombia. In addition, fumigation may be part of a deliberate military strategy of desertification. Such desertification benefits certain groups when it facilitates control of territory or clears the land for megaprojects. In some areas of the country, manual eradication is used instead of aerial fumigation to destroy coca crops (notably in Afro-Colombian and indigenous communities, where the protected status of their territories prohibits fumigation). Both aerial fumigation and manual eradication are often accompanied by violence, as they conflict with the interests of the armed groups involved in the cultivation of coca (Holmes,

Gutiérrez de Piñeres, and Curtin 2006). Military actions linked to fumigation and eradication contribute to civilian insecurity, and additionally eradicators have been known to steal the possessions and produce of the civilian population.

Urban violence is another key feature of the Colombian context, affecting the major cities, in particular Medellín and Buenaventura. This results in insecurity for many urban citizens, and intra-urban displacement as people cross invisible borders in the cities. In 2010, for example, it was estimated that there were around 400 criminal gangs of different sizes in Medellín alone. These are connected to the wider conflict in at least two key ways. First, former AUC paramilitaries form the backbone of these groups, and second, micro-trafficking of drugs links these gangs with the armed actors which control the drug trade. Insecurity for the citizens of Medellín comes in the form of homicides, indiscriminate attacks, forced disappearances, intra-urban displacements, forced recruitment of minors and abuse of minors, restrictions on movement and public transport, extortion of public transport and small shops, restricted access to educational facilities and withdrawal of enrolments because of threats and violence, increased sexual violence, and reduced access to healthcare.

The ICRC has been present in Colombia since 1969, initially visiting detainees, and since 1997 has also been working on the protection of the civilian population. In 2013, the ICRC spent CHF 30.7 million on its operations in Colombia, with over sixty expatriate and nearly 300 nationally recruited staff members (ICRC 2014a: 418). Having previously carried out some operations from what was then the UNHCR regional office in Venezuela, UNHCR first became officially involved in Colombia in 1997, providing advice to the Colombian government on the drafting of IDP legislation, which resulted in Law 387 (UNHCR 2008a: 1).[5] Subsequently the Colombian government requested assistance on protection and the prevention of displacement, and in 1999 UNHCR signed a Memorandum of Intent with the government.[6] This mandates UNHCR Colombia to strengthen national mechanisms for the prevention of displacement and the protection of IDPs (UNHCR 2008a: 1). In 2013, UNHCR spent USD 19.7 million in Colombia, and employed 159 staff members.

[5] República de Colombia. 1997. *Ley N° 387 por la cual se adoptan medidas para la prevención del desplazamiento forzado; la atención, protección, consolidación y estabilización socioeconómica de los desplazados internos por la violencia en la República de Colombia*, N° 387, 18 July 1997.

[6] UNHCR. 1999. *Memorando de intención entre la Oficina del Alto Comisionado de las Naciones Unidas para los Refugiados (ACNUR) y el Gobierno de la República de Colombia, relativo al suministro de cooperación para el tratamiento del problema del desplazamiento forzado*, 28 January 1999.

DRC

Current conflict and violence in the DRC[7] can be understood as a continuation of the First Congo War (September 1996 to May 1997) and the Second Congo War (August 1998 to July 2003). Despite the formal cessation of hostilities in 2003, and a number of subsequent peace agreements, violence has continued largely unabated. Conflict has been fuelled by political and social exclusion as well as the potential for economic gain, and is intrinsically linked to regional dynamics and the aftermath of the Rwandan genocide. Violence is concentrated in the east of the country, and the research for this book focused on the work of the ICRC and UNHCR in the Kivus, and in Katanga. Research for this book was undertaken in the DRC in July and August 2014.

In eastern DRC, several dozen non-state armed groups, of varying levels of organization and professionalization, clash with each other and with the Forces armées de la République démocratique du Congo (FARDC, Armed Forces of the Democratic Republic of the Congo). The armed non-state actors range from localized village militia to transnational armed groups. The Democratic Forces for the Liberation of Rwanda (FDLR) is the largest non-state armed group in the DRC, comprising members of the Rwandan government and army ousted in 1994, Rwandan refugees, and growing numbers of Congolese. In recent years, the 23 March rebel movement (M23) has also been a major cause of insecurity in the Kivus, formed in April 2012 when Gen Bosco Ntaganda, a senior officer in the FARDC, led a mutiny of 300–600 soldiers following discontent over unpaid wages and poor living conditions. M23 fighters took control of Goma, and carried out widespread violations of international humanitarian law (IHL), until the group was defeated in November 2013 after international pressure on its Rwandan backers, and the deployment of MONUSCO's 'intervention brigade'. Some former M23 fighters are thought to have joined the Nduma Defence of Congo (NDC), an armed group established by Ntabo Ntaberi Sheka in 2009. Despite a warrant being issued for his arrest in January 2011, by the end of 2014 he was still at large and his forces continued to commit abuses, including killing, rape, torture, child recruitment, and forced labour in Walikale and Masisi territories in North Kivu (Human Rights Watch 2015). In Katanga, the main non-state armed group is the Bakata Katanga Mai Mai, founded by Gédéon Kyungu Mutanga on his escape from prison in 2011. A demobilization attempt in 2012 did not get very far, but around half of the group demobilized in a subsequent demobilization in October 2013. There is a lot of wealth and power in the

[7] For detailed information on, and analysis of, the historical, political, and conflict context in the DRC, see Clark (2002), Lemarchand (2009), Marriage (2013), Prunier (2009), Stearns (2011), Stearns et al. (2013).

Katanga region, and discontent because the mining revenues tend not to get back there from Kinshasa. In Katanga, there is also conflict between the Batwa and Bantu populations.

In addition, the DRC is host to the largest and most expensive UN peacekeeping operation ever. Established as the United Nations Organization Mission in the Democratic Republic of the Congo (MONUC) in 1999, the mission was renamed the United Nations Organization Stabilization Mission in the DRC (MONUSCO) and given a stronger mandate explicitly including the protection of civilians in 2010. A specialized 'intervention brigade' was authorized in 2014, which has a mandate to carry out offensive operations against armed groups. However, MONUSCO has been frequently criticized for not doing enough to prevent abuses of civilians, even when it knows attacks are ongoing or when its soldiers are witnesses to attacks (Human Rights Watch 2014).

In the Kivus and in Katanga, a range of conflict-related violations against civilians take place, including sexual violence, child recruitment and general forced recruitment, forced displacement, extortion, looting, destruction, and movement controls (barriers and checkpoints set up by both the FARDC and non-state armed groups). In addition, general insecurity and restrictions on movement hamper travel to fields and markets, and thus have a negative impact on livelihoods. State security forces have also been responsible for extrajudicial killings, rapes, and enforced disappearances. In Katanga, there are few major clashes between armed actors, so there is not much in the way of crossfire casualties. However, there have been a number of incidents of the Bakata Katanga Mai Mai burning villages, and it is not always clear what the motivation for this is, particularly given that the militia are from this area, and often have family in the villages they are burning (IRIN News 2014; Katanga protection cluster 2015). The Bakata Katanga has also reportedly recruited large numbers of children into its forces (US State Department 2014: 2). As a consequence of all of this, there are around 500,000 IDPs in Katanga, 1 million in North Kivu, and over 600,000 in South Kivu (Katanga protection cluster 2015: 2; UN OCHA 2015a: 2, 2015b: 2).

Sexual violence represents a major threat to civilians in the DRC. Rape and sexual violence are likely to be massively under-reported; yet government statistics show around 10,000 to 15,000 cases of sexual violence each year (Banza-Nsungu, Kishimba, and Dackam-Ngatchou 2011; Ministère du Genre de la Famille et de l'Enfant 2013). Reporting systems and research studies may be subject to selection bias (as they often rely on case file data related to the provision of particular services or treatments), so identifying trends is difficult. However, UN data suggests that state agents (FARDC and police) perpetrate approximately the same number of rapes as members of all other armed groups combined (MONUSCO/OHCHR 2014). This finding is backed up by analysis of the incidents presented to protection monitors working as part of the protection cluster, of which approximately 20 per cent are attributed to state agents, approximately 20 per cent to other armed groups, and some 50–60 per cent to civilians. The large percentage of sexual violence perpetrated by civilians seems to be a relatively recent trend with data from a smaller-scale research project showing the number of sexual assaults reportedly perpetrated by civilians growing seventeen-fold between 2004 and 2008 (Bartels et al. 2011). Domestic violence, including domestic sexual violence, is also widespread and is deemed to be exacerbated by displacement for two main reasons. First, men are frustrated because they are not working. Second, displacement results in the loss of social networks, and hence of the usual conflict resolution mechanisms, and the social structure (for example, traditional leaders) that would normally punish perpetrators. Impunity is a major problem because of minimal rule of law and high levels of corruption.

The ICRC first worked in what is now the DRC in 1960 during the civil war that broke out after the independence of the former Belgian Congo, and established a permanent delegation there (then known as Zaire) in 1978. ICRC work in the DRC includes classic protection activities on detention and the protection of the civilian population, as well as re-establishing family links and protection of children associated with armed groups. In 2013, the ICRC employed 102 expatriate and 756 nationally recruited staff members in the DRC, and spent CHF 64.7 million, a little under a third of which was on protection and prevention (ICRC 2014a: 135). In the same year, UNHCR employed 351 staff members in the DRC, and spent USD 80.4 million, of which USD 18.5 million was spent on IDP projects (and the rest on the refugee programme, the stateless programme, and reintegration projects) (UNHCR 2014c: 1, 7).

Myanmar

From 1962 to 2011, Burma/Myanmar[8] was ruled by a military junta, and the country was characterized by several concurrent conflicts between different ethnic non-state armed groups and the national armed forces (the Tatmadaw), a repressed democracy movement, and inter-communal violence in Rakhine State. In 2011, a nominally civilian government came to power, and a new peace process was started that same year. Thirty-five non-state armed groups had previously disarmed or transformed into the People's Militia or Border Guard Force (parts of the Tatmadaw), and sixteen main armed groups remained (Zaw Oo 2014: 14). Of these sixteen, fourteen had signed bilateral

[8] For more detailed analysis of the history and conflict context in Burma/Myanmar, see Callahan (2003), Falla (1991), International Crisis Group (2014), Sadan (2013), Smith (1998), and South (2008).

ceasefire agreements with the government by 2014 (Zaw Oo 2014). Despite this positive progress, at the time of interviews (December 2013 and January 2014), the ceasefire armed groups had not demobilized, and on occasion clashes continued to occur between the Tatmadaw and some of these armed non-state actors.

In northern Rakhine State, the main protection concerns were arising from inter-communal violence between Muslim communities and the Rakhine Buddhist majority. Two major outbreaks of violence in 2012 were followed by sporadic lower-scale violent incidents, restrictions on movement, and restrictions on access to livelihoods and basic services such as education and health. While Rakhine Buddhists undoubtedly suffered too, the Muslim communities—in particular the Rohingya Muslims—were bearing the brunt of this violence, suffering not only from the direct consequences of violence, but also from the official response. According to government figures, the two events in 2012 left 58 Rakhines and 134 Rohingyas dead, and destroyed the homes of 1,192 Rakhines and 7,422 Rohingyas (Republic of the Union of Myanmar 2013: 85). Subsequently, the authorities established checkpoints, purportedly for Muslim protection. However, many analysts suggest that the real aim was to restrict movement and to arrest Muslims as much as possible. As a consequence, people were isolated within their communities and could not access markets and other livelihoods activities. In addition, the authorities relocated—somewhat forcibly—some groups. Many from the government and from the population at large would prefer to see Rohingya Muslims leaving, and the government chose to support segregation rather than alternatives as a means to resolve the violence.

In Kachin State and in northern Shan State, renewed conflict actually occurred between 2011 and the time of writing. The Kachin Independence Organization/Kachin Independence Army (KIO/A) had not signed on to the peace process, and there was ongoing armed conflict between the KIO/A and the national military. At the time of interviews, the Tatmadaw was positioning its soldiers at strategic points, and the KIO/A was also fielding soldiers—and so doing recruitment activities. There was child recruitment on both sides. In addition, there was somewhat forced recruitment by the national military into neighbourhood forces, so-called village volunteers. In some cases, for example, displaced families had been told that to retain the right to their land, they had to return and either join the village volunteers or give a percentage of their rice to the army. In addition to child and adult recruitment with varying degrees of force, civilian insecurity was arising from IHL violations, skirmishes, and a few cases of landmines. The majority of IDPs in Kachin were in camps, although some were with host families. In the south-east of Myanmar, conflict-related violence had all but disappeared by the time of interviews. However, some taxation and portering continued. In addition, there was some development-induced displacement, including as a consequence of land grabbing by the military in collusion with big business. In general in the south-east, there was more freedom of movement and access to markets than previously, but insecurity as a consequence of prior conflict lingered in the form of landmines.

The history of the ICRC and UNHCR in Myanmar is somewhat more complex than in Colombia or the DRC. UNHCR began work in Maungdaw in northern Rakhine State with the repatriation of refugees from Bangladesh in 1978, and opened a permanent office there in 1994, running a statelessness operation. The ICRC first opened a delegation in Burma in 1986, with a focus on physical rehabilitation for amputees. Following an aborted effort to begin prison visits in Myanmar in 1994–5, the ICRC eventually began them in 1999 (ICRC 1995, 1999).

In 2002, the ICRC opened an office in Mandalay and also began working on the protection of the civilian population (ICRC 2002a, 2002b). For the next two years, a typical ICRC operation was run in Myanmar, involving classic protection work on behalf of detainees and the civilian population, with around fifty expatriate staff. At the same time, UNHCR sought to establish a presence in the south of Myanmar, taking the view that, in order to get access, they had to be useful, and hence do community assistance projects with the non-displaced population. UNHCR did not do protection work, and all of the projects were in villages in government-controlled areas, but little by little they were getting closer to non-government-controlled areas. Essentially, they sought to buy their way in by undertaking projects which posed no threat to the government—and indeed which fitted with the government's priorities. From an ICRC perspective, however, UNHCR was colluding with the government and working contrary to humanitarian principles. Moreover, it became increasingly difficult for the ICRC to do its own classic protection work. Not wanting to acknowledge the existence of IDPs and of protection needs, the government started pushing the ICRC to be more like UNHCR and IOM, doing community development projects rather than talking about IDPs and protection concerns whose existence the government preferred to deny.

By December 2005, the Myanmar authorities were preventing the ICRC from undertaking its detention visits in line with its standard procedures, and so the ICRC suspended these visits, and then in 2006 the government ordered the ICRC to close its five field offices in Myanmar (ICRC 2006). In the space of a year, the ICRC reduced the number of delegates in Myanmar from fifty-six to sixteen (ICRC 2007d). Finally, in light of the extreme restrictions on its work, in June 2007 the ICRC took the rare step of publicly denouncing IHL violations committed by the Myanmar government against both detainees and civilians affected by armed conflict (ICRC 2007c). After this public denunciation, all ICRC operations in Myanmar were put on hold apart from funding and running an orthopaedic rehabilitation centre in Hpa-an together with the Myanmar Red Cross Society, and paying transport costs for family members to visit their detained relatives.

UNHCR remained in the country and continued to work under restrictive conditions imposed by the government. It was able to carry out programming but did not have free choice as to what programming. Essentially it was limited to the statelessness operation in Rakhine State, and government-authorized practical projects in the south-east of the country. Between 2004 and 2014, UNHCR implemented around 3,000 such projects, from distribution of non-food items to building schools and clinics. Unsurprisingly, then, UNHCR came to be seen largely as an infrastructure and development agency, despite its international protection mandate and the protection needs of IDPs in Myanmar. Only in 2013 did UNHCR's letter of understanding with the government regarding its work in the south-east mention refugees, IDPs, and protection for the first time. This was a big change and allowed for higher budgets, and more international staff. At the same time, UNHCR began to cut back on the more practically focused projects.

UNHCR has been in Myitkyina (Kachin State) since late 2011, and began its Sittwe operation (Rakhine State) in the aftermath of the June 2012 violence, initially dispatching emergency teams from the already existing Maungdaw office, and then opening an office in Sittwe itself. Since then, what was a statelessness operation in Rakhine State has become primarily an IDP operation. For UNHCR, displacement and statelessness are the two major issues in Rakhine State, and both issues affect more or less the same populations.

In the context of reforms initiated by the Myanmar government that came to power in 2011, the ICRC began to grow its Myanmar operation again in 2012, and prison visits restarted at the beginning of 2013. Thus, as in Colombia and the DRC, ICRC protection work in Myanmar includes activities related to detention as well as to the protection of the civilian population. In April 2013, a protection coordinator for the delegation began work in Yangon, and as at December 2013 the ICRC had more than 30 expatriate staff and approximately 280 national staff in Myanmar. The organization was set to grow further in 2014. The pace of expansion is reflected in ICRC expenditure on Myanmar operations, which rose from CHF 3.5 million (approximately USD 3.7 million) in 2011 to CHF 5.3 million in 2012, to CHF 13.2 million in 2013, of which a little over one-third was spent on protection and prevention (ICRC 2012a: 225; 2013a: 250; 2014a: 290). The budget for 2014 was CHF 24.3 million. In 2013, UNHCR had 174 staff in Myanmar, including 24 international staff, and expenditure of USD 29.3 million (UNHCR 2014d: 1, 5).

Despite the fact that the ICRC has a longer history in the country, several interviewees referred to it being 'early days' for the ICRC in Myanmar, or to the ICRC being a 'new' actor. The ICRC's recent absence from Myanmar, and the consequent lack of presence in conflict zones and lack of well-established relationships with both state and non-state authorities, is seen to limit the work of the organization. However, the main problems and limits relating to restarting operations in Myanmar appear to be the same problems and limits associated with *starting* operations anywhere, rather than anything specific to the public denunciation and subsequent exit from Myanmar. For both the ICRC and UNHCR, difficulties arise working with the government because of lack of capacity, and non-democratic, non-participatory styles of working. Projects are slowed down because of the time taken by the government to grant travel authorizations to restricted areas, and in some cases, restrictions prevent access—and therefore protection activities—altogether.

METHODS AND PRESENTATION

The ICRC and UNHCR are treated together in one book—and indeed in each chapter—not to compare their achievements, but as a way to understand better each respective approach to protection, and the challenges and contradictions that characterize humanitarian agency efforts to protect civilians more generally.

The analysis triangulates between secondary literature, policy documents, and interviews with staff from the ICRC and UNHCR at both headquarters and in the field. Being a public international organization, UNHCR is required to publish a great deal more than the ICRC in terms of policy deliberations and statements. Thus, the analysis of UNHCR draws heavily on policy documents to chart the adoption of issue-areas within UNHCR, and to explain the approach undertaken to address the issue-area of in-country protection. Evaluation reports and secondary literature are used to explain organizational culture and structure and the nature of the relationship between UNHCR and states. For the ICRC, the analysis draws more on secondary literature, but a large part of this is written by former or current members of ICRC staff, and in many cases represents a deliberate statement of ICRC policy. In some cases, this literature is not as objective as analytical works written by outsiders free to criticize the ICRC when they see fit, but it provides a useful insight into official policy and into how the organization wishes to present itself. The secondary literature on the ICRC is supplemented with interview data to generate an understanding of the organizational history, structure, and culture of the ICRC.

A central aspect of the analysis concerns the experience of policy implementation, and thus it was important to reveal what the two organizations do in practice in different contexts. However, there does not exist a great deal of literature on the operations of either of these two organizations in the specific contexts of Colombia, the DRC, and Myanmar, or indeed on the detail of what they do in the name of protection anywhere in the world. Thus, much of the analysis in this book is based on interviews conducted during fieldwork in Colombia between July and September 2010, in Myanmar in December 2013 and January 2014, and in the DRC in July and August 2014. As such, it primarily captures snapshots of their work in these contexts in these particular time periods. I travelled to all the field offices in which I was able to set up a meeting, and in most cases I met with the head of the office. In some I also met with other national or expatriate staff. Interviews followed a semi-structured format. The key advantage of these interviews is that they provide original and first-hand accounts of the work of both organizations across Colombia, the DRC, and Myanmar. The disadvantage of relying on data from interviews with staff from the organizations under scrutiny is that they may wish to present a picture of their work which is somewhat at odds with reality. Given this concern, analysis of the interview data takes into account not only what my interviewees recounted but also the 'metadata' (Fujii 2010). In other words, attention is paid not only to their descriptions of their work, but also to consistency or contradictions across the descriptions by different interviewees, to the questions interviewees asked me, and to their confidence or uncertainty in explaining their work.

Over sixty interviews were conducted, mainly with current staff from the ICRC and UNHCR at headquarters in Geneva and in field offices across Colombia, the DRC, and Myanmar, but also with staff from other international humanitarian agencies in the field and with former members of ICRC and UNHCR staff. Many interviewees spoke openly and frankly about the nature of their work and the problems they face, as well as about their perspectives on Colombia, the DRC, and Myanmar, and the different actors in those settings, and I am very grateful for this input. In order to avoid compromising the position of either the ICRC or UNHCR, or of any individual members of staff, and to assure the confidential nature of the interviews, data is not attributed to specific interviewees.

PLAN OF THE BOOK

One of the central arguments of this book is that institutional characteristics of the ICRC and UNHCR go a long way to explaining why each organization has adopted its respective approach to protection. Accordingly, Chapter 1 focuses on explaining the institutional history, structure, and culture of the two organizations. Each of the following five chapters then explains and critiques one particular dimension of the ICRC and UNHCR understandings of protection. Collectively, these five dimensions characterize the ways in which the ICRC and UNHCR conceptualize and practise protection. The analysis shows how institutional factors have been instrumental in shaping each of these five dimensions, and highlights the ways in which they impose limitations on the protection work of both organizations.

Chapter 2 discusses the principles underlying ICRC and UNHCR protection work, namely humanity, impartiality, neutrality, and independence, showing that their respective institutional histories and structures have shaped how each organization interprets and implements these principles. The chapter also argues that as a consequence of a more conservative organizational culture and a greater commitment to consistency, the ICRC applies these principles more rigidly than does UNHCR.

Chapter 3 turns to the legal and normative frameworks employed by the ICRC and UNHCR, explaining not only which frameworks each organization uses but also how those frameworks shape their work. IHL is central to the identity, mandate, and day-to-day work of the ICRC, while UNHCR emphasizes the Guiding Principles on Internal Displacement, domestic legislation, and the rights of IDPs not to be disadvantaged or discriminated against on account of their displacement. Both organizations are more confident and more committed to working on issues that fall squarely within their mandates in international law; yet both are also working increasingly outside the scope of these legal mandates.

Chapter 4 examines the specific objectives pursued by these two organizations in their protection work. Echoing their respective objectives in other issue-areas within their institutional mandates, the ICRC aims mainly to reduce the threats posed by armed actors to civilians, while UNHCR tends to focus on changing policy at least one step removed from the violence and armed actors that are the essence of the protection problem.

Chapter 5 considers the protection roles and responsibilities of other protection actors. In line with the main objectives pursued by each organization, and also in keeping with their normative biases and their modus operandi on other issue-areas within their mandates, the ICRC and UNHCR each prioritize different actors in protection and relate to them in distinct ways. The ICRC emphasizes the importance of armed parties to conflict, both state and non-state, while UNHCR focuses on the civilian agencies of the state.

Chapter 6 sets out the main activities carried out by the ICRC and UNHCR in the name of protection. The activities undertaken by each organization also correspond to the objectives they pursue and the actors they work with, but the ICRC tends to have a clearer conceptualization of how particular activities link to particular objectives than does UNHCR.

1

The ICRC and UNHCR

One of the central arguments of this book is that a number of institutional characteristics are of paramount importance in shaping the ways that the ICRC and UNHCR understand and practise protection. This chapter specifies just what those characteristics are. It is divided into three main sections, each of which deals with a particular dimension of ICRC and UNHCR institutional character: (1) institutional history; (2) institutional structure; and (3) institutional culture. These different aspects are not wholly internal, as they include, for example, the structural relationships between the ICRC or UNHCR on the one hand, and states and other organizations on the other. However, they are characteristics that are specific to each organization. In this chapter the three different aspects are discussed separately for clarity of presentation. This is not to suggest that they are entirely independent of one another. On the contrary, what an organization does is constitutive of what that organization is, and thus the historical experiences and activities of any given organization shape its culture, which in turn affects how current activities are defined and undertaken. Likewise, an organization at its inception is structured with the initial mandate of the organization in mind. That structure then has a lasting impact on how the mandate evolves and expands and how informal processes and culture develop. Those informal processes and the culture then affect future mandate changes or expansion, and may also affect formal structures and external relationships.

Mainstream approaches in the field of international relations have traditionally focused on external factors in determining international organization (IO) behaviour, with a strong emphasis on the role of states. Although the ICRC was not created by states, it is financially reliant on a small number of relatively powerful states and has a particular mandate in international law which is defined by states. UNHCR is both politically and financially dependent on states. Existing literature suggests that state interests have at least been a partial driver of their behaviour (Forsythe 2005; Hutchinson 1996; Loescher 2001). This book does not deny such a perspective, but it does suggest that the influence that states exercise on ICRC and UNHCR policy and practice is not always direct, and that the relationships between states and each organization are not one-way. For example, it is state preferences *combined with* a competitive funding environment that may incentivize these organizations to behave in a particular way. It is not for the most part direct orders from states. In addition, these organizations can and do respond in different ways to such incentives. They are actors themselves and they vary in the extent to which they bow to, or withstand, such indirect pressures from states.

More recent work has shifted attention to factors internal to the IO. The seminal work in this regard is *Rules for the world: international organizations in global politics*[1] by Michael Barnett and Martha Finnemore, and this provides the starting point of my analysis of how institutional factors shape the protection approaches of the ICRC and UNHCR. They argue that the authority, knowledge, and rules internal to an organization are important in explaining that organization's autonomy and behavioural choices, including those behavioural choices that may be dysfunctional (Barnett and Finnemore 2004: 8). Rules and procedures, institutional history and identity, as well as the level of internal contestation and incorporation of external feedback, are all expected to impact on the behaviour of the organization. The rest of this chapter is therefore devoted to exploring these different characteristics of the ICRC and UNHCR, and the following five chapters explain how these different characteristics affect their respective approaches to protecting IDPs and other civilians in the midst of armed conflict.

INSTITUTIONAL HISTORY

Since their inceptions, both the ICRC and UNHCR have been continually expanding, not only quantitatively (in terms of the number and size of operations, staff, and budget) but also qualitatively into new issue-areas. This mandate expansion has important impacts on the way that the new tasks within an institutional mandate are addressed. Indeed this book argues that a major part of the explanation for why the ICRC and UNHCR have adopted their particular institutional approaches to protecting IDPs and other civilians in the midst of armed conflict lies in their organizational history, and specifically in the issue-areas they worked on prior to expanding their mandates into the newer issue-area of in-country protection. The existence of prior mandates means that when they developed their respective approaches to in-country protection, they were not starting from a blank canvas. In Chapters 2–6, we see that to a great extent both organizations have replicated the means,

[1] *Rules for the world* focuses on intergovernmental organizations (IGOs), but much of its analysis and argument is also relevant to an organization like the ICRC, which is neither an IGO nor a 'normal' INGO.

methods, and understandings of protection from older issue-areas within their mandates to new ones. In order to contextualize this replication, this section explains how their institutional mandates have evolved and expanded.

The ICRC was conceived as an organization whose role would be to coordinate national societies tasked with providing medical assistance in the field, but the original 'committee of five' quickly decided it would be necessary for the ICRC itself to be operational, and from World War I onwards the ICRC has continually expanded the scope of its operations. By 2013, the ICRC had an average of 11,784 staff working in field missions (the vast majority of whom are national staff, not expatriates), and 949 staff working at headquarters in Geneva (ICRC 2014a: 93). It is not only the size of the organization, but also the nature of its work that has changed dramatically. The ICRC was set up to work on the protection and assistance of wounded soldiers in international conflicts. In terms of the object of protection, the ICRC extended its activities from wounded soldiers to prisoners of war, to political prisoners, to civilian internees, to civilians in the midst of conflict. In terms of the contexts in which it operates, the ICRC extended its activities from international to internal conflict, first with respect to the war-wounded and political prisoners, and later with respect to civilians. The ICRC has since further expanded the range of contexts in which it works to include internal disturbances and tensions that fall short of armed conflict.

In its second meeting, in 1863, the ICRC had affirmed that it would not involve itself in civil wars (Armstrong 1985: 622). However, the ICRC added internal conflict to its self-devised mandate in the early stages of the break-up of the Ottoman Empire, and with its work in Russia in 1917–18 and Hungary in 1919 (Forsythe 2005: 33). In 1921, the Red Cross conference formalized this role in institutional policy. In practical terms, the role further expanded in the Spanish Civil War from 1936 to 1939, and the application of IHL to internal conflicts and the role of the ICRC were subsequently codified in common article 3 of the 1949 Geneva Conventions and in Additional Protocol II of 1977. More recently, in outlining its strategy, the ICRC states that it 'is determined to pursue its universal humanitarian work to protect the lives and dignity of all persons affected by armed conflict and other situations of armed violence—no matter what form those situations take or what stage they have reached' (ICRC 2007b: 2).

Each of these steps in the expansion of the ICRC mandate was justified on the basis of a moral imperative, and analogies between the predicaments of those whom the ICRC was legally mandated to assist and those whom the ICRC sought to assist (Forsythe 2005: 34). Practical action on the ground came first, and was subsequently formalized in ICRC policy. Institutional policy was then later followed up with codification of the ICRC role in international law, thus formalizing its legal mandate. At each stage, analogies were drawn between the then existing activities and responsibilities of the ICRC, and those that it has sought to adopt. Such a tactic fits with the idea that through the construction of linkages—so-called adjacency claims—between existing norms and emergent norms, norm entrepreneurs can facilitate wider acceptance of the new norms (Finnemore and Sikkink 1998: 908; Price 1997).

There are three key things to note about the way that the ICRC has framed expansion into new issue-areas. First, there is always a strong argument made in terms of the moral imperative to tackle the new issue-area in question. Second, the new issue-area is presented as morally and functionally very similar to the existing issue-areas in the ICRC mandate. Third, it is always emphasized that ICRC efforts in respect of the new issue-area will not and must not impact negatively on the organization's existing work. While parallels have been made in terms of the moral equivalence of the new issue-areas and the pre-existing issue-areas, 'functional spillover' arguments have not played a part in justifying expansion (Haas 1958). Thus, incorporating civilian protection in internal conflict into the ICRC mandate was not justified on the grounds of it being instrumental to the work of the ICRC on other issue-areas (though the other issue-areas may have given the ICRC a comparative advantage in its civilian protection work). However, in expanding the ICRC mandate, and in keeping with the cautious approach to change within the organization, there has always been concern as to whether any potential new issue-area would damage the ability of the ICRC to carry out its existing mandate.

As J. D. Armstrong has explained, 'the invariable sequence of events has seen an ad hoc action by the ICRC develop into a general practice that later achieved the status of a customary norm in international law and was finally codified by treaties and conventions' (Armstrong 1985: 621). This order of expansion, with practical action on the ground preceding legal codification, suggests that expansion has largely been led by the ICRC, with states brought on board for the lawmaking process later on. However, even if states did not exert direct pressure on the ICRC to expand its mandate to include a wider range of categories of person and a wider range of contexts, strategic decisions by the ICRC may have been shaped by expectations about state preferences and a market-based logic. In other words, the ICRC may have anticipated state interests and taken them into consideration when undertaking new kinds of practical action, developing institutional policy, and proposing international legal initiatives, knowing that any such expansion needed to be acceptable to states as the main funders of ICRC work, and as the ultimate decision makers in treaty negotiations.

There are some similarities in UNHCR's expansion story. When UNHCR was created in 1950, it was not for the purpose of protecting IDPs in the midst of armed conflict, but rather to provide or to negotiate international protection and solutions for refugees, specifically Europeans displaced by World War II. Originally conceived as a temporary organization with a mandate to operate until 31 December 1953, by which time it was hoped that the post-war refugee problem in Europe would be solved, UNHCR began life with a limited mandate and correspondingly limited funding. The mandate was repeatedly extended through General Assembly Resolutions which renewed the existence of UNHCR for periods of two or five years until the agency was finally given an indefinite mandate in 2004.[2] UNHCR had an initial annual budget of only USD 300,000, and a total of thirty-three members of staff at the end of its first year of existence (Loescher 2001: 50–1). However, over time the agency expanded massively, both in terms of the number and scale of its operations, and the number of issue-areas within its mandate. In 2013, expenditure reached USD 2.97 billion and UNHCR employed over 7,000 staff members in 123 countries (UNHCR 2014b: 2–3). Moreover, from the late 1990s, UNHCR took on increasing responsibility for IDPs on an ad hoc basis, and this role has now been formalized under the cluster approach through which UNHCR is mandated to play a lead role in coordinating IDP protection at the global level, and at the field level in conflict situations.

Although UNHCR was first involved with IDPs in the 1970s in Africa and Asia in situations where IDPs were mixed with refugees, it was not until the 1990s that UNHCR regularly extended its service to those displaced within their own countries (Mattar and White 2005: 3). UNHCR traditionally worked in third countries, and protection was conceived in terms of the legal principles of *non-refoulement* and asylum, rather than in terms of physical safety for either refugees in camps across the border from the country of origin or IDPs within their own countries. Since the 1980s, the range of activities undertaken by UNHCR has expanded, new populations have been identified as being of concern, and emphasis has shifted. Changes in the character of refugee flows and shifts in the attitudes of states to those flows such that resettlement and asylum became increasingly unrealistic solutions put pressure on UNHCR to prevent outflows, to provide in-country protection and assistance, and to repatriate those who have fled (Loescher 2001: 283; Roberts 1996: 13–14).

In the 1980s, UNHCR began to emphasize repatriation (as opposed to local integration or resettlement) as the preferred solution to the refugee problem. This was a response to increasingly restrictive asylum policies in both industrialized countries and the developing world, and pressure from states to find an alternative durable solution. Prior to 1985, UNHCR considered voluntary repatriation the preferred solution in principle, but resettlement was promoted in practice; from 1985 to 1993, voluntary repatriation was favoured, with emphasis on ensuring its voluntary nature; in 1993 the notion of safe

[2] UN General Assembly, *Implementing actions proposed by the United Nations High Commissioner for Refugees to strengthen the capacity of his Office to carry out its mandate.* 24 February 2004, A/RES/58/153 (2004).

return introduced the possibility for UNHCR rather than refugees themselves to determine when they should repatriate; and 1996 brought the doctrine of imposed return, under which refugees could be sent back to conditions considered less than optimal by UNHCR (Chimni 2004; Loescher 2001: 283–6; Zieck 1997). Conceptually it is a short step from repatriation to seeking to prevent refugee flows altogether, and already in 1985, UNHCR's governing body stated that the 'aspect of causes is critical to the issue of solution and international efforts should also be directed to the removal of the causes of refugee movements. Further attention should be given to the causes and prevention of such movements' (UNHCR 1985, para. c). This shift was in keeping with broader moves within the UN to address the 'root causes' of conflict and human rights abuses within countries of origin, as reflected in the study on human rights and massive exoduses by (former High Commissioner for Refugees) Prince Sadruddin Aga Khan for the UN Human Rights Commission (Aga Khan 1981).

Against this background, UNHCR went from having minimal involvement in countries of origin in the 1980s to become the lead agency for IDPs in 2006. Analysis of General Assembly Resolutions and UNHCR policy documents reveals that three main arguments were made for the expansion of UNHCR into IDP operations. The first is a practical argument, fitting with the idea of functional spillover (Haas 1958). According to this reasoning, UNHCR should expand into IDP protection because IDPs often become refugees, protecting and assisting IDPs may prevent refugee flows, and the prevention of refugee flows is a solution to the 'refugee problem' (UN General Assembly 1993; UNHCR 1994b, para. 15d; 1998, para. 11). The second is a normative argument, based on the fact that refugees and IDPs are often in the same place and the same predicament (UNHCR 2000: 3; 2007c, para. 36). The ethical reasoning is that if UNHCR is protecting and assisting the refugees, it should also protect and assist the IDPs. The third argument cuts across the other two, and identifies the expertise and experience of UNHCR with refugees as qualifying it to provide protection and solutions for IDPs (UNHCR 1994a, para. b; 1998, para. 12; 2000: 5). Indeed, in outlining the particular assets at its disposal with which to undertake the task of IDP protection, 'the expertise, competence and capacity that UNHCR has developed in protecting uprooted populations' is described as the most significant (UNHCR 2007g, para. 11). Whereas UNHCR might have focused on any of the other assets (moral authority, human, physical, and logistical resources, relations with states, IGOs, and NGOs) to make the case for a more general protection role, UNHCR emphasizes its experience and expertise with respect to 'uprooted populations'.

Of course, these arguments are the public justifications for expansion, and they do not tell us the whole story. In the 1980s and 1990s, European and North American states were adopting increasingly restrictive asylum policies and practices. As a consequence of the increasing reluctance of states to accept refugees, IDP protection came to be seen as both a humanitarian solution and as a means to contain would-be refugees in their countries of origin (Dubernet 2001; Duffield 1997; Phuong 2004; Shacknove 1993). The financial and political dependence of UNHCR on states (discussed in more detail in the next section) ensured that the policy pursued by UNHCR has reflected the global move towards containment (Dubernet 2001; Duffield 2008: 154). Nonetheless, these three arguments for the expansion of UNHCR into IDP protection and assistance demonstrate how a link between issue-areas was constructed to justify expansion into the new issue-area. It is logical that these constructions may then have an impact on how the new issue-area is addressed. The second and third arguments rely on adjacency claims which, if taken to their logical conclusion, suggest that the objectives pursued and activities undertaken by UNHCR with respect to refugee protection and assistance would form the template for IDP protection and assistance. In many respects that is indeed what we see in Chapters 2–6.

The historical trajectory of each organization has had a direct impact on its understanding and practice of protection, as the next five chapters of this book detail. The ICRC approach to protecting civilians in the midst of internal armed conflict replicates the institutional approach to protecting other persons of concern to the ICRC, namely wounded and sick soldiers, prisoners of war and others deprived of their liberty, and civilians in international conflicts or occupied territory. Similarly, the approach taken by UNHCR to IDP protection in conflict contexts replicates the institutional approach to refugee protection. However, these new issue-areas or problems that the ICRC and UNHCR seek to address are by definition not identical to the pre-existing issue-areas within their mandates. To the extent that the new 'problems' are different from the old ones, seeking to address them with old solutions is likely to limit the scope of protection that the ICRC and UNHCR are able to provide.

These institutional histories also have an indirect impact on how the ICRC and UNHCR go about the newer task of in-country protection, via their impacts on organizational structure and culture. Their organizational structures were designed for addressing different issue-areas, but those designs continue to affect how they go about their work today on both older and newer tasks. Their organizational cultures and values have also been shaped by historical institutional mandates, and themselves shape the contemporary mandate. These two dimensions—organizational structure and organizational culture—are explored in the next two sections.

INSTITUTIONAL STRUCTURE

The ICRC is *sui generis*, with both public and private characteristics (Forsythe 2001a: 676; Ratner 2011: 464). Technically, it is an INGO, set up by private individuals, without member states, and incorporated as a private body under Swiss law. However, the ICRC is not a 'normal' INGO in that: (a) it derives its mandate in part from the broader Red Cross movement and from international law, and states play an important role in both of these; and (b) it is recognized in international public law as if it were a public international organization. The original 'committee of five' which became the ICRC was a group of five private individuals who proposed their idea (for an international treaty) to a group of states. Unlike intergovernmental organizations which are set up by states and composed of member states, the impetus to set up the ICRC thus came from individuals, and it remains the case that states do not have membership or any direct, formal control over the institutional agenda. This formal independence has been significant in determining ICRC identity and practice, and indeed in shaping organizational culture and the institutional attitude towards states. By contrast, UNHCR is an intergovernmental organization, and was created by states. It is the General Assembly that has the power to make formal amendments to the mandate of UNHCR, and from this perspective it is clear that UNHCR is not an entirely independent actor.

Both organizations are also members of wider institutional structures. The ICRC is part of the International Red Cross and Red Crescent Movement, which comprises the ICRC, the International Federation of Red Cross and Red Crescent Societies (IFRC), and 189 individual national societies (such as the American Red Cross and the Iraqi Red Crescent).[3] The Movement is thus best understood as a network, rather than a single organization, and 'the units of the movement are formally joined in a tenuous way' (Forsythe 1977: 6). They are not wholly independent of one another. For example, National Societies must be recognized by the ICRC and admitted to the IFRC, and the mandate of the ICRC derives in part from the Statutes of the Movement. The IFRC coordinates the humanitarian activities of the national societies, and is governed by a General Assembly comprising national society membership. Nevertheless, each unit has its own legal identity and the ICRC is not subject to the authority of any other unit. Indeed, the intention is that there is a division of responsibility among them, clarified in the 1997 Seville Agreement,[4] which provides for the ICRC to take a lead role in situations of armed conflict and the IFRC in natural disaster contexts.

UNHCR is part of the institutional architecture of the UN and, moreover, is subject to the authority of superior organs of the UN, in particular the General Assembly and the Economic and Social Council (Palley 1996). UNHCR is

[3] For more on the International Red Cross and Red Crescent Movement, see Forsythe (1977: 5–6), ICRC (2013b), and International Red Cross and Red Crescent Movement (1997).

[4] International Red Cross and Red Crescent Movement 1997. *Agreement on the organization of the international activities of the components of the International Red Cross and Red Crescent Movement—The Seville Agreement*, Council of Delegates, Seville, 25–7 November 1997.

politically dependent on states and operates with their consent. As a UN agency, UNHCR also has to conform to broader UN policies, and particular procedures can restrict its ability to act autonomously. For example, UNHCR is subject to the security directives of the UN Department of Safety and Security (UNDSS), and on occasion (as in Lebanon in 2006, for example), the ability of UNHCR to carry out its humanitarian mandate has been compromised by security measures deemed to be unduly restrictive (Sperl, Diagne, and Snider 2006). Furthermore, UNHCR activity may be used to further the objectives of other UN agencies, which thus constrains its ability to act autonomously. Additionally, as part of the UN, UNHCR must act in conformity with the norms that characterize the organization, and must manage the associated tensions between those norms, as for example between sovereignty and human rights.

The institutional setting in which humanitarian action takes place—variously labelled the humanitarian international (de Waal 1997), the international humanitarian order (Barnett 2009), the humanitarian marketplace (Crisp 2002), the humanitarian complex (Hilhorst 2002), and the humanitarian enterprise (Minear 2002)—impacts on the ways in which individual organizations within that institutional setting function (Duffield 1997: 540–1; Hopgood 2008; Ramalingam and Barnett 2010). This institutional setting can be understood as an intervening variable between state preferences and ICRC or UNHCR responses to those preferences. However, the ICRC, UNHCR, and other humanitarian agencies respond differently to this institutional environment, and to the incentive structures that characterize it. Their respective senses of their own identities and roles play an important part in shaping their relationships with states and other external actors, and much of this comes down to organizational culture, which is discussed in the next section.

ICRC policy and practice have always been driven by a combination of state interests on the one hand, and humanitarian motivations on the other (Finnemore 1999; Forsythe and Rieffer-Flanagan 2007: 7; Hutchinson 1996: 29–30, 348). Although not directly an agent of states, the ICRC understands its mandate as derived from IHL and as requiring the further development of IHL treaties. Since treaties are negotiated and signed by states, this requires the ICRC to work to develop IHL in such a way as to be palatable to states. In this way, IHL is driven at least in part by state preferences. Once codified, IHL contributes to defining the mandate of the ICRC, thereby suggesting the work of the ICRC is indirectly driven by the state preferences. Additionally, the ICRC is financially dependent on voluntary contributions, the vast majority of which come from a relatively small group of states, despite ICRC efforts to diversify and expand its range of primary funding sources. In recent years, between 75 per cent and 80 per cent of funding has come from ten governmental donors, including the European Commission (ICRC 2014a: 82).

The relationship between the ICRC and the Swiss government merits special mention. In earlier years, there was something of a revolving door between the top levels of the Swiss confederation and the top levels of the ICRC. The three most recent presidents of the ICRC[5] were former Swiss diplomats, and the Assembly counts Swiss diplomats, politicians, bankers, businesspeople, and academics among its members. This close relationship has at times allowed the Swiss government to exert an influence on ICRC policy (for more on this, see the section on independence in Chapter 2). More generally, the Swiss political culture has undoubtedly affected the internal decision-making processes (discussed below), and the institutional culture (discussed in the next section of this chapter) of the ICRC.

The need for the cooperation of states with the development (and implementation) of IHL, as well as financial reliance on states, thus suggests that the ICRC must take state preferences into account when making institutional policy choices, and in this way states can be expected to have an influence on ICRC policy. Furthermore, states may have a say in ICRC policy through their participation in the International Conference of the Red Cross and Red Crescent Movement. The International Conference takes place approximately every four years and brings together the ICRC, the national societies, the IFRC, and states party to the 1949 Geneva Conventions.[6] The International Conference is a deliberative body and does not exercise formal control over the agenda of any of its participants. However, the Statutes of the International Red Cross and Red Crescent Movement are adopted by the International Conference, and the ICRC sees part of its mandate as deriving from these Statutes. In this way, therefore, states can exercise some direct influence on the ICRC mandate.

UNHCR is financially and politically dependent on states, and is formally mandated by states. However, while the General Assembly defines UNHCR's formal mandate, General Assembly resolutions leave a lot of flexibility for UNHCR to define its own competence and role. Taking advantage of this flexibility, different High Commissioners have autonomously expanded activities in areas that have subsequently been recognized by the General Assembly. That being said, the General Assembly is not the only forum through which states may exercise influence on UNHCR. The Executive Committee of the High Commissioner's Programme (Excom) is the governing body of UNHCR and meets annually in Geneva, with a Standing Committee which usually meets three times per year. Excom started in 1958 with twenty-five member states and has steadily expanded to ninety-four member states (as at the end of 2014). Excom oversees the budget of UNHCR and is a forum for debate

[5] Peter Maurer (2012–), Jakob Kellenberger (2000–12), and Cornelio Sommaruga (1987–99).

[6] The 1949 Conventions have been universally ratified, so this, in effect, includes all (recognized) states.

among member states on issues pertinent to the work of the organization. Excom issues conclusions relating to particular policy issues, which are essentially guidelines both for UNHCR and for states. Through these conclusions, those states which are members of Excom have a direct and formal influence on UNHCR policy. Moreover, UNHCR views itself largely as a servant of states and seeks to demonstrate its relevance to states and to remain competitive in the 'humanitarian marketplace' (Crisp 2001; Ogata 2005).

Reflecting the hierarchical relationship anticipated between states and the organization, the Statute of UNHCR also envisaged a vertical structure internally, investing all the authority in the person of the High Commissioner (appointed by the General Assembly), who would be assisted by a Deputy High Commissioner, and who would appoint staff who in turn would be responsible to the High Commissioner (Gottwald 2010: 11). Additionally there are now Assistant High Commissioners for Protection, and for Operations. Individual High Commissioners have been of the utmost significance in defining the direction of the institutional mandate. It is no coincidence that Gil Loescher's excellent institutional history of UNHCR is structured chronologically by High Commissioner. It charts the evolution of the organization, with a chapter dedicated to the leadership of each High Commissioner from Gerrit Jan van Heuven Goedhart in 1951 through to the end of Sadako Ogata's period in office in 2001 (Loescher 2001). The role of the High Commissioner in setting overall objectives and policy is sufficiently important to merit structuring the book around them. Moreover, throughout the book, Loescher demonstrates the impact of the personality and the personal and professional background of each High Commissioner on institutional direction, mandate expansion, and the relationship between UNHCR and states. In a 2005 evaluation commissioned by UNHCR to review its decision-making processes with respect to IDPs, the High Commissioner was found to be by far the most significant actor in deciding whether UNHCR should be involved in any given IDP situation (Mattar and White 2005: 47). Similarly, analysis of the drivers of mandate expansion through the history of UNHCR has emphasized the role of the High Commissioners (Betts 2012). In many of the UNHCR field offices I visited in the course of the research for this book, a framed photo of the High Commissioner hung in the reception area, and often also in the offices of individual staff members.

By contrast, the formal structure of the ICRC is designed to ensure a system of checks and balances on major policy developments, and to prevent any one individual wielding excessive power in policy and operational decisions.[7] The ICRC is headed by the President and the top policymaking body or governing board is the Assembly, comprising fifteen to twenty-five co-opted members of

[7] For more detail on the organizational structure, and how it has evolved through the history of the ICRC, see Forsythe (2005: 201–41).

Swiss nationality. However, there is a dual executive and daily operational policy is largely made by the Director General and the Directorate (Forsythe 2005: 202). The norm has been to appoint outsiders to the position of President, very often individuals with experience as senior officials in the Swiss administration, who for the most part have come to the ICRC without any humanitarian experience. By contrast, the Directorate comprises the Director General and the heads of the five ICRC departments (Operations, International Law and Cooperation, Communication and Information Management, Human Resources, and Financial Resources and Logistics), all of whom have significant professional humanitarian experience within the ICRC (ICRC 2011b: 60). The nature of relations between the President, the Assembly, and the Directorate is somewhat opaque, as befitting an organization known for its secrecy. However, in a reflection of Swiss political culture, and in stark contrast to UNHCR, there is a preference for deliberation and collective decision-making (Forsythe 2005: 202, 223). Furthermore, there does not exist the same kind of cult of the President as could be said to exist within UNHCR in relation to the High Commissioner.

The structures and relationships discussed in this section both condition, and are conditioned by, institutional culture.

INSTITUTIONAL CULTURE

In addition to formal structures and processes, organizations are characterized by informal rules, norms, and accepted ways of doing things. These are the constituents of organizational culture and this section examines three particular dimensions that are pertinent to understanding how the institutional characteristics of the ICRC and UNHCR have shaped their respective approaches to protection.

Decision-Making and Internal Communication

The first of these relates to decision-making and communication styles within each organization. Michael Barnett and Martha Finnemore characterize bureaucracies as hierarchical organizations organized according to impersonal rules and staffed by professionals with particular expertise, and expect particular types of behaviour to flow from these attributes (Barnett and Finnemore 2004: 17–18). However, among bureaucracies we can observe variation in the degree of hierarchy. The level of hierarchy is institutionalized in the formal organizational structure and processes discussed above, but it also has a cultural dimension. Decision-making processes may be top-down or bottom-up, there may be a culture of secrecy or openness, and there may be significant or minimal delegation to officials at the level of implementation. All of this concerns the distribution of power and authority within the organization. All other things being equal, organizations with more bottom-up decision-making processes based on widespread information-sharing and consultation with field-level operatives can be expected to adopt approaches better adapted to the specific tasks at hand.

In the ICRC, expatriate staff members who are sent on field missions are known as delegates, a unique term among humanitarian organizations, first used by the fledgling ICRC in 1864. It has a diplomatic connotation, and the first two delegates—one sent to approach the Danish belligerents and the other the Austro-Prussians (who were fighting over the duchies of Schleswig and Holstein)—were to act as observers rather than to undertake any particular humanitarian activity (Troyon and Palmieri 2007). There has been a tradition of deferring to delegates in the field and of giving them considerable freedom of action, on the assumption that the person in the field could best diagnose the problem and formulate a solution (Bugnion 2003: 252; Forsythe 2005: 193). Originally the primary role of ICRC delegates was to observe conflict zones and the military medical services operating in those zones, acting as the eyes and ears of the ICRC, and reporting their observations back to Geneva.

Contemporary delegates have more defined activities to undertake, and there are both general delegates and specific professions such as medical delegates. However, they continue with this tradition as ICRC representatives who observe situations of violence and report back, and who are 'are expected to be creative, resourceful, and industrious within legal norms and agency guidelines' (Forsythe 2005: 171). This enables knowledge and experience of the field to be relayed to headquarters and to be incorporated into future policymaking. Current ICRC practice continues a 'long tradition of acting as a bottom-up and consensus-driven organization, with the head of delegation's judgement on the strategy generally receiving deference in Geneva' (Ratner 2011: 470–1). Institutional policy sets preferences on the one hand, and well-defined parameters on the other, and it is between these two that delegates in the field are able to exercise autonomy. Since 1975 the ICRC has communicated clear statements of policy throughout the organization (Forsythe 2005: 193). The rationale for policies is also widely explained, and the practice of delegates in the field is informed and constrained by these policy boundaries and by a number of institutional principles. In conducting interviews for this book, it was very clear that ICRC delegates always knew the party line and the rationale for it. This clarity enables delegation of responsibility, and also appears to inspire self-confidence in individual delegates.

UNHCR's financial dependence on donor states and its status as a UN agency both place top-down pressure on the decision-making dimension of organizational culture (Mattar and White 2005: 11). In UNHCR, strategic decisions tend to be made by senior management with little meaningful input from lower- or middle-ranking headquarters staff, and even less input from field staff (Gottwald 2010). Thus, decisions about protection policies are made by those who are often far removed from the people they seek to protect, and the contexts in which they seek to protect them. In particular, those in senior management who are not career UNHCR staff may lack experience of the operational realities of the field, and may be insensitive to the needs of those of concern to the organization, as well as lacking understanding of the internal structures and processes at lower levels (Gottwald 2010: 19; Loescher 2001: 2). A similar pattern of top-down decision-making emerges even at the field level in terms of country-specific policies. 'Protection strategies and country operations plans are often drafted by the senior management of UNHCR field offices without involving front-line staff—such as national staff, junior professional officers and United Nations Volunteers' (Gottwald 2010: 18).

This lack of experience and understanding at the top might be mitigated with effective information and participation from field staff. However, the top-down influence of states and other UN bodies is not countered by a significant flow of influence from the field level. Minimal staff input into decision-making and poor information-sharing make for a system in which strategic decisions on policy direction and the overall approach to protection are relatively uninformed by empirical reality. Policy criteria and information from the field level are employed by senior management to legitimize decisions already taken rather than to inform decisions (Gottwald 2010: 21; Mattar and White 2005: 9). The UN internal audit service flagged weak and ineffective information-sharing between management and staff in UNHCR as a significant cause for concern (UN OIOS 2008: 22).

Poor information flows naturally impact on monitoring, evaluation, and learning within the organization. Thus, Gil Loescher explains that 'UNHCR is confronted with persistent problems of lack of learning and policy effectiveness' (Loescher 2001: 2). The UN internal audit risk assessment study highlighted weak monitoring and evaluation as a significant risk, anticipating it 'may result in the inability of UNHCR to adapt its strategies to changing operational realities' (UN OIOS 2008: 10). Weaknesses in internal communications and information-sharing also came to light in the course of field research for this book. As compared with ICRC delegates, UNHCR interviewees were much less likely to explain the rationale for particular policies and approaches, and in some cases seemed unsure where particular directives had come from. In one or two cases, interviewees even asked me for information on what their colleagues were doing in other field offices within the same country.

Confidence, Certainty, and Consistency

The second dimension concerns the levels of confidence, certainty, and consistency across staff members, policies, and decisions in each organization. Consistency is not necessarily a virtue. Indeed, 'bureaucratic universalism', identified by Barnett and Finnemore as one of five mechanisms through which international organizations may engage in dysfunctional behaviour, occurs when 'one-size-fits-all' policies are adopted in contexts for which they are not well suited (Barnett and Finnemore 2004: 39). However, confidence goes hand in hand with certainty and consistency, as well as with good internal communications and information-sharing. Both individual ICRC staff members and the ICRC as an organization come across as much more confident than UNHCR and its staff.

Consistency is arguably part of the very identity or value set of the ICRC; certainly it is a key part of organizational culture. In the course of the research for this book, this was clearly evidenced in three particular ways. First, some ICRC interviewees explicitly emphasized how their priorities, work, and approach were consistent across different contexts. As one delegate put it, 'With the ICRC, one certainty you have is it never really changes.' Interviewees reported that although individual delegates have different styles, their interlocutors could be sure to hear a consistent message even when staff rotated. Second, ICRC staff members always tell the same story. They all know, understand, and repeat the same rationale for institutional policies. It seems to be the case that there is some scope for internal dissent and debate while a proposed policy is being discussed, but that once that policy is adopted, then ICRC staff members—at least when communicating with non-ICRC people—must support that policy. Third, there is strong policy coherence within and across countries. The ICRC has a clearly defined modus operandi which is applied in every context in which the ICRC works.

By contrast, a number of inconsistencies could be identified in the positions of UNHCR staff in each of the three country contexts in which the research for this book was undertaken. For example, there was some uncertainty among UNHCR staff members as to what the principle of neutrality means in practice, with the consequence that it is interpreted and implemented inconsistently within and across Colombia, the DRC, and Myanmar. This is explored in more detail in Chapter 2. In addition, there was a lack of clarity as to the precise relationship between UNHCR and the governments of the states in which UNHCR is operational. In Chapters 3 and 5 we see how this uncertainty as to how far the organization should defend its own positions and hold the government to account plays out in shaping the UNHCR mandate and UNHCR–state relations in particular contexts. The inconsistencies identified in the course of the field research for this book seem also to be characteristic of UNHCR headquarters, where other research has highlighted a desire among staff members for more coherence among the senior management team (Wigley 2006).

Conservatism and Pragmatism

The third dimension of institutional culture concerns whether an organization is more conservative (resistant to change, and committed to a principled or rule-based approach) or more pragmatic (quick to change, and content to eschew its own principles and rules in response to external pressures). All organizations incorporate various rules and principles, but officials may face uncertainty as to which, if any, existing rules will solve new problems, and particular rules may be interpreted differently by different individuals within an IO (Barnett and Finnemore 2004: 19). The role played by rules and principles thus depends on their interpretation and application by the organization and individuals in question. Different organizations may vary in the extent to which they emphasize a particular set of rules and principles in their operations. In other words, they may take a more rigid or more flexible approach to the application of such rules and principles. The attitude to change within the organization also determines its level of conservatism or pragmatism. Some organizations are resistant to change, while others will adapt quickly in response to new information and new pressures.

The institutional culture of the ICRC is conservative in the sense of adhering to traditional values and being averse to change, or at least slow to change. The conservatism and cautiousness within the ICRC has been reinforced by the dominance for much of the IO's history of a highly legalistic approach to protection, as discussed in Chapter 3. Nonetheless, the ICRC has also been an innovator in terms of the development of IHL to encompass an expanded range of conflicts and other situations of violence, and an expanded range of categories of protected person. This innovation and expansion has occurred through a process of practice-led, incremental, and principled change. What we see is an organization that is often innovative in terms of practice, while remaining cautious in developing policy. New activities may be implemented in one particular setting and lessons can be learned very quickly to inform practice in other settings, but they will not be incorporated into institutional policy until they have been tried and tested in multiple settings. ICRC policy will not be designed on the basis of single experiences but on a whole body of experience, and it takes time to build up such learnings. In addition, the organization has been slow to reform internal structures and processes, and wary of questioning its own internal principles and traditions (Forsythe 2007: 89–91). The ICRC is cautious in nature, demonstrating a preference for tried-and-tested methods. Where change occurs, it is incremental and slow-paced, testing reactions at each increment. Further, any such change takes place within a clear framework of principles which are largely non-negotiable (see Chapter 2).

UNHCR is at the same time characterized by pragmatism and by 'an organizational culture that makes innovation and institutional change difficult' (Loescher 2001: 2). This apparent paradox is explained in two ways. First, UNHCR is pragmatic in response to direct pressure from states and to incentives created by the external institutional environment, but not in response to the field-level experience of UNHCR staff or the needs of refugees and IDPs. As Amy Slaughter and Jeff Crisp[8] acknowledge, 'the organizational culture of the UN can be one that encourages "safety first" approaches that are acceptable to states, and which provides inadequate incentives for the rethinking and reorientation of long-established activities' (Slaughter and Crisp 2009: 6). Second, pragmatism may be evident in terms of the issue-areas adopted by UNHCR and the specific contexts in which it undertakes operations, while at the same time there is a lack of innovation in terms of how to address these issue-areas.

In sum, the ICRC organizational culture is characterized by consensus-led decision-making, and strong internal information-sharing combined with a tendency to secrecy externally. UNHCR has a much more hierarchical culture with weaker internal communications. Within UNHCR, the lack of clarity on various issues seemed to create a sense of uncertainty and lack of confidence among staff members, which may make UNHCR susceptible to pressures from states (or other actors) to act in a particular way.

CONCLUSIONS

Table 1.1 summarizes the main explanations of this chapter, providing an overview of the key institutional characteristics of the ICRC and UNHCR that are pertinent to the rest of this book. The next five chapters show how these institutional characteristics have shaped how the ICRC and UNHCR understand and approach the protection of civilians (ICRC) and IDPs (UNHCR) in the midst of armed conflict.

In both the ICRC and UNHCR, a combination of moral and institutional imperatives has driven mandate expansion. While the public justification tends to rest on the moral case for incorporating the new issue-area, a more market-based logic can often also be identified. In the following chapters, we see that the prior issue-areas within each organization's mandate, combined with the logics and discourses of expansion, have led to a replication of the understandings, means,

[8] Jeff Crisp was then Head of the Policy Development and Evaluation Service at UNHCR.

Table 1.1. Institutional characteristics of the ICRC and UNHCR

	ICRC	UNHCR
Institutional history	Object of protection: wounded and sick soldiers → prisoners of war → political prisoners → civilian internees → civilians at large	Object of protection: Europeans displaced by WWII → all refugees worldwide → IDPs → those at risk of displacement
	Contexts of operations: international armed conflict → internal armed conflict → 'other situations of violence'	Context of operations: refugee-receiving countries → countries of return/origin (repatriation/prevention) → armed-conflict contexts
	Order of expansion: practical action on the ground → institutional policy → codification in international law	Order of expansion: ad hoc responses → GA resolutions or Excom conclusions → institutional policy
	Expansion discourse: (1) moral imperative; (2) adjacency claims between new and older issue-areas; and (3) assurance the new issue-area will not negatively affect older issue-areas	Expansion discourse: (1) functional argument; (2) adjacency claims (moral imperative); (3) adjacency claims (UNHCR capacity)
Institutional structure	Private organization	Intergovernmental organization
	Formally independent of states	Formally subordinate to the UN General Assembly
	Member of the Red Cross movement	UN agency
	Checks and balances	Hierarchical structure
Institutional culture	Consensus-led decision-making	Top-down decision-making
	Strong information-sharing internally	Weak information-sharing internally
	Confidentiality and secrecy with external actors	
	Confident, consistent, and slow to change	Uncertain, inconsistent, and pragmatic

and methods of protection from prior issue-areas to the newer issue-areas of in-country protection of IDPs and other civilians. This is particularly evident in the legal framework of the ICRC (see Chapter 3), and the emphasis placed by UNHCR on the role of states in protection (see Chapter 5), as well as in how both organizations define their protection objectives (Chapter 4), and in the activities they undertake in practice (Chapter 6). The variation in institutional structure and culture between the ICRC and UNHCR also helps to explain variation in how they interpret and implement particular principles of humanitarian action, which is the subject of Chapter 2.

2

Principles of Humanitarian Action

Both the ICRC and UNHCR seek to inject certain principles into global politics, and their own actions are also guided by a number of values and principles. Like most major Western humanitarian organizations, they subscribe to broadly the same set of principles of humanitarian action—humanity, impartiality, neutrality, and independence. However, the precise meaning and content of these principles has varied across time and across different humanitarian agencies. Furthermore, the effect of these principles on their protection work is mediated by external influences and their respective organizational cultures. The ICRC believes that strict adherence to principles will enable it to be more effective in its protection work in the long term, whereas UNHCR is more pragmatic on a case-by-case basis, seeing less connection between its adherence or non-adherence to principles in one context today, and its ability to work in another context now or in the future. As a consequence, in the face of obstacles to their implementation, or competing influences and objectives, UNHCR is more likely than the ICRC to abandon, ignore, or flexibly interpret one or more of these principles. This chapter takes each of these four principles in turn, analysing how these principles are explicitly or implicitly contested, how the ICRC and UNHCR interpret and implement them in practice, what challenges they face in seeking to apply them in Colombia, Myanmar, and the DRC, and how these interpretations and challenges affect their protection work.

HUMANITY

The principle of humanity requires that all humans, simply by virtue of being human, be treated humanely. Reflecting the *raison d'être* of humanitarian action, it is a moral principle, the ultimate end of such action, and it emphasizes the universality of the human condition and the importance of empathy. It is our shared humanity that both inspires and requires us to help others; we should do so because they are human and we are human. Their lives should be saved and their suffering alleviated with dignity and respect. According to the 'fundamental principles of the Red Cross', articulated in 1965, and on which other humanitarian agencies have drawn, the principle of humanity requires its adherents 'to prevent and alleviate human suffering wherever it may be found. Its purpose is to protect life and health and to ensure respect for the human being. It promotes mutual understanding, friendship, co-operation and lasting peace amongst all peoples' (Pictet 1979).[1]

It is generally uncontroversial to suggest that we should value human lives and dignity, and treat all human beings with respect. It is a principle which, in its abstract form, is subscribed to by all international humanitarian agencies and meets little explicit resistance from affected communities, states, and armed groups. However, Craig Calhoun has argued that such a principle is not in fact universal, resting as it does on modern, Western conceptions 'of individuals as equivalent to each other, all deserving of modern recognition . . . To imagine human beings in the abstract, as it were, in their mere humanity, disembedded from kinship, religion, nationality and other webs of identity is not universal' (Calhoun 2009: 5). Moreover, if it is largely uncontroversial in theory, there does exist some contestation over the interpretation of the principle in practice. Specifically, Hugo Slim has highlighted two 'heresies' in the way that this principle has been interpreted—or, in his words, distorted—by several international humanitarian actors, the first of which 'commodifies humanitarianism and relates it solely to material help', and the second of which 'tends towards making humanitarianism non-negotiable in war' (Slim 1997: 345). He argues that the principle of humanity should be understood as requiring respect for the whole human being, rather than just his physical welfare, and that the notion of a non-negotiable 'humanitarian imperative' may 'undermine the very serious negotiation which needs to take place between warring leaders and humanitarians to ensure that humanitarian action is fair' (Slim 1997: 346).

Both of these heresies are especially relevant in thinking about protection. The first heresy is salient because the 'humanitarian protection agenda is not susceptible to the commodity-based approach that tends to characterise humanitarian assistance, nor to the kind of quantitative analysis that may underpin it' (Darcy and Hofmann 2003: 6). Protection is not a physical item and cannot be equated with material help or understood as a commodity to be delivered. Humanitarian action that emphasizes material help and the provision of commodities risks interpreting humanity in such a way as to produce well-fed dead, raped, or intimidated. Furthermore, even protection efforts that

[1] Jean Pictet joined the ICRC as a legal secretary in 1937 and remained with the organization until his retirement in 1984, by which time he held the position of vice-president. He proposed the Movement's seven Fundamental Principles. The other three are voluntarism, unity, and universality, but these three apply more to the national societies than to the ICRC.

do move away from the purely material may emphasize bare life and de-emphasize dignity and respect, ignoring the whole being. The second heresy is pertinent because protection activities are, almost by definition, carried out in insecure areas. They may also be more likely to be perceived as political (Pantuliano and O'Callaghan 2006: 18). Such insecurity and perceptions of political involvement are expected to increase the need for negotiation between armed actors and humanitarian agencies.

In theory, the ICRC does not commit these heresies. Indeed, Slim defines the heresies against the orthodoxy of the ICRC articulation and understanding of humanity. Thus, some of the interviewees for this book emphasized the holistic approach taken by the ICRC, highlighting the connections between different aspects of their work, and how that enables them to devise a multidisciplinary response to the concrete needs of the victims: one victim can have several needs, and the ICRC may not be able to address all of them, but they would try to give a multidimensional response, and perhaps also refer the victim to other actors. In practice, however, providing material help is often more achievable than initiatives focused on physical safety, and negotiating with armed actors is not always straightforward. Therefore, while the ICRC may remain true to humanity as an objective, the principle is just that—an objective and an ideal, rather than something that is always (or ever) achieved. UNHCR, like many agencies, sometimes emphasizes material assistance, as we shall see in Chapter 6. Moreover, much of what it sets out to achieve is at least one step removed from those it ultimately seeks to help, focusing instead on legal and public policy initiatives (see Chapter 4). Such an approach risks offering a one-size-fits-all solution for everyone, regardless of individual needs and questions of dignity and respect.

When it comes to negotiation with armed actors, the ICRC is also usually ahead of other international humanitarian agencies. As shall be seen in Chapters 5 and 6, the ICRC engages in constant dialogue with armed actors, both for the purposes of negotiating access, and with the aim of improving the conduct of those actors towards civilians. UNHCR also recognizes the need for negotiation with warring parties in order to secure access. Indeed, for UNHCR this is the primary purpose of any such negotiation. However, UNHCR does not engage with armed actors anywhere near as consistently as does the ICRC, and often sees negotiating access as the responsibility of other UN actors.

IMPARTIALITY

The principle of impartiality further specifies and operationalizes the principle of humanity. It does so by making explicit the universality of the humanity principle, and by providing concrete criteria to guide its practical application

(Slim 2015). Impartiality in humanitarian action requires that humanitarian action be undertaken on the basis of need and need alone, with no discrimination as to nationality, race, religious beliefs, class, or political opinions. We can see the principle of impartiality in Henri Dunant's efforts to provide assistance to wounded soldiers *of both sides* at the Battle of Solferino. It is based on notions of non-discrimination and proportionality of response, requiring the prioritization of the most urgent needs. As such, impartiality can be understood as both a means and an end, and as of a higher order than the principles of neutrality and independence, which are primarily operational rather than moral principles. Impartiality can be applied at different levels: at the global level or in specific countries or even sub-country contexts; and in terms of the sector-wide response or the response of an individual agency. Implementing impartiality at the global level is primarily a question of how human and financial resources are allocated to different country contexts. At the global level, then, the headquarters of each organization can make a global comparison, incorporating needs assessments from all countries of operations to set a budget and work programme for the year which allocates resources according to the level of need in each country. Within any given country, impartiality is a question both of how to distribute resources geographically, and of what kinds of sectors and activities to focus on in each location. Impartiality is uncontroversial in contemporary mainstream (Western) discourses of humanitarianism, and is implicitly understood as being of both intrinsic and instrumental value. While the value or desirability of the norm is thus largely uncontested, its application in practice reveals (mainly implicit) contestation over its content and meaning.

Interpretations of Impartiality

Different agencies often have different specializations in terms of both populations of concern and the kinds of needs addressed, and the resulting division of labour across the sector is not necessarily in accordance with need. At the level of each individual agency, these specializations can be seen to impose certain parameters on their interpretations of impartiality. For example, UNICEF and Save the Children focus on the rights and needs of children, regardless of whether adults in a particular context have greater needs. The Mines Advisory Group works specifically to clear landmines and other unexploded ordnance, regardless of whether guns pose a greater threat than mines. Similarly, the ICRC and UNHCR are mandated to protect particular categories of person, and thus they understand impartiality vis-à-vis those categories of person, rather than in reference to humankind as a whole. The categories of person with whom both the ICRC and UNHCR are concerned have expanded over time, but they remain far from universal. As such, the mandates and specializations of the ICRC and UNHCR imply particular interpretations of impartiality.

The ICRC mandate was originally limited to wounded and sick combatants, and subsequently expanded to include prisoners of war and civilians. The ICRC interpretation of impartiality now entails institutional concern with all victims of armed conflict, as well as many victims of organized violence that falls below the threshold for armed conflict. With respect to the civilian population specifically, the ICRC is concerned with all civilians affected by conflict or violence. Singling out a subset of conflict victims such as IDPs is seen to contradict the principle of impartiality, because it may result in IDPs being prioritized over non-displaced civilians with greater needs (Aeschlimann 2005: 26; ICRC 2011b: 49). Nonetheless, the ICRC does restrict its activity to assisting those affected by violence. In other words, the ICRC views impartiality through a conflict and violence lens.

UNHCR is concerned with people affected by displacement, originally refugees narrowly defined, then refugees more broadly defined (in terms of the reasons for which they left their country, but nonetheless still limited to those outside their country of origin), and subsequently including those displaced within their country of origin (IDPs). Having taken on coordination responsibilities for IDP protection under the cluster approach, UNHCR has two overlapping populations of concern, and differing responsibilities for each. Those at 'risk of displacement' fit within the coordination responsibilities of UNHCR as cluster lead for protection, whereas the personal responsibilities of UNHCR (and hence its own protection policies and programmes) are first and foremost for actual IDPs, albeit including support for host communities or non-displaced populations in areas of return (UNHCR 2007c: 6). As the mandate of UNHCR has expanded, there has been a discursive shift regarding the objects of its protection work. While the organization once limited itself to the terms 'refugees' and 'asylum seekers', from the mid-1990s to the mid-2000s it commonly referred to 'persons of concern to UNHCR', and by 2010 the favoured phrase was 'people on the move' (Crisp 2010). In defining who is of concern to UNHCR, the cross-border and persecution elements of refugeehood have lost their salience, but the notions of movement and forced displacement remain central. Impartiality is thus understood through a forced migration lens: UNHCR seeks to attend to forced migrants according to need, but not to those unaffected by displacement, even if they have equal or greater protection needs.

Beyond focusing on particular categories of person, the ICRC and UNHCR also focus on particular types of needs, again in keeping with the respective lenses through which they understand protection and impartiality. For the ICRC, the victims of conflict are to be protected from 'danger, suffering or abuse of power' (Bugnion 2003: xxxii). In other words, they are to be protected from the threats posed by the perpetrators of violence, in particular those in power, or in ICRC terminology, the authorities (which, for the ICRC, extends beyond legal authorities to include non-state parties to conflict). The ICRC was inspired by the witnessing of a battle. From the outset, its *raison d'être* was mitigating the consequences of organized violence, and central to its vision for doing so was the idea of working in the midst of conflict. Thus, within the issue-area of civilian protection, the ICRC seeks to protect all civilians, and it seeks to protect them from the negative consequences of conflict and organized violence. This understanding of the objectives of protection runs through all of the issue-areas the ICRC addresses. Indeed, issues relating to conflict and violence are core to the identity of the ICRC, and also key to how they define their aims.

Likewise, the notion of forced displacement is central not only in defining who is of concern to UNHCR, but also in defining the understanding of what those people are to be protected against. The note of a May 2007 consultative meeting between UNHCR and Excom sums this up: 'The overall goals of UNHCR's protection activities are to assist governments to ensure that IDPs are not discriminated against for reasons related to their displacement, have access to the same rights as other citizens, and that their specific displacement related protection needs are met' (UNHCR 2007f, para. 31). While this notion is rarely stated so explicitly, implicit in UNHCR doctrine as a whole is the idea that IDPs and those at risk of displacement are to be protected from forced displacement and the impact of forced displacement. It is not the impact of violence or conflict per se, but the impact of displacement with which UNHCR is primarily concerned. The underlying idea here is that those affected by displacement should not be adversely affected by that displacement, and should be able to enjoy the same rights as those unaffected by displacement.[2] In sum, the ICRC focuses on needs arising from conflict and violence, while UNHCR focuses on needs that are specific to displacement.

Challenges to Working Impartially

Beyond institutional mandates, impartiality may be modified or compromised when it comes into conflict with other goals or norms, and, in some cases, implementation is constrained by other actors. At all levels, allocating resources in proportion to need depends on a number of factors.

First, it requires information on the level and type of needs. However, needs assessment usually depends on physical presence in a country, which may lead to a bias in favour of those countries in which humanitarian agencies are

[2] I refer to those 'affected by displacement' rather than simply IDPs, as UNHCR also concerns itself with communities which host IDPs and refugees and which may be adversely affected by the inflows.

already operating (Olsen, Carstensen, and Høyen 2003). Even when the level of analysis is the country rather than the global level, impartiality depends on comprehensive needs assessment, which in turn depends on complete information about needs. Such information is not a very realistic prospect in most conflict contexts (Knox Clarke and Darcy 2014: 19–21). For example, one of the interviewees for this book cited an incident in which an international NGO operating in Rakhine State in Myanmar had taken some Muslims for medical treatment. Later, the Rakhine community complained that they did not take some Buddhists who also required treatment. However, no one had alerted the NGO to the fact the Buddhists needed medical care. When we move from thinking about individual agencies to the whole humanitarian sector, the picture is further complicated. Implementing impartiality at the sector-wide level requires each agency to have knowledge not only about what needs exist, but also about what needs other agencies are meeting. At the local or country level, agencies do seek to fill gaps, avoid overlap, and think about how and where they can add most value, but often lack sufficient information.

Second, implementation of the principle of impartiality requires that the measures of needs are comparable, in order to know which to prioritize and where to devote more or less resources. However, it is not at all clear whether people with acute malnutrition, for example, are more or less 'in need' than people facing daily threats of violence from an armed group. Furthermore, needs assessment with respect to protection as opposed to material needs may be more problematic and less amenable to quantification: theoretically, it is possible to rank a population in order of nutritional needs, for example, but it is much more difficult to determine whose security is most at risk. Even if it were possible to assess and rank needs, funding is often earmarked for specific activities and for specific parts of a given country.

Third, then, impartiality requires that donors either fund different country operations and different sectors in proportion to their respective levels of need (and the different costs of meeting those needs) or that they provide flexible funding that operational agencies can allocate in accordance with their own needs assessment. Certainly such an approach would be in line with the principles on Good Humanitarian Donorship (Harmer, Cotterrell, and Stoddard 2004). However, in practice it often does not work like that. Thus, in June 2014, for example, the ICRC sought to highlight its top six underfunded operations, which included Colombia and Myanmar. With respect to Myanmar, interviewees noted that there is a particular challenge in raising funds for a country which previously barely featured on the ICRC budget, and the ICRC does not want to commence activities that it will not be able to sustain. Even with un-earmarked funding, humanitarian agencies may face incentives to allocate that funding otherwise than according to need. A desire to maintain or increase their level of funding may lead agencies to base their decisions about which countries to operate in more on market-based considerations than on where there is insufficient coverage by other organizations. Hence we see a scramble by international humanitarian organizations to be present and visible in the most high-profile contexts, and a relative lack of interest in so-called forgotten emergencies.

Fourth, access to affected populations—necessary not only for the purposes of needs analysis but also for the provision of aid or the practice of protection activities—is in many cases limited by geographical and logistical constraints, by legal and bureaucratic restrictions, or by violent opposition. Different combinations of these types of constraint have limited the work of both the ICRC and UNHCR in the three country operations that are the focus of this book.

In Colombia, there was little explicit objection to the work of humanitarian agencies in general, though in parts of the country the label 'NGO' was equated with 'left-wing', 'guerrilla-sympathizer', which made NGOs unpopular with certain segments of the population and sometimes subject to threats from certain armed actors. While this had not directly affected the ICRC or UNHCR, it demonstrates the potential for opposition to humanitarian work. Individuals and organizations working on sensitive issues such as land reform often faced threats and restrictions on their work. Nonetheless, both the ICRC and UNHCR considered Colombia to be a near ideal working environment, and part of the reason for this was the relatively good access they both had. In 2010, when interviews for this book were undertaken in Colombia, both organizations had access to almost every part of the country. However, this had not always been the case. In 2002, for example, the ICRC stopped moving in certain areas because of security concerns. Beyond security concerns, the distances and terrain in some regions made access difficult.

Access is not simply a matter of being able to be physically present in a particular place: it is also a matter of being able to interact with those actors deemed important in protection. For both the ICRC and UNHCR, access to communities and interlocutors from within the Colombian state was relatively easy, while access to armed non-state actors was more difficult. UNHCR, together with all organizations apart from the ICRC and at times the Catholic Church, was prohibited from having contact with the non-state armed groups. The ICRC could liaise with any of the armed groups, and sought to engage with all of them. However, contact with the guerrilla groups was in practice more limited than contact with the army because the guerrillas were on the defensive and would not stay in the same place for long. At the time the interviews for this book were undertaken, the AUC had formally demobilized and relations between the ICRC and the neo-paramilitary groups were at an early stage.

In the DRC, for both the ICRC and UNHCR, there was very little formal restriction on access to communities and interlocutors, and challenges to access had more to do with terrain, weather, and military operations. In general, targeted attacks were not an issue for teams in the field, but if there were military operations, then security concerns prevented access. In other words, the problem was general instability rather than threats directed specifically at humanitarian workers. Indeed some interviewees specifically reported that they had no problems getting security guarantees from both the military and armed non-state actors in the DRC. Nonetheless, access to parts of the DRC was restricted by the terrain and the weather. In the rainy season in particular, many places were rendered inaccessible. Among armed groups, the state, and affected communities, there did not seem to be specific objections to impartial humanitarian action in the DRC. However, in the context of vast inequality between wealthy Western organizations such as the ICRC and UNHCR on the one hand, and local communities on the other, the act of prioritizing those with greatest need can generate hostile reactions from those who seek assistance but have lesser needs, and who are disappointed to receive little or no support from these rich organizations.

Of the three countries under study, the ICRC and UNHCR both faced the greatest challenges to impartial action in Myanmar. In some parts of the country, for example in Kachin state, the terrain and weather also made access difficult for at least some of the year. Across the country, access to many places was made more difficult by bureaucratic restrictions and in some places also because of security concerns. International actors such as the ICRC and UNHCR were not permitted to travel to many non-government-controlled areas or to parts of Rakhine state without travel authorizations from the government. It could take two months for a travel authorization to be granted, and in some cases access to particular areas was denied. Consequently, ICRC and UNHCR activities were sometimes delayed or cancelled. The official reason for this travel authorization policy was to ensure the security of the staff of the international humanitarian organizations, but in reality it was a way in which the government could exercise control over their movements. In Rakhine state, government restrictions were compounded by hostility from several among the Rakhine community. Some Rakhine Buddhist hardliners did not want any assistance to be provided to the Rohingya Muslim population, and there were many within the Rakhine population who were hostile to international humanitarian action. In March 2014, the Sittwe offices of a number of international humanitarian agencies, including the ICRC, were attacked.

Getting agreement on the principle of impartiality proved difficult or impossible in a context of enormously unequal needs. Although reliable numbers were hard to come by, it was estimated that less than 5 per cent of IDPs in Rakhine state were Buddhist, with the vast majority being Rohingya Muslim. There were also a number of isolated villages, both Buddhist and Muslim, whose populations faced restrictions on movement, and consequently lacked access to livelihoods. Muslim villages may have been affected in greater number, but Rakhine residents were also affected by the deteriorating economy, and by movement restrictions, including curfews in some places, or de facto restrictions where their own village was surrounded by Muslim villages. In short, there were needs on both sides, but those needs were highly unequal. As such, the principle of impartiality requires that the Muslim population receives correspondingly greater support and assistance. However, impartiality is international humanitarian-speak. The local authorities and Buddhist community did not talk in terms of impartiality but in terms of a 'balanced approach'. They insisted that humanitarian organizations should assist the communities equally, but would not discuss what 'equal' meant. For many, it clearly represented a demand to offer the same level of support and assistance to the Buddhist communities as was provided to the Muslim communities.

ICRC and UNHCR Strategies to Overcome These Obstacles

While external factors certainly pose a number of obstacles to impartial action, these obstacles are not entirely exogenously determined, and in the face of such obstacles and objections to impartial humanitarian action, the ICRC and UNHCR adopt a number of strategies to overcome them, in particular in order to gain access and acceptance for their work. Some of the strategies sometimes involve compromising other principles, and sometimes impartiality itself may be compromised in pursuit of other goals.

With respect to obstacles to collecting adequate information for needs assessment, for example, the ICRC might look to different sources from normal. Ordinarily, the ICRC conducts its own needs assessments, and in doing so draws mainly on information gained by being present in, and talking to, affected communities. However, at the time of interviews in Myanmar, the ICRC was just beginning to establish itself in the north-east of the country, and lacked sufficient presence and contact with communities to assess needs. In the absence of first-hand information, the ICRC was relying on the government for information on where the most significant needs existed. Such an approach carries with it the risk that the needs identified by the government—or indeed by any actor with a stake in the conflict—are not the greatest and most urgent, but rather those that the government itself prioritizes. There are two aspects to this risk. On the one hand, there is a danger that the government may direct the ICRC to communities that do not have pressing needs. If this happens, it should quickly be apparent to delegates, and if they realized through their own assessment that the government information was wrong, they would rethink their reliance on the government for needs assessment. On the other hand, there is a danger that the government may *not* direct the ICRC to communities that do have extremely pressing needs. However, given the scale of needs and the limits of the ICRC response at this early stage, delegates were in any case fully aware that there were many serious needs that they could not yet address.

In terms of access, presence, and acceptance, different protection actors gain different levels of access as a result of different methods, reputations, and attitudes. Humanitarian space is something to be proactively created by humanitarian agencies (Abild 2010). The ICRC and UNHCR undertake different strategies in their efforts to secure access to populations in need of protection, and other actors deemed instrumental to that protection. In many contexts, UNHCR has less access than the ICRC, and often UNHCR regards negotiating access as the responsibility of UN OCHA rather than a task for UNHCR staff themselves. Furthermore, access to populations of concern is not generally seen as so important for UNHCR as for the ICRC. However, it is not clear whether access restrictions have shaped the approach, or whether an approach less centred on access to affected communities and armed actors has led UNHCR to pay correspondingly less attention to negotiating and generating access.

Access to populations at risk and proximity to victims and armed actors are central to the ICRC approach, and delegates described access as 'pre-protection' and a 'condition *sine qua non*'. Presence is seen as necessary for four main (and interrelated) reasons: (1) to be able to undertake political and conflict analysis; (2) to build trust with the communities and the armed groups; (3) to collect information from the communities; and (4) to be able to present that information to the armed groups and to persuade them to change their behaviour. The ICRC takes access not as a given, but as an objective that the organization must work to achieve. ICRC delegates have a clear idea of how they generate acceptance through effective programming, neutrality, confidentiality, and transparency, and the sense that it works fairly well in Colombia and the DRC. However, it is seen as a constant work in progress. UNHCR also does not consider access to be entirely exogenously determined, but UNHCR does not have such a clear strategy, nor does it take such a proactive stance, for generating that access. Indeed, UNHCR staff often talk about access as something beyond their control. ICRC strategies are more deliberate and thought out, while UNHCR has a less clearly defined and articulated strategy for generating acceptance and access. We can, nonetheless, observe three general methods employed by both organizations, namely effectiveness, communications, and reliance on partner organizations.

For the ICRC, access is understood to be determined by acceptance of the organization by the government, armed actors, and local communities themselves. Acceptance, in turn, is perceived to result primarily from demonstrating the benefits of ICRC work—both for the communities and the combatants—and by maintaining neutrality and confidentiality (Geremia 2009: 5). Presence and visibility are also seen as vital, so that something of a cycle is constructed: access facilitates presence, visibility, and practical humanitarian action; and that visibility and action also generate acceptance and trust, which in turn contribute to further access. Access is thus dependent on adherence to principles but also on trust and effectiveness. At the time of interviews, this virtuous cycle of access–presence–action–visibility–trust–acceptance was seen in Colombia, but was not yet in spin in Myanmar, and so delegates there placed greater emphasis on strategies aimed specifically at extending access and anchoring presence.

While UNHCR does not for the most part conceptualize effectiveness as a means to securing access and acceptance quite so clearly and consistently as does the ICRC, it does in fact adopt related strategies. In Colombia, for example, one UNHCR interviewee reported that for the communities in that particular zone, it was so important that UNHCR could go on missions there that community leaders would always check with the relevant armed groups, and if there was something going on that made it unsafe for UNHCR to come, the communities would tell them to postpone the mission. Implicit in this, then, is the idea that because UNHCR's work is valuable to affected communities, those communities will do what they can to make it safe for UNHCR, hence extending access. In Myanmar in the early years of the twenty-first century, a more explicit logic underpinned UNHCR efforts to extend access and (government) acceptance of its work by being useful to the government and by not engaging in any activities that the government wanted to avoid. While being useful in this way is not the same as being effective, the idea that certain activities can help extend access and presence is nonetheless related.

On the one hand, the ICRC sees effectiveness as key, and the work of the ICRC is expected to speak for itself. On the other hand, ICRC staff emphasize the importance of communications activities with military forces, non-state armed groups, and affected communities. These communications activities encompass explaining the work of the ICRC and its principled approach, and are aimed at gaining acceptance for its work. Again, UNHCR does not appear to have such a consistent policy on communication, and in some cases relies on OCHA to undertake such communication and negotiation on its behalf. However, in some contexts UNHCR does seek to increase access and acceptance for its work through communicating directly with affected populations, community groups, and—on occasion—armed actors.

In both Colombia and the DRC, the ICRC seems to be generally well received as a neutral, impartial actor, but interviewees emphasized that acceptance was a perpetual work in progress. Delegates always bear in mind the perceptions of different stakeholders, and these perceptions are not fixed. For example, interviewees noted that young people in the army or a non-state armed group may not know the ICRC and its mandate, even if their leaders do. ICRC staff thus always stop and talk to people to explain who they are and what they do. In parts of the DRC, for example, there are not really objections to principles, but what is easily understandable for ICRC staff internally has to be explained to interlocutors in the field because there are potential misunderstandings that need to be avoided. In Myanmar, much of the dialogue the ICRC was engaged in with the authorities was really a pre-protection dialogue focused on gaining acceptance for ICRC presence.

In Rakhine state in particular, there were objections to impartiality, as explained above, but there was also a lack of understanding by both the local community and the government of what impartiality entails. In order to address both the misunderstanding of, and objections to, impartiality, one method employed by both the ICRC and UNHCR was constant communication with local authorities and communities to reiterate the meaning of impartiality. Both organizations were constantly explaining their impartiality, but it was unclear how much currency this had in Rakhine state. Notably, in February 2014, MSF was ordered to leave Myanmar, with the government claiming that the organization prioritized the treatment of Rohingya Muslims over Buddhists in Rakhine (BBC News 2014). For the ICRC, a key difference from other contexts was that communications activities were directed primarily at the communities instead of armed actors. As anywhere else, delegates would explain the fundamental principles of the Red Cross and the mandate of the ICRC. Although the interlocutors were different from 'normal'—monks' organizations and women's groups do not look much like armed groups—the dialogue regarding the ICRC history, mandate, and principles was exactly the same. Ultimately, ICRC staff members would explain that it is the authorities who validate ICRC presence, and that as the authorities had validated it, the communities had to accept it. In addition, they would ask whether these community groups or representatives had any suggestions of where assistance was needed; if needs were identified and the ICRC deemed them to be valid, then it would respond to those needs with the aim of generating acceptance.

Both the ICRC and UNHCR also work with partner organizations where that is expected to help extend access. In the case of the ICRC, this is primarily the national societies of the Red Cross and Red Crescent Movement, and for UNHCR, this includes other UN agencies as well as NGOs that are either members of the protection cluster or implementing partners of UNHCR. In government-controlled areas of Myanmar, for example, the Myanmar Red Cross Society (MRCS) was very useful for the ICRC in terms of security, information, and access, and this institutional relationship was deemed to be a big advantage for reaching areas that UN agencies and INGOs might not be able to go to. UNHCR tends to rely heavily on OCHA to negotiate access. In Myanmar, OCHA was coordinating and applying for travel authorizations on behalf of many humanitarian actors, including INGOs, UN agencies, and local NGOs. In addition, UNHCR interviewees made it clear that OCHA was responsible for contacts with extremist elements in Rakhine state. In the DRC, UNHCR interviewees also saw access as being the responsibility of OCHA, particularly with reference to gaining access and establishing contact with non-state armed groups. UNHCR was also using MONUSCO transport and escorts to access areas it would otherwise have had problems getting to. In Myanmar, as in many contexts, UNHCR was delegating work to national NGOs. Given that UNHCR had little or no access to most non-government-controlled areas in Myanmar, national NGOs were UNHCR's eyes and ears on the ground. However, this approach was not deemed to be entirely satisfactory, given that, in Kachin state, for example, the NGOs did not offer sufficient coverage.

In many cases, there are tensions between different principles and goals, and compromises must be made. For instance, at the level of implementation, a trade-off may be struck between impartiality on the one hand, and efficiency and effectiveness on the other. In 2005, for example, the ICRC changed its approach in Colombia from generalist coverage of the country to priority zones. The organization then began to focus its presence and activities on areas in which there are greatest needs or risks, and where the ICRC can have greatest impact. This, in turn, is seen to depend on where the ICRC can develop contacts with the armed groups, and where there is an absence of other international actors undertaking similar work. On the one hand, such an approach is based on an assessment of needs, and to that extent it is in keeping with the principle of impartiality (which requires the ICRC to focus its efforts according to, and in proportion to, need). On the other hand, incorporating consideration of impact may be at odds with impartiality if the greatest needs are also the hardest to address.

Given the extreme inequality of needs in Rakhine, it was a challenge for humanitarian agencies to work impartially. As one interviewee put it, it was a 'bit of an art' to make sure both sides got the assistance they needed. In practice it seems that, in order to facilitate acceptance of the agencies and their work, some kind of compromise is often struck between providing assistance in proportion to need and providing equal assistance to each community. Thus, in addition to providing assistance to those with the greatest needs, they may also offer visible assistance to those with lesser needs but from the other community, in order to demonstrate that they are committed to an approach that does not favour either community.

The explicit objections to impartial humanitarian action were specific to Rakhine state. However, elsewhere in Myanmar, there were other challenges to working impartially, relating in particular to relations with the government. In Kayah state, for example, UNHCR wanted to install water points in five particular villages, where the greatest needs were identified, and the government wanted them to install them in five other villages. UNHCR staff negotiated to do all ten villages, demonstrating pragmatic flexibility, rather than a rigid commitment to impartiality. In a sense this kind of compromise can be seen as a second best to responding directly in proportion to needs, operating a sort of maxi-min principle, whereby in order to meet the most severe needs (i.e. maximizing the welfare of the worst off), they expend additional resources on other activities which do not necessarily respond to the next greatest or most urgent needs, and which may thus divert resources which could otherwise be used to address the next greatest needs. Elsewhere, government restrictions meant UNHCR did not have regular access to non-government-controlled areas. Thus, UNHCR was operating cross-line missions in Kachin state. These missions were used to do workshops, deliver assistance, and to talk to the KIO/A. They were distinguished from convoys to indicate longer-term or more regular delivery of assistance, but they were not considered a good substitute for regular presence

In sum, the meaning given to the principle of impartiality is shaped by the core identity of the organization, itself a product of institutional history. Thus, the ICRC understands impartiality as pertaining to the violence-related needs of those affected by conflict and other forms of organized violence, while UNHCR understands impartiality in terms of the displacement-related needs of those affected by, or at risk of, displacement. Whatever the basic meaning, implementing the principle of impartiality is far from straightforward. Imperfect information about needs and a variety of financial, political, and practical constraints make it difficult or impossible to act impartially at every level. Some of the paths taken by both the ICRC and UNHCR in an effort to overcome these obstacles risk compromising neutrality, which suggests that the envisaged relationship between these two principles is not straightforward in practice. In theory, neutrality and impartiality work together. Certainly, a lack of impartiality can be perceived as non-neutral. But on the other hand, implementing impartiality often depends on the staff of humanitarian agencies getting physical access to affected populations and, as we shall see in the next section, the methods they employ to achieve such access sometimes sit uncomfortably with the practice of neutrality.

NEUTRALITY

The principle of neutrality requires that its adherents do not take sides with any of the warring parties in a conflict, and that their work and assistance do not lend support to any one side or another. In contrast to the principle of impartiality, the appropriateness of neutrality for international humanitarian organizations is often explicitly contested. In addition, the meaning and content of the principle is implicitly—and occasionally explicitly—contested by those who seek to apply it. Different organizations interpret and implement the principle in different ways. Indeed, Barbara Ann Rieffer-Flanagan suggests that neutrality is an essentially contested concept: it implies not lending support to one or other side in a conflict, but beyond that its contents are context-specific and contested (Rieffer-Flanagan 2009: 892).

Perspectives on Neutrality

As the value and appropriateness of neutrality have increasingly been questioned, some agencies have chosen to abandon the principle in favour of taking a political stand, sometimes rearticulating their position as one of solidarity or political humanitarianism (Fox 2001; Leader 2000; Slim 1997; Weiss 1999). Arguments in favour of neutral humanitarian action mainly revolve around access. Neutrality is not usually deemed to be of intrinsic value, but rather as instrumental to the access and presence demanded by impartiality, itself an operationalization of the principle of humanity. Arguments for abandoning the principle of neutrality take various forms. On the one hand, many have made the case that it is impossible to be truly neutral, and that humanitarian actors will always affect the contexts and conflicts in which they operate, whatever their intentions. A good deal of existing work has shown how the provision of material assistance and protective measures for the victims of war can and does impact on the course of war (Anderson 1999; Lischer 2005; Stedman and Tanner 2003; Terry 2002). This inability to be neutral in practice combined with the Kantian ethical notion that 'ought implies can' can be taken to suggest that humanitarian agencies ought not to be neutral. However, if we understand neutrality as an operational principle that facilitates acceptance and access rather than an ethical choice in itself, applying the Kantian maxim is inappropriate.

If neutrality is an instrumental rather than a moral principle, the salient question is whether or not neutrality (or trying to be neutral) does in fact facilitate access. There is a lack of compelling evidence as to whether neutrality has any significant impact on staff security and humanitarian access in general (Fast 2010). A further argument against neutrality suggests that it is intrinsically undesirable, on the basis that humanitarians should speak out against abuses (de Waal 1994). Despite significant rhetorical contestation over the value of neutrality, many, if not most, of the major international humanitarian agencies maintain a commitment to neutrality, even if each interprets the principle differently in practice.

The ICRC in particular has consistently sought to defend its commitment to neutrality against such criticism (Harroff-Tavel 1989, 2003; Sommaruga 1999). The central role of neutrality in the work of the ICRC can be traced to two particular roots. First, from the very first discussions in Geneva in 1863 regarding the provision of aid to wounded soldiers on the battlefield, the question of whether belligerent nations would accord neutral status to hospitals and ambulances was an issue (Hutchinson 1996: 35–8, 43–4). In this sense, neutrality is not a principle of conduct of the medical staff but rather a protected status, or an undertaking *by belligerents* not to attack medical facilities. However, such an undertaking would not be upheld for very long by one side in a conflict if the medical staff and facilities were seen to be operating to the military advantage of the enemy side. Hence, the corollary of this undertaking by the combatants is an undertaking by those medical staff—and in contemporary operations by all ICRC staff—to operate without supporting or conferring advantage to one side over another. Second, the ICRC is a Swiss organization which has historically had very close links with the Swiss government, and has undoubtedly been shaped by the norms of Swiss society and politics, including that of neutrality. Neutrality in the ICRC can thus be understood through analogy to neutral states (such as Switzerland) in the context of international conflict, the defining characteristics of neutrality being: a duty of abstention (not providing military assistance to belligerents); a duty of prevention (not allowing its resources to be used for military purposes); and a duty of impartiality (applying equally to all sides in a conflict those rules according to which it conducts its relationship with combatants) (Plattner 1996). The ICRC only began to employ non-Swiss professional staff in 1992. Even then, it was decided that the Assembly, the top policymaking body of the ICRC, should remain all-Swiss, 'primarily because it guaranteed that in a conflict—assuming the neutral Swiss state was not involved—no one from a fighting party would have any representative on the Assembly' (Forsythe and Rieffer-Flanagan 2007: 4).

In UNHCR, the principle of neutrality is less central, and less absolute, and has been arrived at via a different route, given that the organization's original mandate did not include working in the midst of armed conflict. The Statute of UNHCR stipulates that 'the work of the High Commissioner shall be of an entirely non-political character; it shall be humanitarian and social.'[3] The meanings of the terms 'political' and 'humanitarian' are both contested, as is the distinction between them, and their interpretation by UNHCR has changed over time (Sugino 1998). Originally included in the Statute to minimize tensions between East and West, the non-political nature of the mandate was interpreted as characterizing the institution of asylum and implied that the granting of asylum was not to be seen as a hostile act and was not supposed to create tensions between the sending country and the receiving country. For UNHCR specifically, it meant not criticizing countries of origin and not seeking to manipulate the causes of refugee flows (Sugino 1998: 50–4). This stance changed through the 1980s, and by the end of the Cold War, UNHCR was increasingly involved in countries of origin, and increasingly outspoken about human rights violations. General Assembly resolutions and Excom

[3] *Statute of the Office of the United Nations High Commissioner for Refugees.* 14 December 1950, A/RES/428(V) (1950) para. 2.

conclusions continue to assert the 'non-political and humanitarian' character of UNHCR, but the interpretation of non-political has shifted, and the 1990s saw a new emphasis on neutrality and impartiality (Sugino 1998: 56–8).

ICRC and UNHCR Interpretations of Neutrality

In theory, there are a number of similarities between ICRC and UNHCR interpretations of neutrality. For both, neutrality prohibits involvement in partisan politics and international realpolitik (Forsythe 1977: 1, 2001b: 1; Forsythe and Rieffer-Flanagan 2007: 92). This means that they do not make direct and explicit pronouncements on who should govern, or on the content of public policies and (domestic or international) laws that are not directly related to their respective mandates. However, both the ICRC and UNHCR seek to influence public policy and international law (Forsythe 1977: 2, 2001b: 2). Furthermore, in many cases, lobbying for particular public policy affects power struggles and thus impacts on who governs, because lobbying for acceptance and implementation of public policy to safeguard the worth and welfare of individuals in distress can very often intersect with the strategic or partisan goals of governments (Forsythe 2001a, 2001b: 2). In this sense, then, lobbying for policies to protect IDPs and other civilians cannot be totally separated from the question of who governs. Similarly, the idea that the ICRC and UNHCR do not engage in international politics even as they seek to influence international law rests on an artificial distinction between international law and international politics. In reality, the process by which international law is made is a political process which both impacts on, and is impacted by, state interests (Lowe 2007).

In sum, the ICRC and UNHCR do not seek to engage in partisan politics and international realpolitik, but their pursuit of much narrower protection goals inevitably sometimes has the effect of influencing domestic and international politics. In these abstract terms, ICRC neutrality appears very similar to UNHCR neutrality. However, in practice there are important differences between the two organizations in their interpretation and implementation of neutrality, relating to confidentiality, support for affected states, and relationships with military actors.

For much of the history of the ICRC, the principle of neutrality was mediated by an institutional inclination towards secrecy, and understood as a commitment to confidentiality and discretion. This aspect of the ICRC is in part a product of its Swiss origins. The Swiss commitment to confidentiality, as evidenced by banking and business practices, can also be seen to have influenced the ICRC approach to protection in terms of the institutional preference for confidential, bilateral, and non-confrontational dialogue. The 1975

Tansley Report[4] found that the uncritical commitment to discretion within the ICRC was dysfunctional, and that the ICRC sometimes maintained discretion not because it was necessary (to gain access to conflict victims, for example) but because it was comfortable (ICRC 1978: 326). Thus, the Swiss tradition of discretion and confidentiality can be seen to have been inherited by the ICRC. The ICRC response to the Tansley Report on the issue of discretion was to clarify its policy as to when it should maintain discretion, and when it should speak out about violations of IHL (ICRC 1978, 2005).

Thus, in the contemporary ICRC, confidential dialogue is preferred practice, but not an absolute principle; rather, it is seen as 'proportional to the willingness of the authorities to take into account the ICRC's recommendations' (ICRC 2008b: 758). This conditional confidentiality reflects a rethinking of the ICRC understanding of neutrality in the light of the many criticisms it faced after World War II and in the Tansley Report. It remains the case that discretion is key to ICRC work, but in exceptional circumstances, where confidential bilateral dialogue with those responsible for IHL violations fails to yield tangible results, the ICRC may share information with other actors (for example, third-party governments or human rights organizations) who may be able to influence the behaviour of the relevant (state or non-state) authorities or, in more extreme circumstances, may make a public denunciation of one or more of these authorities (as in Myanmar in 2007). UNHCR does not attach the same importance to confidentiality as does the ICRC, and is more likely to share information with other UN agencies, other non-UN humanitarian agencies, and other non-UN political actors, including other states and their diplomats. At the very least, UNHCR is more open than the ICRC about sharing information externally, but as we shall see in Chapters 5 and 6 both organizations do sometimes share information with other actors.

The ICRC and UNHCR have the same broad objectives with respect to changing state policy and behaviour, but their differing interpretations of neutrality imply two key differences. First, UNHCR sees its role primarily as one of supporting the state, and in many cases offers a much greater level of support than does the ICRC. UNHCR works with states to seek permanent solutions to displacement and in this regard 'is engaged in strengthening national protection capacity, working closely (although not exclusively) with governments' (Tennant, Doyle, and Mazou 2010, para. 30). The emphasis on solutions within UNHCR and the pre-eminence of the state in any such solution result in relationships which would not be considered as neutral by the ICRC, but which are central to the work of UNHCR. Indeed, UNHCR

[4] The Tansley Report, published in 1975 and formally titled 'An Agenda for the Red Cross in 1975', was the final report of a study by a team led by Donald Tansley that reviewed the state of the Red Cross and Red Crescent Movement, and explored the future of the Movement as a whole.

itself recognizes that in internal conflicts, 'such engagement may contribute to a perception that UNHCR is not entirely neutral, and may even be seen as endorsing a particular political or institutional model, or aligning itself with a party to a conflict' (Tennant et al. 2010, para. 31).

In Colombia, for example, UNHCR staff members acknowledged that the mandate to work with the government made it more difficult for UNHCR to remain neutral than for the ICRC. UNHCR seeks to ensure its neutrality by emphasizing that it works with the state, not with the government, and that this means relating to officials as occupiers of a particular role or position, and not as individuals. Such a distinction reflects a Western conception of statehood that assumes that the government is temporary and the state apparatus is distinct from, and independent of, the government. In Colombia, this assumption is relatively unproblematic, but in many of the contexts in which UNHCR operates, the state and government are in fact conflated and this distinction does not hold true. Even in those contexts in which UNHCR provides less direct support to the government, building up health, education, and social services often comprises part of UNHCR's work, and such activities may lend support to the relevant authorities in the area, either because they win the authorities' support among the local population who have better services available, or because they free up the authorities' own resources to be employed in military action. Since UNHCR more often works in government-controlled areas, it is more likely to lend such support to the government than to opposition authorities.

While the state-centric approach of UNHCR makes neutrality particularly difficult, the ICRC is not immune to the difficulties involved in applying neutrality in practice. As we have seen earlier in this chapter, in much of Myanmar, the ICRC was relying heavily on the national society to help expand its reach into new areas. However, the MRCS was very close to the government, and was sometimes seen as part of the state. Indeed, the MRCS would march with the military on parade (MoeOo 2013). This created a potential impediment to ICRC neutrality and perceptions of ICRC neutrality, though the organization had not seen its frequently close working relationship with the MRCS as problematic. Whether or not armed non-state actors in Myanmar perceived the ICRC as less than neutral on account of its relationship with the MRCS was unclear. At the time of interviews, the ICRC had only limited access to non-government-controlled areas in Myanmar—primarily KIO/A-controlled areas. However, the organization had been well received in those areas and this was taken to suggest that the mandate of the ICRC and the corresponding institutional commitment to neutrality had been understood by the KIO/A.

Second, the ICRC counterbalances its interaction with, and support to, the state with interaction with, and support (for the implementation of IHL) to, non-state parties to conflict. For the ICRC, neutrality means maintaining a distinction between military and humanitarian action but does not proscribe contact with military actors; on the contrary, the ICRC seeks as much contact as possible with the armed groups in the contexts in which it is working, and much of its protection work is premised on such contact. For UNHCR, the implications of the institutional commitment to neutrality for its relations with armed actors are context-specific and contested. In Colombia, for example, UNHCR staff are not allowed to interact with the non-state armed groups. Interestingly, several staff members were not aware that this was not the result of a UN directive, but rather a stipulation of the Colombian government.[5] Moreover, many seemed to have merged this ban with their understanding of neutrality, and not talking to armed non-state actors was often described as a way to ensure institutional neutrality.

For some UNHCR staff in Colombia, neutrality also precluded interaction with the police and national military, except to inform them of missions for security purposes. Others felt that there were no such restrictions, but that at the local level they would be careful with contacts with the police and the national military, as well as with extremist leftist elements, because they did not want to be seen as leaning too much to one side or the other. In parts of the country, UNHCR was running workshops on human rights and humanitarian principles with the public forces, and holding meetings with them. However, it would never go out on mission with the military, and if the public forces arrived in a community while UNHCR was there on mission, the UNHCR team would leave. That said, UNHCR did go out on missions with several of the civilian agencies of the state, in particular the Defensoría del Pueblo (Office of the Human Rights Ombudsman), Registraduría (Registry Office) and Procuraduría (Office of the Inspector General). However, in an effort to be perceived as neutral, in many areas UNHCR avoided joint missions with Acción Social, a state agency which plays an important role in the territorial consolidation plan and is a target in some guerrilla areas. In general, UNHCR work with civilian branches of government depended on the context, and in some places security concerns prevented such joint missions altogether. In certain areas of Putumayo department, for example, government projects were banned by the FARC, and in such areas UNHCR would undertake UNHCR-exclusive projects.

In contexts where UN peacekeeping forces are present, UNHCR works with them, whereas the ICRC would not ally with a military force in this way. In the DRC, this means UNHCR was working a lot with MONUSCO. From 2013, with the creation of the 'intervention brigade', MONUSCO had a very strong mandate to eliminate armed groups. The implications of this for UNHCR

[5] The Colombian government prohibited all organizations other than the ICRC (and, at times, the Catholic Church) from having contact with the non-state armed groups (see *El Tiempo*, 15 June 2005).

neutrality were considered to be most critical in the east, because elsewhere MONUSCO was not engaged in military operations. Some UNHCR staff deemed that neutrality obliged the organization to keep a distance from MONUSCO, and sought to put limits on working together, but this view was not universally shared. Ultimately the UN mission in the DRC was an integrated mission, and Joint Protection Teams undertook missions in which UNHCR and other civilian agencies of the UN were working together with MONUSCO.

Two particular concerns about the implications of UNHCR's relationship with MONUSCO were highlighted in interviews. The first relates to the acceptance by UNHCR staff of armed escorts and helicopter transport provided by MONUSCO in the field. One interviewee reported that while he generally refused to go on protection assessments in the field with MONUSCO, because he believed UNHCR should not be seen on mission with a military and non-neutral actor, sometimes 'it's too convenient to go with MONUSCO, in their helicopter, to places you know there are IDPs but wouldn't otherwise be able to access'. UNHCR staff generally sought to work with UNDSS to avoid or minimize the need for MONUSCO escorts, but ultimately there were many red zones they were not allowed to go to without a MONUSCO escort. As a consequence, there was something of a trade-off between neutrality and impartiality. The second concern was about sharing information with MONUSCO. On the one hand, it was understood that they had to share information for a number of reasons. UNHCR staff considered that they needed MONUSCO to inform UNHCR if they were planning an attack, so that UNHCR staff could avoid the area, and potentially evacuate civilians. In addition, UNHCR staff felt they needed to inform MONUSCO if they thought an area was at serious risk, because, if MONUSCO did not go to the area, people would be killed. However, in providing information to MONUSCO, they were giving intelligence to the military, and hence compromising neutrality.

In the DRC these concerns about how UNHCR relations with MONUSCO affected neutrality were described as issues of principle rather than practical issues (whereas in Afghanistan, for example, they would have been seen as practical issues). In other words, UNHCR had not found that working with MONUSCO had created any security problems for staff in the DRC. Some staff security incidents had occurred—but these were judged to have been economically motivated (that is, because UNHCR had big cars and other valuables), not because of UNHCR-specific motivations. Whereas in Colombia, UNHCR deemed neutrality to be of paramount importance to access and staff security, in the DRC this was not seen to be the case. In such a context, where adherence to the principle of neutrality is not seen to be a practical question, UNHCR is content to take a flexible approach to interpreting and implementing the principle.

For the ICRC, then, neutrality is more tightly defined and more strictly adhered to, whereas for UNHCR there is greater flexibility and pragmatism in its application. However, for both organizations there may be a trade-off between neutrality and impartiality, and in most contexts they are faced with a number of challenges to working neutrally and to ensuring that armed actors perceive their work as neutral. Each adopts similar but distinct strategies to work in a way that is both neutral and perceived as such.

ICRC and UNHCR Strategies to Ensure and Demonstrate Neutrality

One way in which the ICRC has traditionally sought to ensure neutrality is by ensuring that most contact with armed actors is by international staff. The rationale behind this is that there is a greater likelihood of national staff members being forced not to be neutral. International staff (and their families) can be out of a country within a few hours if they are seriously threatened, whereas national staff often cannot leave so easily. In addition, national staff may not want to expose issues to their own authorities, and some work may expose them and their families to risk. However, relying on international staff to interact with armed actors also has its drawbacks and in some places the ICRC is moving to be more localized, to have longer expatriate postings, and to emphasize contextual knowledge. Giving more responsibility to local staff is deemed to be advantageous in the sense that they often have greater knowledge and understanding, being part of the situation, and in some contexts these advantages are deemed to outweigh the risks. UNHCR does not have such a fixed policy regarding national and international staff as does the ICRC. Thus, while the head of each ICRC delegation, sub-delegation, and field office is always an expatriate, UNHCR country and field offices may be headed by either national or expatriate staff members. In particular contexts, however, UNHCR does pay careful attention to staffing for reasons of impartiality, perceptions of neutrality, and staff safety. National staff in Myanmar have generally worked for the UN because they were anti-regime, and as such they have been under heavy suspicion from the government. In Rakhine state, national staff were recently arrested and detained for up to six months for the very reason that they were UNHCR staff. In light of this perceived bias against UNHCR, international staff were used as buffers and in that context it would have been very rare to send national staff on mission alone.

The ICRC perspective is that neutrality is necessary, but not sufficient. On the one hand, being neutral is not enough to enable ICRC operations, and the *perception* of neutrality is also assumed to be a precondition for the cherished access to victims and armed actors. On the other hand, genuine neutrality is seen as absolutely essential, because, in the long run, the perception of neutrality is seen to be dependent on being completely neutral in practice. In addition to acting in accordance with the principle of neutrality, the ICRC thus seeks to ensure perceptions of neutrality by maximizing the visibility of its work. ICRC staff do not travel or work in secret; they seek to demonstrate that they have nothing to hide, and in many places they do not travel at night except in an emergency, in which case they contact all the armed groups that they can to let them know. They also seek to be transparent with the armed groups about ICRC activities and to give the armed groups the opportunity to raise any objections to those activities. This is seen as critical to building confidence and trust with the armed groups. In some areas of Colombia, the guerrillas had said the ICRC was not neutral because they would take wounded combatants to the hospital, and the hospitals were obliged to report certain injuries and illnesses to the police, so the combatants risked arrest. In an attempt to remedy this, the ICRC would explain the procedure and let the group decide if it wanted to go ahead with a medical evacuation or not. However, this problem reflects a general difficulty of acting with neutrality in internal conflicts in which states often have greater resources and facilities that non-state armed groups, and in a world in which states are legitimate actors and non-state armed groups are not.

The ICRC also considers it important to be trusted by the communities in which the organization works, and staff tell people only about projects they are actually going to undertake, not what they are thinking about doing. They seek to avoid making promises they cannot keep, and operational effectiveness is seen not only as of intrinsic importance but as instrumental to acceptance by communities and armed groups (Geremia 2009; ICRC 2010b: 13). In short, visibility, transparency, and reliability are all seen to contribute towards trust and the perception of neutrality, which, in turn, are seen to facilitate access. Communication is thus an important element of ICRC work, and delegates explicitly explain the nature of their work, the meanings of neutrality and impartiality, and the importance of these principles. The general consensus among ICRC interviewees was that getting understanding of these principles is always a challenge, but not impossible. In most contexts in which the ICRC works, delegates have the sense that neutrality is broadly understood, and some suggested that after explaining the difference between the ICRC and other actors, it is easier for the ICRC to articulate and demonstrate its neutrality. It is also seen to help that the ICRC is separate from the rest of the humanitarian system, and in particular from the UN.

UNHCR interviewees reported difficulty in getting either government representatives or members of non-state armed groups in Myanmar to understand the principle of neutrality. One interviewee told me that he explained it by saying that UNHCR does not take sides, and does not think the government is better than the non-state actors. However, it may well be the case that actions speak louder than words and that the armed non-state actors struggled not to understand, but to believe, such a sentiment in light of the actual conduct of UNHCR. At the time of interviews, for example, UNHCR always went into the non-government controlled zones in the south-east of Myanmar with an armed government escort. Thus, while the letter of understanding between UNHCR and the government concerning UNHCR work in the south-east specifically mentioned building the capacity of non-state actors, and UNHCR would refuse a government escort (and hence not go themselves) if it meant taking government officials to an area they had never been to before, it is easy to see how UNHCR may have been perceived by non-state actors as non-neutral.

The principle of neutrality is both enabling and constraining, but the particular constraints implied by a commitment to neutrality depend on how that principle is interpreted. For the ICRC, the principle of neutrality is mediated by the organizational tendency towards confidentiality, discretion, and even secrecy, and the resulting interpretation proscribes public denouncement of the behaviour of particular armed actors. The silence thus imposed by the principle of neutrality (though even the ICRC has, on rare occasions, broken this silence, as in Myanmar in 2007, for example) is deemed unacceptable by many agencies (Plattner 1996: 269). On the other hand, it is the same principle of neutrality—and, importantly, the perception of neutrality by combatants and civilians in a conflict context—that is seen to facilitate access to populations in need. It is widely accepted that the ICRC does have greater access to populations in most contexts than other major humanitarian organizations. However, the ICRC does not have unimpeded access across the globe, and there have been deliberate attacks on ICRC staff and compounds, for example, in Chechnya in 1996 and Iraq in 2003 (Stoddard, Harmer, and Haver 2006: 4), with two delegates held hostage in Darfur in 2009–10 (ICRC 2011b: 85), and with the Sittwe office attacked in 2014. Further, even to the extent the ICRC has better access than other organizations, this may be for a variety of reasons, though most assume it is related to the institutional commitment to, and interpretation of, neutrality. Thus, ICRC neutrality is instrumental to the principle of impartiality, and to all of the field-level activities undertaken by the ICRC in the name of protecting and assisting the victims of conflict.

For UNHCR it is clear that neutrality means different things, and that the institutional commitment to it is less absolute. However, it is not always clear when differences arise because the ICRC and UNHCR are interpreting the principle of neutrality differently, and when they arise because UNHCR has sacrificed neutrality to other ends. What is clear is that UNHCR is less restricted than the ICRC in some ways. For both organizations neutrality is seen as being of instrumental rather than intrinsic importance, but the ICRC has a longer-term, more global view. Therefore, even in a context where strict neutrality may not be necessary for reasons of access and staff security, as in the DRC, for example, the ICRC maintains a commitment to strict neutrality, whereas UNHCR is more flexible. As we have seen, for example, UNHCR staff travel with MONUSCO escorts and share information with MONUSCO. Ultimately, getting acceptance of their presence and work does not seem to have been very problematic for either the ICRC or UNHCR in the DRC, and in such a context UNHCR is much more flexible in its application of neutrality. In contexts such as Colombia and Myanmar, UNHCR attaches greater importance to institutional neutrality but, nonetheless, understands it differently from the ICRC, given that it sees its role as one of supporting the state, and given that it does little or no work with armed (state or non-state) actors.

INDEPENDENCE

The principle of independence entails operating independently of influence from other actors, including states and international organizations. This is intended to enable international humanitarian organizations to operate as they see fit, rather than to further the aims of others. In essence, the idea is that if such an organization can act in a way that is free from the influence of other actors, it will be free to work in a neutral and impartial manner. But what does it mean to be free from the influence of other actors? It means having the power to set an agenda according to needs (that is, according to the principle of impartiality), as the organization assesses them, without outside influence. As with all these principles, there is an element of interpretation involved in translating the principle into practice.

One interpretation of independence emphasizes financial independence. Notably, MSF considers its ability to respond independently to any given crisis to derive from its independent funding, approximately 90 per cent of which comes from private sources rather than governments or intergovernmental organizations (MSF 2014: 13). By contrast, both the ICRC and UNHCR rely heavily on voluntary contributions from states, and in practice are financially dependent on a small number of governments. Given their need to compete for these contributions, those donor states may exert an indirect influence on the programming decisions of the ICRC and UNHCR, as they seek to attract funding. In other words, the external institutional environment may incentivize a focus on particular regions, countries, and activities. Furthermore, through earmarking of funding for specific activities or contexts, states may exercise direct influence on the focus of UNHCR operations. In 2012, 60 per cent of ICRC funding was tightly earmarked, and this increased to 64 per cent in 2013 (ICRC 2014a: 530). For UNHCR, the percentage of funding that was tightly earmarked increased from 47 per cent in 2011 to 64 per cent in 2013 (UNHCR 2014b: 113).[6] This kind of earmarking naturally imposes constraints on the scope and focus of ICRC and UNHCR operations.

For the ICRC, independence entails the separation of humanitarian action from political and military action. Independence enables the ICRC to focus its attention on the contexts in which the needs are greatest and without providing support for one or another side in a conflict, because political actors are unable to pressure the organization into directing its efforts elsewhere. The ICRC seeks to ensure its independence through formal independence from any states or political institutions. Thus, the ICRC is not a member of any organization which would require it to yield any formal control of decision-making. The ICRC has observer status at the UN, but would not engage in any relationship that required it to be bound by the decisions of other actors, be they states, IOs, or NGO-coordination bodies. Being part of the UN undoubtedly does impose constraints on UNHCR independence. For example, UNDSS restrictions limited 'access to affected populations, even under escort' in several locations (UNHCR 2007b, para. 31). Moreover, UNHCR may be pressured to undertake particular activities (at the expense of other priorities) in order to support the strategic objectives of other parts of the UN. For example, operations in Afghanistan were expanded in the first half of 2001 because UN partners hoped to use humanitarian assistance by UNHCR to revive failing negotiations with the Taliban (Mattar and White 2005: 11).

While the ICRC is a part of the International Red Cross and Red Crescent Movement, its formal independence within this network does seem to have insulated it from the kind of pressures UNHCR experiences from its status as a UN agency. That said, the ICRC has not always acted independently of influence from the Swiss state (Forsythe 2005: 205–6). In response to criticisms of its silence about the holocaust in World War II, the ICRC admitted that its caution partly arose from a desire not to antagonize Hitler both because that might endanger the work that the ICRC was doing in accordance with existing conventions (for example, for prisoners of war), and because a lack of independence with respect to the Swiss state resulted in a failure to uphold the principle of neutrality because Berne feared German retaliation against the Swiss state if the ICRC spoke out about the concentration camps (Junod 1996: 19; Rieffer-Flanagan 2009: 899). However, I am not aware of any evidence of Switzerland or any other individual state exercising particular influence on ICRC policy and focus since the end of the Cold War. Collectively, of course, states directly and indirectly shape the direction of IHL, and this in turn shapes ICRC policy and practice, as we will see in Chapter 3.

In addition, the work of both the ICRC and UNHCR depends on the consent of the states in which they operate, and this can restrict their ability

[6] See Loescher et al. (2008: 91–7) for analysis of the politics of funding for UNHCR.

to operate in accordance with the principles of impartiality and neutrality. This is discussed in more detail in Chapter 5.

CONCLUSIONS

While humanity is generally seen to be a moral principle or an end in itself, impartiality, neutrality, and independence are mainly understood as operational principles—the means through which humanitarian agencies and their staff can work according to the principle of humanity. Taken together, impartiality, neutrality, and independence are seen to construct humanitarian space, conventionally understood as a space in which humanitarian agents can operate (Thürer 2007). That is to say that they generate access through 'a "deal" whereby the belligerents agree to respect humanitarian principles, and humanitarians will not interfere in conflicts' (Leader 2000: 2). The logic underpinning this deal is that, because activities undertaken according to these principles do not (in theory) pose a threat to combatants, the combatants in turn agree not to pose a threat to humanitarians, and allow them access to particular territory or populations in order do their work. However, as we have seen, in practice these principles do not always work in concert with one another, and adherence to these principles is no guarantee of access.

In addition to tensions between different principles, there can also be tensions between one or more of these principles, and other incentives facing the ICRC and UNHCR. Humanitarian agencies—like other 'moral' agents at the international level—are not *purely* principled actors (Diagne and Entwisle 2008; Prakash and Gugerty 2010). In addition to these principles, the actions of the ICRC and UNHCR are shaped by more interest-based and market-driven motivations. Humanitarian agencies compete for funding, and the 'market' for their services affects what they do and where they do it, sometimes creating perverse incentives such that the agencies in question compete for market share at the expense of their own principles and stated goals (Cooley and Ron 2002; Hopgood 2008; Weiss 2013). Different operational contexts also pose particular challenges to the implementation of these principles in practice. Thus, the ICRC and UNHCR—and indeed all international humanitarian agencies—are constantly balancing principles, practical constraints, market-based considerations, short-term objectives, and long-term objectives.

Institutional culture plays an important mediating role in determining how the organization balances principle and pragmatism, and the balance struck subsequently affects how that organization goes about its protection work. The conservatism and consistency that characterize the organizational culture of the ICRC come into play here. Known for taking a highly principled approach, the ICRC is often said to be the most 'classical' of all contemporary humanitarian agencies (Barnett 2005; Weiss 1999). The ICRC takes a long-term view and seeks to assure its access to the victims of all future conflicts by keeping to its principled approach and operating on the basis of discretion in order to gain the trust of combatants, not only in the contexts in which it currently operates but also in those contexts in which it may need to operate at a later date. Principles will not be put aside even when doing so might produce beneficial results in the short term, for fear of jeopardizing ICRC protection capacity in the long term. For the ICRC, these principles are seen as a means not only to acceptance and access in a given context, but also to acceptance and access in other contexts both now and in the future. Thus, the ICRC seeks to operate in a predictable manner and to avoid confrontation, particularly public confrontation.

By contrast, and in keeping with its own organizational culture, UNHCR has for the most part emphasized pragmatism over caution. While the organization maintains a principled stance in its rhetoric, seasoned commentators have noted an increasingly pragmatic stance since the 1990s, as UNHCR expanded into non-traditional activities, becoming more a general humanitarian organization and less a specialized refugee protection agency. For example, Dennis McNamara and Guy Goodwin-Gill have argued that UNHCR 'is no longer guided by clear principles. The senior leadership sincerely believes that it can contribute effectively to humanitarian crises by being pragmatic rather than basing its actions on traditional principles' (McNamara and Goodwin-Gill 1999: 3). Unlike the ICRC, then, UNHCR often seeks to focus on immediate solutions, sometimes at the expense of honouring its own institutional principles (Roxström and Gibney 2003). This pragmatic organizational culture mediates the principles guiding the work of the organization, making for more flexible interpretation and implementation.

In addition to using the principles of humanity, impartiality, neutrality, and independence to guide their own work, both the ICRC and UNHCR seek to improve protection outcomes by encouraging other actors—primarily combatants in the case of the ICRC, and states in the case of UNHCR—to adhere to a number of legal principles. These are discussed in Chapter 3, which focuses on the ways that the ICRC and UNHCR use different legal and normative frameworks in their efforts to protect IDPs and other civilians during armed conflict.

3

Legal Frameworks for Protection

The principles of humanitarian action discussed in Chapter 2 incorporate standards of appropriate behaviour for the ICRC and UNHCR. Both organizations additionally use a range of norms with the aim of influencing the behaviour of other actors. This chapter explores how protection-related laws and norms shape the work of the ICRC and UNHCR, and with what implications for the effectiveness of that work. It proceeds in three main parts. The first section introduces the main legal and normative frameworks that have a bearing on the protection of civilians in armed conflict, with an emphasis on those frameworks most closely linked to the ICRC and UNHCR. The second section analyses the relationships between these frameworks and the institutional mandates of the ICRC and UNHCR. It argues that the legal frameworks do not strictly delineate the issues which the organizations seek to address, but that both the ICRC and UNHCR have greater commitment and confidence to address those issues that fall within the legal frameworks linked to their respective mandates. Finally, the third section asks how useful the ICRC and UNHCR find these legal frameworks in their protection work in order to draw some conclusions as to the adequacy and appropriateness of existing laws and norms.

KEY LEGAL AND NORMATIVE FRAMEWORKS FOR THE PROTECTION OF CIVILIANS

The ICRC bases much of its work on a number of international legal principles concerning the conduct of hostilities, and the impact of hostilities on different categories of protected person. UNHCR, on the other hand, emphasizes principles that facilitate the movement of people away from persecution, and from the very hostilities that the ICRC seeks to regulate. Both organizations have particular responsibilities for a body of international law—IHL in the case of the ICRC, and international refugee law (IRL) in the case of UNHCR. The ICRC is the self-styled 'guardian of IHL' (Sandoz 1998).

UNHCR has supervisory responsibilities for the 1951 Convention relating to the Status of Refugees (hereafter the 1951 Convention), its 1967 Protocol, and the 1969 OAU Convention governing the specific aspects of refugee problems in Africa (Goodwin-Gill and McAdam 2007: 426, 430, 532; Simeon 2013; Turk 2002). Of course, these responsibilities do not mean that the ICRC and UNHCR are the only actors that can work with these respective bodies of law, but two characteristics suggest a relationship akin to ownership. First, there is an aspect of territoriality, in the sense that each organization can be protective of its particular domain, fearing encroachment by others could diminish its own expert authority and market share. Second, each organization is less expert in, and less likely to use, bodies of law other than 'its own'. Thus, while the ICRC could draw heavily on IRL and international human rights law (IHRL), and UNHCR could draw on IHL, mostly they do not. Furthermore, IHL and IRL have played central roles in shaping the respective institutional identities and mandates of the ICRC and UNHCR.

International Humanitarian Law

For the ICRC, IHL is the most important body of law. Currently in force are four Geneva Conventions, dated 12 August 1949 and pertaining to: (I) wounded and sick in armed forces in the field; (II) wounded, sick, and shipwrecked members of armed forces at sea; (III) prisoners of war; and (IV) civilian persons. In 1977, these were supplemented by two Additional Protocols, relating to the protection of: (I) victims of international armed conflicts; and (II) victims of non-international armed conflicts. In 2005, a third Additional Protocol was agreed. However, this concerns the emblems used by National Societies and is not part of the substance of IHL. The development of these treaties was driven in no small part by the ICRC. In addition to the Geneva Conventions and their Additional Protocols, there are a number of other IHL treaties, many of which prohibit the use of particular weapons, and some of which the ICRC had some involvement in developing.[1] Additionally, there exists a body of customary law, much of which is articulated and explained in the 2005 study by the ICRC on customary IHL (Henckaerts and Doswald-Beck 2005). In respect of civilian protection in internal armed conflict, common article 3 of the four Geneva Conventions of 1949, Additional Protocol II, treaties banning particular weapons and methods of warfare, and customary law are all applicable, relevant, and employed by the ICRC.

[1] For a list of other key treaties, see <https://www.icrc.org/ihl>.

Underpinning the different strands of IHL—relating to both international and non-international armed conflict—is a set of legal principles. These legal principles run through the four Geneva Conventions of 1949, the two Additional Protocols of 1977, and the rules set out in the ICRC's 2005 customary IHL study, and they are central to the ICRC approach to civilian protection.

IHL Principles

According to the principle of *distinction*, means and methods of warfare that do not distinguish between legitimate targets of attack (combatants) and protected persons (in this case, civilians) are prohibited. Distinction is described as the cornerstone of the 1977 Additional Protocols (ICRC 2007a). However, the centrality of this principle to the work of the ICRC far predates the institutional expansion into the issue-area of civilian protection in internal armed conflicts.

The principle of distinction was codified in the first Geneva Convention of 1864, though this did not apply to civilians but to wounded or sick combatants.[2] Over time, the categories of protected person to whom the principle of distinction applied expanded to include military seamen in the 1906 Geneva Convention, prisoners of war in the 1929 Geneva Convention, and civilians in international armed conflicts in the fourth Geneva Convention of 1949.[3] With respect to internal conflicts, the principle of distinction is codified in Article 13 (2) of Additional Protocol II,[4] and is the subject of rule 1 of the 2005 ICRC study on customary IHL.[5] This notion of distinguishing protected categories of person in armed conflict has existed for centuries, even if the definition of the categories has varied significantly (across time, and indeed across and even within different armed forces and non-state armed groups), and has often been anything but precise (Kinsella 2011). Certainly, the meaning of civilian has been contested, and the principle has frequently been ignored in practice (Keen and Lee 2009: 11; Melzer 2009).

The principle of *proportionality* prohibits attacks even where there is a clear military target, if the expected military advantage does not outweigh the risk to civilians and civilian property. The principle is codified in Articles 51(5)(b)

[2] Article 1 states: 'Ambulances and military hospitals shall be recognized as neutral, and as such, protected and respected by the belligerents as long as they accommodate wounded and sick.' Article 6 states: 'Wounded or sick combatants, to whatever nation they may belong, shall be collected and cared for.'

[3] Aside from Article 3 (which is also common to the other three Geneva Conventions of 1949), the fourth Geneva Convention of 1949 applies only to international armed conflict.

[4] 'The civilian population as such, as well as individual civilians, shall not be the object of attack. Acts or threats of violence the primary purpose of which is to spread terror among the civilian population are prohibited.'

[5] 'The parties to the conflict must at all times distinguish between civilians and combatants. Attacks may only be directed against combatants. Attacks must not be directed against civilians.'

and 57 of Additional Protocol I of 1977, and is articulated as rule 14 in the 2005 ICRC study on customary IHL, which states: 'Launching an attack which may be expected to cause incidental loss of civilian life, injury to civilians, damage to civilian objects, or a combination thereof, which would be excessive in relation to the concrete and direct military advantage anticipated, is prohibited.'

The principle of *precaution* supplements the principle of distinction and requires that combatants take into account the presence of civilians or civilian objects prior to any attack. Codified in Article 57(1) of Additional Protocol I[6] and implicit in Article 13(1) of Additional Protocol II,[7] the principle is articulated in rule 15 of the 2005 ICRC study on customary IHL: 'In the conduct of military operations, constant care must be taken to spare the civilian population, civilians and civilian objects. All feasible precautions must be taken to avoid, and in any event to minimize, incidental loss of civilian life, injury to civilians and damage to civilian objects.'

In sum, the IHL framework is characterized by a number of principles with which the ICRC seeks to regulate conflict and change the behaviour of armed parties. These principles, though articulated in greater detail in the provisions governing international armed conflict than in those governing internal conflict (primarily Common Article 3 and Additional Protocol II), are understood to apply across international and non-international armed conflicts, and with respect to different categories of protected person.

The Centrality of IHL in the Work of the ICRC

Although at times the ICRC also draws on international human rights law (IHRL), domestic legislation, and the internal regulations of the armed groups, IHL is far and away the primary legal framework employed by the organization at the global level. This is also true in most field contexts in which the ICRC operates, including Colombia and the DRC, where the main focus is on Additional Protocol II of 1977 and customary IHL. Both countries are party to the four Geneva Conventions of 1949 and their two Additional Protocols of 1977. Despite the Uribe government (2002–10) characterizing the Colombian context as *post*-conflict, the ICRC was able to invoke IHL with respect to the state, and continues to do so. Indeed, the Colombian Constitution states that IHL is applicable at all times, regardless of the existence of conflict (Kalshoven 1998). The ICRC also views the DRC as a classic IHL context.

[6] 'In the conduct of military operations, constant care shall be taken to spare the civilian population, civilians and civilian objects.'

[7] 'The civilian population and individual civilians shall enjoy general protection against the dangers arising from military operations. To give effect to this protection, the following rules shall be observed in all circumstances.'

For a number of reasons, the work of the ICRC in Myanmar has been much less defined by IHL than it has been in Colombia or the DRC. First, at the time of writing, Myanmar was not party to many of the key IHL treaties. For example, Myanmar had ratified the first three Geneva Conventions of 1949, but not the fourth Geneva Convention or the 1977 (or 2005) Additional Protocols, the Ottawa landmine treaty, or any of the other treaties banning particular weapons. Of course, regardless of gaps in international treaty ratification, customary IHL is applicable where the threshold for armed conflict is reached.[8] However, in some parts of Myanmar where the ICRC was working—namely in Rakhine state—the context was one of communal violence and the minimum thresholds for armed conflict were not met, so IHL did not apply. Moreover, even if other parts of the country where the ICRC was working did indeed meet the criteria for armed conflict, the ICRC had not publicly classified the context. Given its more limited relevance, the ICRC placed less emphasis on IHL in Myanmar than in Colombia or the DRC, but it nonetheless drew on IHL more than any other legal or normative framework, as reflected by its 2013 annual report entry for Myanmar, which mentions IHL ten times in five pages (ICRC 2014a).

International Refugee Law

Just as the ICRC mandate is intrinsically linked to IHL, so IRL is central to the mandate of UNHCR. Although IRL is not directly relevant to IDP protection, it has a number of indirect effects on UNHCR efforts to protect IDPs, both in shaping the way that UNHCR understands the meaning of protection, and in shaping UNHCR organizational culture. The 1951 Convention and its 1967 Protocol define who is a refugee and assign a set of rights to refugees and a set of corresponding obligations of states. The content of protection laid out in these treaties is largely defined by analogy to the rights and benefits accorded to nationals or to other aliens in the country of refuge. Essentially, they provide for a refugee to reside legally in the country of refuge, and not to be discriminated against in terms of economic and social rights.

There are two key components of the refugee definition set out in Article 1A(2) of the 1951 Convention: a refugee is someone who (1) is outside his/her country of nationality or former habitual residence, (2) owing to a 'well-founded fear of being persecuted for reasons of race, religion, nationality, membership of a particular social group or political opinion'. States in Africa and Latin America found that the refugee definition in the Convention and Protocol was too narrow to capture the reality of contemporary refugee flows,

[8] For an ICRC opinion and explanation of minimum thresholds for different parts of IHL to be applicable, see ICRC (2008a).

which were not for the most part the result of persecution, but of insecurity associated with armed conflict and generalized violence. As a result, regional approaches to refugee protection were developed.

In 1969, the OAU Convention Governing the Specific Aspects of Refugee Problems in Africa expanded the refugee definition in member states to include not only those fleeing persecution for reasons of being members of a particular group, but also those fleeing occupation, conflict, and serious public order disturbances (Article 1.2). While those who come within article 1.2 of the 1969 OAU Convention are not 'Convention refugees', the OAU Convention entitles them to the same protection and rights. In Latin America, following the Central American crises of the 1970s and early 1980s, the 1984 Cartagena Declaration on Refugees also sought to expand the refugee definition within the region to include 'persons who have fled their country because their lives, safety or freedom have been threatened by generalized violence, foreign aggression, internal conflicts, massive violation of human rights or other circumstances which have seriously disturbed public order' (Conclusion N.3). As a declaration rather than a treaty, the expanded definition is not binding on Latin American states, but several have incorporated it into domestic legislation.

Like much of international law, IRL can be viewed as a pragmatic response to an imperfect world. It accepts that states will not always treat their citizens perfectly, and seeks to deal with this largely inescapable fact. It thus offers an alternative solution whereby another state offers legal protection to those who have fled their own state because it was unwilling or unable to protect them. While there has not been significant replication of the international legal framework from refugee protection to IDP protection, particular aspects of that framework have been mirrored, and an attempt has been made to draw on the same underlying principles in the work of UNHCR within conflict contexts.

IRL Principles

Two fundamental principles underpin the IRL framework that is at the heart of the traditional work of UNHCR: *non-refoulement* and asylum. *Non-refoulement* is intrinsically linked to the definition of a refugee—a state cannot send back a refugee on its territory or at its border 'to the frontiers of territories where his life or freedom would be threatened on account of his race, religion, nationality, membership of a particular social group or political opinion'.[9] Formal recognition of refugee status is not required for the application of the principle of *non-refoulement*; protection from *refoulement* is the

[9] *Convention Relating to the Status of Refugees*, 28 July 1951, United Nations, Treaty Series, vol. 189, p. 137. Article 33(1).

right of an asylum seeker, not only of a refugee. The rights of refugees and the obligations of states do not stop at the principle of *non-refoulement*. Refugees also have the right to a solution, in other words eventually to cease to be a refugee.[10]

The right of states to grant asylum contradicts sovereignty, because a component of state sovereignty is the right of the state to exercise jurisdiction over its citizens. A refugee-receiving country takes on the jurisdiction of refugees on its territory, distinguishing refugees from any other kind of international migrants, and denying the state of citizenship the right to exercise jurisdiction over them. Asylum can be understood through analogy to foster care for children. In normal circumstances, children will be cared for by their parents and, providing they comply with certain norms and standards of care, parents are free to decide how to raise them. However, if parents are unwilling or unable to take proper care of their children, social services may take children into foster care until they can either be returned to the care of their parents or adopted. Like taking away the custody of children from their parents, the granting of asylum involves confiscating an element of sovereignty from the state of origin. Refugees maintain their citizenship, but the state of which they are citizens is deprived of its right to exercise jurisdiction over them.

These principles cannot easily be applied to IDPs, except in terms of the principle that they have the right to seek asylum if they cross an international border (at which point in any case they cease to be IDPs). The inapplicability of these principles to IDPs reflects the significant differences between the situation of refugees and IDPs. A parallel with *non-refoulement* can exist along the lines that IDPs should not be forcibly returned to regions within their country where they will be in danger. The problem is that in the context of conflict, IDPs often continue to be in danger even in the places to which they have fled, and in many cases the state in question does not have the will or capacity to prevent such dangers. As such, a principle analogous to *non-refoulement* means little in practice without an equivalent to the principle of asylum enabling the IDP to live in safety in the place to which he or she has fled. However, it is harder to draw a clear parallel with asylum. In the case of IDPs, the state in question is not deprived of the right to exercise jurisdiction over them. It may be that some parts of a country are safer for particular individuals than other parts of the country, but the level of safety does not depend on the legal jurisdiction, because the *de jure* authority is the same—the

[10] There are three ways to end being a refugee: (1) a new state may actually be created, as was the case with Timor Leste and Eritrea, where the returnees were previously refugees from Indonesia and Ethiopia respectively, and then they got citizenship in the new country; (2) refugees may re-avail themselves of the protection of their country of origin; and (3) refugees may gain citizenship of a new country through naturalization.

state—throughout the country. To only a limited degree, therefore, can notions of asylum and *non-refoulement* apply by analogy in the context of internal displacement. Nonetheless, these legal principles, together with the operational principles set out above, are constitutive of UNHCR identity and indeed of the way in which UNHCR addresses the tasks within its mandate.

International Human Rights Law

IRL is a subset of IHRL, a broader body of law, some of which has a bearing on the protection of IDPs and other civilians during armed conflict. Key treaties which incorporate provisions that are pertinent to protection in times of conflict include the 1966 International Covenant on Civil and Political Rights (ICCPR), the 1979 Convention on the Elimination of all Forms of Discrimination against Women (CEDAW), the 1984 Convention against Torture and Other Cruel, Inhuman or Degrading Treatment or Punishment (CAT), and the 1989 Convention on the Rights of the Child (CRC). At the time of writing, Colombia and the DRC had either ratified or acceded to all of these, while Myanmar had only acceded to CEDAW and the CRC. In addition to treaty-based human rights law, the 1948 Universal Declaration of Human Rights (UDHR) includes a number of rights relevant to protection in armed conflict. It is a declaration rather than a treaty, and, as such, its articles are not binding in and of themselves, but many are now considered to be customary law and hence binding on all states.

At times both the ICRC and UNHCR will reference IHRL. For example, the ICRC draws on the CAT in its work to protect detainees, and UNHCR can use IHRL and UN-based human rights protection mechanisms in its refugee and IDP protection work (Gorlick 2000). Until relatively recently, the ICRC was averse to talking about human rights in its efforts to protect civilians, but since the late 1990s this has changed. In theory, there is now an emphasis on pragmatic effectiveness, drawing on whichever normative framework is expected to be most effective in any given situation. UNHCR has a general preference for drawing on domestic legislation for IDP protection, with the expectation that states are more likely to be convinced to comply with their own laws than with international law. However, it will also use IHRL pragmatically, particularly where domestic legislation does not offer much in the way of legal protections for IDPs. For example, in Myanmar, UNHCR was using the CEDAW and the CRC, among other treaties. Staff would not necessarily quote these Conventions, but they were drawing on them. Given Myanmar was not party to many IHRL treaties, UNHCR was also emphasizing the UDHR and customary law.

International and Regional Legislation on IDPs

The Guiding Principles on Internal Displacement[11] constitute the most important *international* normative framework for the work of UNHCR with respect to IDP protection during armed conflict. They are soft law, but they are based on hard law, reflecting, and consistent with, IHL, IHRL, and, by analogy, IRL (Deng 1995; Kälin 2008). At the regional level, the African Union 'Kampala Convention'[12] is the first binding Convention on IDPs (African Union 2009). The Convention was adopted by the African Union in 2009 and came into force in 2012. While these frameworks play an important role in UNHCR IDP protection efforts, they are nowhere near as central to those efforts as IRL is to the refugee protection role of UNHCR. They are not 'owned' by UNHCR in the same way that IRL is, and they do not assign a particular mandate or role to UNHCR. The Guiding Principles were not developed by, or at the instigation of, UNHCR. The Office of the UN High Commissioner for Human Rights (OHCHR) requested that the UN Secretary-General, Kofi Annan, appoint a representative on IDPs and in 1992 Francis Deng was appointed to this role, publishing the Guiding Principles in 1998. However, UNHCR has since been designated the UN agency with primary responsibility for IDP protection under the cluster approach, and envisages incorporating the Guiding Principles into 'all IDP activities and operations' it undertakes (UNHCR 2007e, para. 26).

Domestic Law

For both the ICRC and UNHCR, use of domestic legislation naturally depends very much on what domestic law exists in any given context. Where domestic law deals with issues that they are concerned with, they may draw on it, and indeed for UNHCR, this is often the first port of call in IDP protection. By contrast, the ICRC has a preference for working with IHL, but domestic legislation or the internal rules of armed groups can play an important supplementary role.

An increasing number of states have drawn up—or are in the process of drawing up—IDP-specific legislation based on, or consistent with, the Guiding Principles. In Colombia, for example, there is a very developed legal framework for IDPs, and that framework is absolutely central to the work of

[11] UN Commission on Human Rights. Report of the Representative of the Secretary-General, Mr Francis M. Deng, submitted pursuant to Commission resolution 1997/39. Addendum: Guiding Principles on Internal Displacement, 11 February 1998, E/CN.4/1998/53/Add.2.

[12] African Union Convention for the Protection and Assistance of Internally Displaced Persons in Africa ('Kampala Convention'), 22 October 2009.

UNHCR. Law 387, the core of IDP legislation in Colombia, predates the Guiding Principles. However, it provides 'comprehensive cover for most if not all the principles set out in the Guiding Principles' (Carr 2009: 38). International law played a minimal role in the UNHCR approach to protection in Colombia, in part because reference to international law alone carried little weight in getting the social institutions of the state to respond at the local level, and in part because in any case the national legislation was so well advanced that there was seen to be little need for recourse to any other body of law. In the DRC, domestic IDP legislation was nowhere near as advanced as in Colombia, but in 2014 was in the process of being developed, and UNHCR was supporting its development. Additionally, domestic legislation more generally may be relevant for the protection of IDPs and other civilians during armed conflict. This may include, for example, laws on land and property ownership, or on social welfare or human rights more broadly.

The ICRC preference for IHL and its focus on armed actors means the organization places much less emphasis on domestic law than does UNHCR. However, the ICRC also seeks to draw on the internal rules of armed groups (where they exist and are in line with IHL), and may also draw on domestic legislation in situations where some or all of IHL does not apply because the context falls below the threshold for IHL, or because a country is not party to certain IHL treaties. Of course, very often the same countries that are not party to key international treaties have only limited domestic law with the potential to support protective interventions. To compound the gaps in Myanmar's international law commitments, for example, there is little in the way of domestic legislation on issues relating to human rights or the conduct of hostilities.

Geneva Call Deeds of Commitment

Finally, it is worth introducing a non-state-based normative framework which has the protection of civilians as its central concern, but which is not routinely employed by either the ICRC or UNHCR. Geneva Call is an NGO which has negotiated with several non-state armed groups to sign 'Deeds of Commitment' which are based on IHL treaties (which only states can sign up to), or on parts of such treaties, and commit their non-state signatories to the same or similar obligations as states which have signed the relevant treaties. The Deeds of Commitment can best be described as 'quasi-IHL'. The rationale is that armed non-state actors 'may not feel themselves bound by conventions that they have not been involved in drafting, nor been allowed to sign', and that being able to sign up to a commitment to respect particular humanitarian norms should increase compliance, because 'they take ownership of rules that they might otherwise consider not applicable to them or biased in favour of States' (Bongard 2008: 111–12).

At the time of writing, there were three Deeds of Commitment. None of the non-state armed groups in Colombia had signed up to any of these, although Geneva Call was engaged in dialogue on these issues with some of the armed groups there. Six armed groups in Myanmar, of which the Chin National Front (CNF) and the Palaung State Liberation Front (PSLF) were still active, had signed the Deed of Commitment banning antipersonnel mines, four armed groups—the Karen National Union (KNU), the Karenni National Progressive Party (KNPP), the Chin National Front (CNF), and the New Mon State Party (NMSP)—had signed the Deed of Commitment on the protection of children from the effects of armed conflict, and the CNF and the KNU had also signed the Deed of Commitment prohibiting sexual violence in armed conflict and gender discrimination. As at early 2015, Geneva Call was in dialogue with a number of armed groups in the DRC, but none of them had yet signed any of the Deeds of Commitment.

Given the relevance of these commitments to the protection of IDPs and other civilians, it is perhaps surprising that they are not employed by either the ICRC or UNHCR. It is especially surprising in the case of the ICRC, given the institutional commitment to engaging armed non-state actors in dialogue, and the potential utility of these commitments with those groups that have signed up to them.

In sum, a multitude of international laws and norms have a bearing on protection, but the ICRC emphasizes IHL and constraints on the conduct of hostilities, while UNHCR emphasizes the Guiding Principles, domestic legislation, and the rights of IDPs not to be disadvantaged or discriminated against on account of their displacement. The next section explores the relationship between these legal frameworks, the mandates of the ICRC and UNHCR in international law, their de facto mandates, and the activities they carry out in practice.

LAWS, NORMS, AND THE MANDATES AND ACTIVITIES OF THE ICRC AND UNHCR

Some humanitarian agencies—including the ICRC and UNHCR—have specific international mandates that are legally recognized by states and imply a certain kind of international legitimacy and 'delegated authority' to address the issues that come under those specific mandates (Barnett and Finnemore 2004: 22–3; Slim and Bradley 2013: 3). Such mandates usually also imply an obligation to address those issues. In many cases, these mandates are defined in, or explicitly linked to, particular treaties or international legal frameworks.

However, institutional mandates are also often broader than the specific legal mandates bestowed by states. In general terms, the mandate of an organization can refer simply to the legitimate scope of an organization's work, with that legitimacy deriving from implicit or explicit acceptance by states or other relevant actors (Betts 2012: 118). In what follows, therefore, the relationships between the respective legal mandates, institutional mandates, and practical work of both the ICRC and UNHCR are examined.

The legal mandate for the work of the ICRC is seen to comprise three parts: in international armed conflict, it derives from the 1949 Geneva Conventions and Additional Protocol I of 1977; in non-international armed conflict, the ICRC maintains a right of humanitarian initiative codified in common article 3 of the 1949 Geneva Conventions; and in internal tensions and disturbances, the ICRC maintains a right of initiative recognized in the Statutes of the International Red Cross and Red Crescent Movement (ICRC 2010c). The right of initiative is deemed to have become customary law, and it is not restricted to situations covered by IHL or to persons protected by IHL (Bugnion 2003: 355). In this way, the mandate of the ICRC centres on, but also extends beyond, the supervision and development of IHL.

The legal mandate of UNHCR derives from its 1950 Statute and subsequent General Assembly Resolutions. UNHCR is specifically mandated to supervise IRL, the core of which is the 1951 Convention and its 1967 Protocol. The 1951 Convention only applied to people who were refugees as a consequence of events prior to the Convention, and states parties had the option to restrict it to events in Europe. The Statute of UNHCR envisages a greater role for UNHCR than the 1951 Convention, and carries no geographical or temporal restriction on the definition of a refugee. However, the difference between the two definitions has lost much significance over time, particularly since the 1967 protocol removed the geographic and temporal restrictions of the 1951 Convention.[13] General Assembly resolutions are only valid until the General Assembly produces an amendment or replacement. Through such amendments and replacements, the formal mandate of UNHCR has expanded significantly over the past sixty years. Additionally, UNHCR has been able to expand its de facto mandate through autonomous activity (Betts 2012). Whereas UNHCR has a clear legal mandate for refugee protection, it has no such mandate in international law for IDP protection. Therefore, its formal mandate in any given IDP context depends on the activation of the cluster system, and on any agreement UNHCR has entered into with the host government.

While these legal frameworks are central to the protection work of both the ICRC and UNHCR, the scope of their work is not strictly delineated by these

[13] It is still possible for states which took the geographical limitation to maintain it, but in practice very few states do. A notable exception is Turkey which, therefore, is not obliged to take refugees from Iraq or Syria, for example.

frameworks. If IHL precisely dictated the issues addressed by the ICRC, we would expect the ICRC to be concerned with issues if and only if they reflected violations of IHL. In other words, the ICRC would address everything within the IHL framework and nothing beyond that framework. Similarly, if the work of UNHCR was strictly delineated by IRL, the Guiding Principles, and domestic legislation, UNHCR would deal with all issues covered by those bodies of law and nothing else. As we shall see in the sections below on working outside the relevant legal frameworks and on ignoring issues within those frameworks, this is not the case for either organization. At different times the different legal frameworks have been used in a more or less restrictive manner both in terms of defining the issues which the ICRC and UNHCR seek to address, and the ways in which they seek to address them. While their mandates in international law can and do have a constraining influence on the work of the ICRC and UNHCR, in many cases they have worked in contexts and on issues not covered by their legal mandates, and they certainly do not work in every context and on every issue that those mandates pertain to. Moreover, the legal frameworks themselves are not absolutely fixed, and both the ICRC and UNHCR have played a role in extending and developing them.

Law Restricting Issues that the ICRC and UNHCR Will Address

When the mandate of an organization derives from a particular body of international law, it can be argued that contexts and issues not covered by that body of law are also outside that mandate. In line with such arguments, a number of historical examples show how the legal mandates of the ICRC and UNHCR can and have been used to restrict their de facto institutional mandates and practice. In both organizations, we also see greater compulsion to work on those issues that fall within the remit of their legal mandates. This plays out slightly differently in each organization. In the ICRC, it means that when needs relating to IHL violations exceed ICRC capacity in a given context, other issues are unlikely to be addressed. In UNHCR, it means that in the face of limited resources, refugee protection may be prioritized over IDP protection. Furthermore, with respect to in-country protection in particular, the issues that UNHCR addresses are very often constrained by the terms of engagement agreed between UNHCR and the relevant government.

In its early years, the ICRC was cautious in working beyond its legal mandate from states and, 'when it embarked upon the first major extension of its work, with its first visits to prisoner-of-war camps in 1870, the ICRC initially created a separate organization to undertake the task' (Armstrong 1985: 621). This shows that while the organization could be pragmatic in finding a way to undertake work it believed to be important, it did view its own institutional mandate as equivalent to its (then narrow) legal mandate. At times, this perspective led the ICRC to avoid addressing certain issues altogether. For example, during the Italo-Ethiopian War of 1935–6, the ICRC response to Italy's use of poison gas was restricted to requesting National Societies to donate gas masks for medical personnel and for wounded and sick combatants, but not for civilians, because at this time there was no Geneva Convention concerned with civilians (Baudendistel 2006: 290). Internal debate within the ICRC on this issue came down on the side of the lawyers, who argued that the ICRC could take action only on behalf of those categories of person who were the objects of the then existing Geneva Conventions. Furthermore, despite the illegality of poison gas, the ICRC would not speak out against its use. Rainer Baudendistel explains that in the opinion of the lawyers, 'the ICRC had to base its action exclusively on the Geneva Conventions of 1929, for which it had a specific responsibility and not on Conventions regarding methods of warfare, such as the Gas Protocol of 1925' (Baudendistel 2006: 290). Similarly, in World War II, the ICRC remained silent about the Holocaust, among other issues.[14] In the face of fierce criticisms levelled against it by the USSR and Yugoslavia after the war, the ICRC sought to defend its silence with a number of arguments, including reference to the fact that there was at that time no convention relating to the protection of the civilian population (Junod 1996: 17–18).

It was only after World War II, in response to these experiences and criticisms, that the ICRC took the explicit decision that conforming to the Geneva Conventions did not require the ICRC to restrict itself to the specific activities or persons of concern or contexts detailed in those treaties, but rather meant applying the spirit of those treaties for the victims of all types of armed conflict through activities which may be unforeseen (Junod 1996: 11). In theory, the contemporary ICRC sees itself as the guardian of IHL generally, not only those treaties which it helped to develop, or which explicitly mention its rights and duties. However, long-time senior ICRC staff member, François Bugnion,[15] has criticized the ICRC for being overly reliant on the 1949 Geneva Conventions and the 1977 Additional Protocols when there are many other legal sources on which it could usefully draw in its protection work, and for too often taking 'refuge behind semantic or literal readings [that] frequently fall short of the practice that the Committee itself has developed on the basis of the Conventions' (Bugnion 2003: 398).

Similarly, at times the legal framework underpinning the work of UNHCR has been interpreted in such a way as to restrict the institutional mandate. For

[14] For more on the work and criticisms of the ICRC during World War II, see Favez (1999), Forsythe (2005: 41–50), Moorehead (1999: 371–529), Vonèche Cardia (2012).

[15] François Bugnion joined the ICRC in 1970 and served as Director of International Law and Cooperation from 2000–6. Since 2010, he has been a member of the Assembly.

a long time, UNHCR considered its mandate was restricted to those defined in the UNHCR Statute, which was adopted by the General Assembly on 14 December 1950. Notably, UNHCR never used the same definition as that contained in the 1951 Convention, which only applied to people who were refugees as a consequence of events prior to the Convention and could only be applied in Europe. Nonetheless, UNHCR deemed that a refugee was someone outside their country owing to a well-founded fear of persecution. Thus, despite the more expansive refugee definitions adopted in Africa and Latin America, it was only in the 1990s that UNHCR finally came to the conclusion that, for UNHCR, a refugee includes anyone defined as a refugee in the UNHCR Statute, the 1969 OAU Convention, or the 1984 Cartagena Declaration, depending on the particular context in which the organization is working. Arguments based on the limits of UNHCR's legal mandate were also used to restrict UNHCR involvement with IDPs. For example, under the leadership of Prince Sadruddin Aga Khan in the 1960s, UNHCR assumed a policy of non-involvement in major internal conflicts on the basis that the displacements were largely internal, and that these situations were not of direct concern to UNHCR for constitutional and legal reasons (Loescher 2001: 145).

Since UNHCR took on the role of cluster lead for IDP protection, there are two key ways in which its work is sometimes limited by its institutional mandate or by the agreements it has entered into with the governments of affected states. First, UNHCR has an obligation to respond to refugees, and the High Commissioner is accountable for refugee protection, whereas for IDPs staff have the understanding that they have to do their best, but if there is no funding, there is no response. Second, there is the question of who is an IDP in different contexts. The Guiding Principles contain a descriptive definition of an IDP; they do not define a legal category. As such, governments have significant scope to define who counts as an IDP on their territory, and hence to set the parameters of UNHCR's competence and work. This was evident in Colombia, where the government had, for example, excluded those displaced within cities from the national programme of support for IDPs. In Rakhine state in Myanmar, the government only defined those whose houses were destroyed as IDPs, and limited UNHCR to assisting them, so that UNHCR could not assist those in the same communities who were still in their own homes. In Kachin state, the work of UNHCR was largely restricted to IDP camps, as per the Memorandum of Understanding between UNHCR and the government.

In sum, the specific mandates of the ICRC and UNHCR in international law can and have been used to limit their de facto mandates—that is, what is understood to be the legitimate scope of their work. However, both the ICRC and UNHCR have also sometimes willingly worked beyond the confines of their mandates in international law. As such, it cannot be the case that it is the legal mandates per se that restrict what activities the organizations undertake, but rather their interpretation of those mandates. For both the ICRC and UNHCR, this has changed over time, generally moving from more restrictive interpretations of their mandates to more flexible interpretations. Even much earlier, however, examples can be found in which each organization demonstrated creativity in its use of the law, and undertook practical activities beyond the boundaries of the relevant legal framework.

Working in Contexts and on Issues outside the Relevant Legal Frameworks

The ICRC works beyond its legal mandate when delegates observe humanitarian consequences of actions that are not IHL violations, and where there are similarities or spillovers between the ICRC response to those consequences and its traditional IHL work. This most commonly occurs in contexts in which the ICRC is already operational and delegates are present. UNHCR has worked on issues beyond its legal and institutional mandates where clear analogies could be constructed between its core refugee protection responsibilities and other issues such as IDP protection, or where working on other issues has been seen to have a positive spillover effect on its refugee protection mandate. UNHCR does not have an international legal mandate for working in IDP contexts, but rather a mandate to lead the protection cluster, and to conform to the agreements it has entered into with the states within which it operates.

Every new convention the ICRC has developed was the offspring of practical action in accordance with the spirit, but beyond the letter, of prior treaties. Thus, the ICRC has always found ways to work beyond the legal frameworks that were understood to define its mandate. On occasion, during the early years of the ICRC, restrictions on the institutional mandate implied by IHL as it then stood were pragmatically bypassed by tasking individuals or agencies that were officially independent but in practice organized and directed by the ICRC to undertake activities which went beyond its legal mandate (Forsythe 2005: 24–5). The institutional mandate of the contemporary ICRC includes a right of initiative to undertake its traditional activities in situations not covered by IHL, which is interpreted in particular to apply to situations of violence below the threshold of armed conflict, thus including, for example, internal disturbances and political violence (Bugnion 2003: 355; Forsythe 2005: 255). Additionally, in those contexts in which IHL is applicable, the ICRC may work on issues beyond those covered by IHL.

Likewise, UNHCR does not restrict its work to what is covered in international or domestic legislation. International refugee law, including the various regional agreements on refugees, is applicable only to those who have crossed an international border. While the work of UNHCR in the context of armed conflict may include refugee protection (particularly in the context of regional conflicts), the main populations of concern in armed conflicts are made up of IDPs. They are not covered by refugee law, and the legal protection capacity of UNHCR does not extend to them. Consequently, there is a divergence between the functional responsibilities of UNHCR and the legal obligations of states, and this middle ground has been characterized by a lack of specific legal obligations (Goodwin-Gill 1989: 16; Zieck 2010). Working in IDP contexts without a binding legal framework at the international level, UNHCR is thus increasingly dependent on domestic legislation. As we have seen, the scope of UNHCR action may be somewhat limited by domestic legislation and especially by any agreements UNHCR has entered into with the government of each state in which the organization is working. However, in some cases, UNHCR actively pushes to work beyond the boundaries of such legislation and agreements.

Historical examples demonstrate that, on occasion, both organizations have worked beyond the boundaries of their legal mandates. For example, during World War I, ICRC work developed to encompass inspecting prisons and negotiating with authorities to obtain improvements in conditions for detainees; operating a tracing agency to exchange information about prisoners; and providing relief assistance to prisoners (Baudendistel 2006: 246–7). This role was then codified in the 1929 Geneva Convention and again in the third Geneva Convention of 1949. After 1917 the ICRC devoted considerable efforts to the victims of civil war in Russia (Forsythe 2005: 33). However, the Russian Revolution occurred in the context of an international war and from the outset included foreign involvement, so the ICRC had a legal mandate to be present, if not to be assisting victims of the civil war. 'True to its traditions, the ICRC and Red Cross societies from various neutral countries left discussion of the legal niceties until later. Indeed, they had little choice: the hospital wards that ICRC delegates visited in 1917–18 contained wounded from both the civil war and the international conflict' (Armstrong 1985: 623). Subsequently, in Hungary in 1919, the ICRC made reference to those 'detained by reason of events' in order to negotiate visits to those detained in a situation that fell short even of internal conflict (Forsythe 2005: 34). In that context, 'the ICRC delegate, Rodolphe Haccius, acting to a considerable extent on his own initiative, organized relief activities for political detainees as well as for the wounded, providing the ICRC's first unambiguous and deliberate action on behalf of political prisoners' (Armstrong 1985: 623). After World War I, the ICRC was involved in efforts to help civilian refugees (not only former prisoners of war) in Europe, and without regard to whether the context was one of internal or international conflict (Blondel 1987: 309).

Acceptance of the roles of IHL and the ICRC in internal conflict made significant advances in the Spanish Civil War. The 'ICRC fielded ten delegations on both sides of the bloody conflict, arranging prisoner exchanges, caring for displaced children, ameliorating the conditions of prisoners and hospital patients' (Forsythe 2005: 39). As it was a conventional civil war with two sides and a clear front, the ICRC was able to draw clear analogies with international war, and negotiated with both sides to permit the ICRC to undertake many of its traditional activities. Additionally, in caring for displaced children, for example, the ICRC worked beyond its mandated activities, justifying its approach on the basis that it was morally obliged to respond to such needs as it observed in the course of its work. Despite mounting a large operation and successfully implementing several activities, notably prisoner exchanges, the ICRC was unable to have significant impact on a brutal conflict. However, the fact remains that the ICRC operated in a context not covered by then existing IHL (non-international armed conflict), and indeed on issues that would not have been covered by IHL (protection of civilian children) even if the conflict had been of an international nature. In justifying working on these issues in this context, the ICRC drew analogies with the contexts and issues that fell clearly within its legal mandate to facilitate a creative interpretation of its institutional mandate.

There are also historical examples of UNHCR working beyond the confines of its legal mandate. For instance in 1956, when the legal mandate of UNHCR still limited its involvement to refugee flows from before 1951, High Commissioner Auguste Lindt responded to the Hungarian refugee crisis with the creative argument set out by his legal adviser that this refugee flow related not only to the 1956 Hungarian uprising, but also to the changes that took place in the country as a result of the establishment of a people's republic in 1947–8 (Loescher 2001: 86). In the early 1960s, much reference was made to the 'good offices' of UNHCR. The so-called good offices formula was first used in 1957 to provide a basis for UNHCR action other than the statute that would enable UNHCR to assist Chinese refugees in Hong Kong without making any evaluation of the causes of their flight (Loescher 2001: 95). The UN General Assembly requested High Commissioner Auguste Lindt to 'use his good offices', and the formula was subsequently much used under High Commissioner Felix Schnyder from 1960 until in 1965 the UN General Assembly requested the High Commissioner to assist all groups within his competence, thus abandoning the distinction between mandate and good offices refugees (Loescher 2001: 113).

Turning to their contemporary work, two particular issues in Colombia provide a helpful illustration of how both the ICRC and UNHCR at times work beyond the boundaries of existing legal frameworks. Aerial fumigations and urban violence have both been major causes of insecurity and displacement for Colombian civilians in several regions of the country. The aerial fumigation of coca crops causes displacement because (a) it destroys livelihoods, both illicit (coca) and licit (as a result of inaccuracy); (b) the chemicals cause health problems in local populations; and (c) it is usually accompanied by clashes between the public forces and other armed groups.

Morgane Landel makes the case for at least some such fumigations in Colombia being violations of IHL, though she acknowledges that scientific and technical evidence which is not currently available would be required in order to prove this point (Landel 2010). In any case, the ICRC position is that fumigations per se are not violations of IHL. As such, the source of the ICRC legal mandate to work on this issue is unclear, and the ICRC has no legal capacity to judge whether any particular incident of fumigation is acceptable or not, but the organization took the view that it could, should, and would support the affected populations. As protection cases must refer to violations of IHL, the ICRC did not formally document incidents of aerial fumigation for presentation to the alleged perpetrators in the way of its classic modus operandi. Furthermore, fumigation was considered to be a particularly sensitive subject; it clearly served political and strategic objectives for the Colombian government and military, as well as being strongly supported by the USA (and indeed carried out by the US firm Monsanto). Thus, it was thought that if the ICRC acted quickly and exerted a lot of pressure on the Colombian government with respect to this issue, the organization would simply be perceived as anti-fumigation. Instead, the ICRC spent some time collecting cases, following the usual ICRC process of documentation, followed by a review of the cases, and from 2011 made representations to the government at the Bogotá level aimed at drawing the authorities' attention to the potential humanitarian consequences of aerial fumigation (ICRC 2012a: 332, 2014a: 419). This reflects the cautiousness inherent in the ICRC bureaucratic culture, and the institutional preference for building up a solid information base before taking action.

The mandate of UNHCR to assist those displaced by aerial fumigations was also unclear. The Colombian government did not recognize those displaced as a result of destroyed livelihoods or health risks as IDPs entitled to the benefits stipulated in Law 387. In Bogotá, UNHCR was working with the state and the constitutional court, arguing that fumigation was part of the conflict, undertaken by a party to the conflict, and that those displaced by fumigation should thus be recognized. Additionally, UNHCR was advocating for those displaced by fumigation to be registered as displaced, at least for the purposes of developing policies to prevent displacement (UNHCR/ACNUR 2007: 52). Across the different field offices, UNHCR staff members held varied stances. Three broad positions could be identified: (1) it was not for UNHCR to say whether or not fumigation was a cause of conflict-related displacement; (2) the UNHCR position on fumigation was dependent on whether fumigation came on its own or was linked to military activities, and in the Colombian case it was almost always linked to military activities; and (3) fumigation in and of itself was part of the conflict because it was about taking away the FARC's means of survival. However, at the local level UNHCR was not for the most part engaging with the state institutions on the issue of fumigation.

Despite numerous connections between urban violence in the cities and the wider armed conflict in Colombia, issues around urban violence were not considered to be part of the armed conflict or covered by IHL. In part because of this, expanding operations to include protection from urban violence was not uncontroversial within the ICRC, but in 2010 a pilot project was underway in Rio de Janeiro, and two initial projects were planned for Colombia, in Medellín and Buenaventura. The Medellín project started in 2011, and was ongoing at the time of writing. Working in an infra-IHL context is nothing novel for the ICRC, and the institutional protection methodology explicitly covers 'other situations of violence' (ICRC 2008b, 2012b). In such contexts, the ICRC can and does draw on other relevant normative frameworks, which can include domestic or international human rights legislation. However, working in cities does represent a departure from traditional ICRC activities, which have been largely focused on armed conflict in rural areas. Thus, urban violence presents two particular challenges for the ICRC: working without the support of the IHL framework; and adapting an approach based on rural experience to the specificities of violence within cities. Nonetheless, at the time of interviews there seemed to be consensus among ICRC staff in Colombia that if the most serious humanitarian consequences from violence were in the city, then the organization must work in the city. This consensus was not automatic and was arrived at after a debate. The decision to expand ICRC work to encompass urban violence was reached after internal discussion and participation from delegates at the field level. The subsequent decision and the rationale behind it were communicated to staff members, who consistently recounted the same explanation.

There is an expectation that the conflicts of the future will more and more be infra-IHL, with more humanitarian consequences arising from internal disturbances and tensions or 'other situations of violence' that fall short of the definitions of armed conflict in the Geneva Conventions. Expansion into the issue of urban violence can thus be seen in the light of needing to stay relevant as the incidence of conflict declines. In Colombia, the ICRC justified its involvement in this issue with three lines of argument: (1) that there were significant links between urban violence in Colombian cities and the wider conflict; (2) that the ICRC had the capabilities and was in a good position (via prison work) to establish contact with the perpetrators of urban violence; and (3) that the ICRC could not ignore the humanitarian consequences of urban violence. In other words, there may be both ethical and market-based rationales underpinning ICRC decisions to work beyond the boundaries of the legal and formal institutional mandates.

With respect to urban violence in Colombia, UNHCR was working to increase recognition of intra-urban displacement. The Colombian legal framework for IDPs was designed for rural displacement, and normative gaps existed with respect to intra-urban displacement. Acción Social claimed that individuals were not IDPs, and thus not entitled to assistance, if they were not displaced by a party to the conflict. However, in a city such as Medellín, there was a high level of intra-urban displacement caused by the urban gangs which the government did not classify as connected to the conflict. UNHCR sought to make the existence of intra-urban displacement more visible, to have the phenomenon recognized by the state, and to ensure that its victims were able to claim the same assistance entitlements as those displaced by armed conflict in rural areas.

Just as in Colombia the ICRC was working on infra-IHL issues relating to urban violence, in Myanmar the ICRC was operating in Rakhine state—a context of communal violence which is not covered by IHL. One delegate explained that humanitarian consequences were the same, but because IHL did not apply in Rakhine, the tools at the ICRC's disposal were different. As a consequence, in their dialogue with the communities in Rakhine, delegates were not referring to particular rules and norms. However, in their dialogue with the police, they were making explicit reference to international standards. The ICRC had held seminars for the police at the national level and in Rakhine itself, and such training was based on international policing standards for riot and crowd control, and on the ICRC 'bible' on policing, 'To serve and protect', a document which deals with issues at the overlap of IHL and human rights (ICRC 2014c, 2014d).

In the DRC, the ICRC was not for the most part working outside IHL. However, this did not seem to relate to concerns about the limits of the institutional mandate, but rather was a consequence of there being more than enough IHL issues for the ICRC to work on, and of IHL issues being the first priority. Certainly delegates were not proactively looking for non-IHL issues to address, but sometimes the line between IHL and non-IHL issues is not so clear. For example, the ICRC had previously worked to support people expelled from Angola. More generally, the ICRC would think twice before addressing an issue outside IHL if other actors were already addressing that issue—but if there were humanitarian consequences of a sufficient level and no one else was doing anything, and if delegates thought they had real added value, then they might do something. In comparison with either Colombia or Myanmar, UNHCR was less restricted in the DRC, where it seemed to be quite free to work on those issues it chose without objection from the government. Thus, it seems to be the interaction between the relevant legal and normative frameworks and the institutional mandate on the one hand, and restrictions imposed by the affected state on the other, that set the parameters for UNHCR work in any given context.

In sum, as well as sometimes being restricted by their legal mandates, both the ICRC and UNHCR have always also found ways to work beyond their particular mandates in international law. However, the way that they have done so has changed over time. Historically, working beyond the confines of their respective legal mandates tended to be in the form of ad hoc responses to concrete events or situations which, in the case of the ICRC and to a lesser extent UNHCR, were often followed up by changes in policy and subsequently by developments of the legal framework. By contrast, they have now explicitly incorporated into their formal mandates certain contexts and issues that fall outside the international legal frameworks they are mandated to oversee. Even when the ICRC and UNHCR work on issues outside the frameworks that help to define their mandates, those issues have to be connected in some way to their core legal mandates, so the respective legal frameworks still have a constraining influence, just not such a strict one. Moreover, when either organization works beyond the boundaries of its legal mandate, it tends to do so with less confidence than that with which it addresses its core mandate.

Ignoring Issues within the Boundaries of the Relevant Legal Frameworks

Where an organization has an international legal mandate to address particular issues globally, or where it has entered into an agreement to do so in a particular context, we might expect that organization to be bound or obligated to address those issues. The legal mandate of the ICRC requires it to address IHL violations, and UNHCR has certain responsibilities under the cluster system and in line with country-specific agreements it enters into with their respective governments. Neither organization would be expected to deal with all the issues in *all* of the potentially relevant legal and normative frameworks, but it might be expected that each would address all those issues that relate to its particular responsibilities. In practice, however, neither organization takes quite such a comprehensive approach.

The Guiding Principles are seen as having 'played a significant role in shaping UNHCR's operational responses for IDPs' (Diagne and Entwisle 2008: 33). However, the issues covered by the Guiding Principles, and indeed the broader frameworks of IHL and IHRL, are best understood as a menu from which UNHCR selects issues to work on rather than a prescriptive list. Thus, there are issues covered by the Guiding Principles and the other applicable frameworks that are not addressed by UNHCR, even in contexts where they are relevant. For example, the Guiding Principles are applicable to non-state armed groups as well as to governments (Deng 2006: 221). This means that those issues which are not specifically about state responsibility imply obligations of non-state armed groups. To take just one example, Principle 13 states that 'In no case shall displaced children be recruited nor be required or permitted to take part in hostilities.' This applies equally to their participation on behalf of a non-state armed group and to their participation as part of a state military force. Thus, addressing these issues implies changing the behaviour of armed non-state actors to increase their compliance with international law. However, UNHCR focuses on the rights of IDPs with respect to the state, and not on the obligations of all armed actors (see Chapter 5).

Both the ICRC and UNHCR are working with limited resources and are thus compelled to prioritize some issues at the expense of others. Often this includes prioritizing some issues over others which they are specifically mandated to address, hence ignoring issues which fall within the legal frameworks that define their mandates. Thus, in the case of the ICRC, for example, while representations to armed parties must relate to violations of IHL, delegates do not make a representation just because a violation of IHL has occurred. As one interviewee explained, there is an 'almost infinite array of issues you have to address and you have to make choices'. In other words, an IHL violation is a necessary but not a sufficient condition for the ICRC to make a representation to the alleged perpetrator. Delegates want to address the most severe humanitarian consequences first, and this might mean ignoring harassment and minor extortion, for example. In such cases, however, the ICRC would aim to check with the community whether or not they want the ICRC to present an allegation, or whether letting it pass would be preferable—to avoid aggravating the alleged perpetrators and to be able to focus on more violations with more severe consequence. UNHCR often prioritizes issues that are explicitly linked to displacement, that is to say, threats resulting from or exacerbated by the predicament of displacement, and issues for which UNHCR envisages a state-based solution.

The ICRC at times also avoids addressing what may be priority issues when delegates deem that addressing them—specifically in the form of representations to armed actors—is likely to damage relations with those actors, or to impede ICRC work on other issues. In Colombia, for example, both the FARC and the ELN commonly used landmines and took hostages, despite both practices being illegal under IHL. Since these were sensitive topics with the guerrilla groups, and the ICRC did not want to compromise its dialogue with them on other topics, delegates sometimes chose to ignore particular violations of IHL. Where they did not expect to have much or any impact on a particular violation, then, they focused instead on fostering a stronger dialogue and changing the combatants' behaviour with respect to other IHL violations. Thus, in respect of these kinds of sensitive issues, ICRC delegates at the local level would weigh up institutional priorities and the obligations imposed by the ICRC's mandate to promote IHL against the damage it could do to their relationship with the relevant armed group. As the head of one office explained, 'It's one thing to come to a FARC zone with health brigades and another to talk about weapons contamination. Geneva, Bogotá and [the sub-delegation in charge of this office] are all pushing to do weapons contamination because it's an institutional priority. My response is yes, when we have the green light from the groups.' Potentially, avoiding the discussion of sensitive issues could entail departing from the principle of impartiality in the short run (ignoring the needs of those affected by landmines, for example) in order to assure access to all areas (itself a prerequisite for impartiality) in the long run. However, if interventions on a specific issue are expected to have zero impact, then avoidance of that issue does not seem to contravene impartiality.

In a similar vein, UNHCR for many years accepted strict limits on its operations in Myanmar, in particular in the south-east, where only in 2013 did its Letter of Understanding with the government mention IDPs for the first time. In order to maintain its operations, UNHCR did not push to be allowed to work with IDPs or to do protection work, and as a consequence has been seen largely as an infrastructure and development agency rather than an IDP protection agency.

As we have seen, both the ICRC and UNHCR have a stronger commitment and greater confidence when working on issues for which they have a clear legal mandate. Such commitment and confidence are undoubtedly important, and in this sense the frameworks are undoubtedly useful. In addition, the relevant laws and norms can also serve as tools with which the ICRC and UNHCR can seek to effect the protection outcomes they are aiming for. However, the different legal frameworks may not be effective tools in all contexts. This does not necessarily imply a particular framework should be easily discarded in those cases where it is ineffective, because that could devalue that framework in other cases, but it does mean that the relationship between law and the ends it is supposed to serve merits our attention.

THE USE AND USEFULNESS OF THESE FRAMEWORKS

This section, therefore, turns to the question of how far these frameworks are adequate and appropriate tools for achieving the ends they are designed for. The analysis starts from the assumption that the strategies adopted by the ICRC, UNHCR, and their staff members in seeking to achieve protective outcomes for the victims of conflict are rational and not misguided, and that we can thus draw inferences about the nature and effectiveness of the relevant legal frameworks from the strategic choices they make in their efforts to implement those frameworks.

General Preference for Legalistic Approaches to Protection

On one level, the experiences and preferences of both the ICRC and UNHCR appear to support the notion that legal norms are distinctive and carry greater persuasive power than more abstract appeals to moral principles and arguments, or at least that consent is an important determinant of the compliance pull of any norm (Chayes and Chayes 1998; Finnemore 2000; Franck 1995). Both organizations have a preference for making legal-based arguments.

Within the ICRC, there is a strong institutional preference for legal argumentation and for reference to the internal codes of conduct of armed forces and non-state armed groups. In contexts in which IHL is applicable, it is seen as a key protection tool (Aeschlimann 2005: 26). In such contexts, the core of ICRC protection work consists in presenting allegations of IHL violations to the alleged perpetrators in the hope of stopping ongoing violations and preventing future violations. In documenting these violations, the ICRC always refers to a specific rule of IHL, contained in one of the treaties or in the ICRC customary IHL database. In discussing the violations with their alleged perpetrators, there is an institutional preference for referencing IHL rules, but there is flexibility.

The ICRC emphasizes the development of IHL for the very reason that an agreed legal framework is expected to improve combatant behaviour, and hence to yield more effective protection outcomes for civilians. In a 2011 statement, Jakob Kellenberger, then President of the ICRC, explained that, 'Based on its long experience, the ICRC is convinced that the very existence of legal rules is essential for the protection of victims of armed conflict' (Kellenberger 2011). The ICRC approach to protection is thus underpinned by the assumption that an approved legal framework will make protection wider-reaching and more systematic than would otherwise be the case (Forsythe 2005: 259). This assumption has underpinned ICRC activity from the very origins of the organization with Dunant's *A memory of Solferino* and his proposal for the first Geneva Convention of 1864. Since then, the ICRC has continually sought to develop and expand the legal framework, and expects that, whether enshrined in treaties or customary law, specific rules rather than general appeals to morals will be more effective in generating the compliance of combatants with the underlying protective principles. This perspective explains the emphasis the ICRC places on the development of such rules, and was reinforced by a 2004 study by the ICRC which concluded that combatants are not morally autonomous and are therefore more likely to change their behaviour in response to explicit rules rather than appeals to their own ethics (Muñoz-Rojas and Frésard 2004).

Similarly, the Guiding Principles and domestic legal frameworks are the favoured protection tools of UNHCR. UNHCR officials invariably prefer to make legal arguments in their efforts to change state behaviour, in particular legal arguments based on domestic law. There are also numerous examples of how the Guiding Principles are used by UNHCR as a tool with which to educate states as to their responsibilities and individuals as to their rights, and with which to persuade states to meet those responsibilities (Diagne and Entwisle

2008). Emphasizing both the rights outlined in the Guiding Principles and the rights enshrined in national legal frameworks is the core of UNHCR protection work in many contexts.

Legal and Non-Legal Argumentation in ICRC Interventions with Armed Parties

ICRC delegates can only document and present protection cases to perpetrators when the cases involve an alleged violation of IHL. When making such a presentation, however, they do not have to use the language and argument of IHL. Different delegates have different styles, and in verbal dialogue some prefer to discuss humanitarian consequences rather than IHL, even where an IHL-based argument may be effective. Additionally, an individual delegate's understanding of which approach is most effective in getting a particular interlocutor to change his or her behaviour will shape that delegate's approach in any given interaction. Where military manuals or codes of conduct contain rules or guidance which reflect general IHL principles, it is sometimes seen to be more effective to remind combatants of these internal regulations from their own armed group. In other situations, the ICRC may choose to emphasize moral principles and arguments, and to de-emphasize IHL, focusing on the humanitarian consequences for civilians of particular conduct, rather than the illegality of such conduct. Thus, the ICRC has a preference for legal argumentation, but its aim is to change behaviour, and it does not always see the legal frameworks as the only or best tool for doing so. For example, ICRC delegates reported that where they are faced with a complete unawareness of IHL, a low level of instruction, and a loose chain of command, but the armed group in question abides by community rules, then an argument focused on humanitarian consequences might be quite effective.

Where the applicability of a particular legal framework is disputed, concrete appeals to that framework are likely to be ineffective or even counterproductive. This may occur where one party to the conflict denies the existence of conflict, the legitimacy of IHL in general, or its applicability to themselves.

In some cases, an actor (usually a state) denies that IHL (or a particular body of IHL) applies to a particular conflict. For example, although the ICRC (and indeed most of the world) considered that the 1990 Iraqi invasion of Kuwait was an international conflict to which most of IHL applied, Iraq claimed that Kuwait was an Iraqi province and hence that the context was not one of international conflict. In this case, then, the ICRC considered explicit references to the Geneva Conventions would be counterproductive, and focused instead on negotiating changes in Iraqi policy that were in line with, but without reference to, IHL (Forsythe 2005: 103). In other cases, the state does not want to acknowledge non-international armed conflict for fear of conferring rights and legitimacy on armed opposition groups. On the one hand, it is not necessary for the ICRC to classify any given context, even internally, because delegates can work under the ICRC's right of humanitarian initiative, and they do not need to talk in terms of IHL. Furthermore, since the ICRC sometimes seeks to use IHL even when it does not apply, they can draw on it for guidance even without classifying a particular context. On the other hand, in many cases ICRC delegates do seem to be less confident of their mandate and role in contexts in which IHL does not apply.

Often, the ICRC has prioritized its humanitarian protection functions over its IHL guardianship functions, choosing not to make public its assessments of the nature of particular conflicts or the violation of particular IHL rules, sometimes not even providing its legal assessment to the violators of IHL in question, and this risks compromising its claim to be an authority on IHL (Ratner 2011). However, the ICRC increasingly does not defer to states on this kind of issue. For example, when President Uribe took office in 2002, he denied the existence of armed conflict in Colombia, but the ICRC went ahead and publicly classified the context as one of non-international conflict. In the 2004 ICRC report of its activities in Colombia, Yves Giovannoni, the Head of Operations for Latin America and the Caribbean, officially stated that all the characteristics of conflict of a non-international character existed in the country (CICR 2005: 6). In Syria, the ICRC also stated that non-international armed conflict existed, contrary to the views of the Assad government (ICRC 2012c). In Myanmar, the ICRC had not made any public classification of the context at the time of interviews. The government did talk about conflict in the border areas, but did not always use the language of conflict, and the ICRC was not insisting on using IHL terminology. However, official ICRC publications did refer to armed conflict in parts of Myanmar, albeit somewhat cautiously and ambiguously, referring to 'conflict/violence' rather than making any explicit reference to a particular legal classification (see, for example, ICRC 2014a: 290–4).

Alternatively, an actor may accept the existence of conflict but deny that IHL applies to them. Most commonly, it has been non-state armed groups that have disputed the applicability or relevance of IHL to themselves. Only states can sign up to international treaties, and thus non-state groups can and sometimes do argue that such treaties are not applicable to them. As it is based on state practice, non-state armed groups can also question the applicability of customary IHL. Where the applicability of IHL is disputed, legal argumentation can be seen to be a hindrance rather than a help. In such cases, rather than simply supplementing legal argumentation with non-legal argumentation, ICRC delegates often choose to avoid legal argumentation altogether. ICRC reports on its work in Colombia demonstrate how the organization relates the humanitarian consequences experienced by conflict victims in Colombia to violations of (mainly customary) IHL rules, wherever possible (ICRC 2010b, 2014b). Protection cases must be based on alleged violations of specific rules, but since the 1990s the ICRC has become more open to talking about IHRL and other legal and normative frameworks as well as IHL. Thus, in Colombia, for example, the ICRC has begun to document alleged 'violations of IHRL and other transgressions against the population' in addition to violations of IHL (ICRC 2014b: 9). However, the extent to which other legal frameworks are cited in representations to armed actors remains relatively limited.

With all parties to the conflict in Colombia, ICRC delegates tended to open dialogue with reference to the humanitarian consequences of the actions of the relevant party. With the public forces, delegates would then employ legal argumentation, generally using IHL together with national legislation, and might also make reference to internal decisions and decrees of the military. Where internal rules existed in line with the spirit of IHL, ICRC delegates reported that they carried more persuasive power than IHL. For any given intervention, delegates can use multiple methods, with the objective being to end a particular violation, or particular humanitarian consequences. With the non-state armed groups in Colombia, delegates generally focused their dialogue on humanitarian consequences rather than violations of IHL, and also sought common ground between the internal rules of the armed group and IHL. The preference for non-legal argumentation suggests that ICRC delegates in Colombia found the legal framework unhelpful for changing the behaviour of armed non-state actors. The focus on internal rules in particular suggests that delegates expected to have more success convincing members of an armed group to change their behaviour in accordance with rules the group itself had created or signed up to. If this is correct, then it seems likely that if non-state armed groups were given the opportunity to sign up to a normative framework for civilian protection, and to play a role in the development of that framework, it might provide a more effective protection tool. However, unlike Geneva Call, the ICRC does not work to develop such agreements with non-state armed groups.

Finally, legal argumentation may be deemed to threaten or undermine relationships with a particular interlocutor in some contexts. For example, the ICRC deems that reference to IHL in general may be inappropriate at the early stages of building a relationship with some authorities, and that reference to specific IHL violations that are sensitive in a particular context may endanger the ICRC relationship with the relevant party.

Even in contexts in which IHL is generally known and accepted, and where the ICRC is dealing with issues that are not especially sensitive, the approach taken depends a lot on the degree of cohesion, the command and control chain, and the motives of the group, as well as the level of instruction of the individual interlocutor. The message is always the same, but the way it is articulated varies. Regardless, delegates almost always put humanitarian consequences up front, and even when they do not refer to concrete IHL rules, they may refer to IHL principles. Because IHL is very closely linked to ICRC identity, it is also seen as a way delegates can introduce themselves, and IHL and humanitarian consequences arguments are very much seen to be complementary.

Guiding Principles, Domestic Legislation, and Non-Legal Argumentation in the Work of UNHCR

In many contexts, UNHCR largely expects appeals either to general moral arguments or to the international soft law framework that is the Guiding Principles to be ineffective. Certainly this was the case in Colombia and Myanmar.

Appealing to national legislation was central to the work of UNHCR in Colombia, on account of the understanding within UNHCR that the only method of persuasion likely to have any impact on the Colombian state was explicit appeals to its obligations as enshrined in domestic law, and because the domestic legal framework was deemed to be largely sufficient. Interviewees explained that UNHCR could not ask more of the state than its obligation—or at most it could ask a little more, with the argument that the state has the capacity to do extra. In negotiating with state agencies for them to improve their provision of services to IDPs and those at risk of displacement, UNHCR staff members confirmed they would never start by asking state agencies to help because it would have benefits for the displaced, but rather they would always start with the obligation. The expectation was that appeals to a logic of appropriateness alone would have little effect—the argument of the needs of the victims was deemed insufficient. In lobbying the state, the language was normative and the discussion was all about obligations, constantly citing laws and constitutional court rulings.

In Myanmar, UNHCR also generally considered that the government would only respond to appeals to domestic law, and not to international standards. Interviewees reported that local officials loved the phrase 'the law of the land', and that referring to a specific clause of national legislation carried some weight with judges, but that international standards simply did not hold much sway. Thus, where domestic law existed and aligned with the objectives of UNHCR, staff members sought to use it. In Rakhine state, for example, there were many local orders (administrative orders from the Rakhine state government) issued since the 2012 violence, that tightened restrictions on Muslims' movement, marriage, number of children, religious practices, etc. At the time of interviews, UNHCR was conducting an analysis of these orders, and cross-referencing them with national legislation and the report of the governmental Rakhine Investigation Commission (Republic of the Union of

Myanmar 2013). The idea was to highlight discrepancies and thus to use national legislation to argue against the local orders. In addition, UNHCR was engaging in advocacy on the Myanmar citizenship law. Despite pressure for change from the General Assembly, the Special Rapporteur, the Office for the High Commissioner on Human Rights, and other international actors, the response from the government to suggestions to change the law was consistently negative. Having done an analysis of the law as it stood, UNHCR took the position that some people could get citizenship with the current law, so the first aim was to have it applied properly, and the more ambitious aim was to get the law changed.

However, domestic legislation relating to IDP protection concerns was very limited in Myanmar, and the Guiding Principles were central to the work of UNHCR, albeit not always as an advocacy tool. The effectiveness of using international standards in dialogue was seen to vary across the country. Interviewees reported that there was no ear for the Guiding Principles in Rakhine, but that they could be useful in Kachin. At the Rakhine state level, there was thus very limited reference to international norms. There, UNHCR action was guided by international norms and principles, but staff members did not use them in their dialogue with the government. In Kachin state, by contrast, all UNHCR advocacy work was based on the Guiding Principles, and UNHCR was working to develop an advocacy document for the government based on international standards as well as doing a similar thing with the non-state armed groups in the non-government-controlled areas. Given the expectation that international laws and standards would have little effect, this focus on the Guiding Principles may have been more a consequence of there being no domestic law to draw on, than of any expectation that this approach would actually be effective.

In the DRC, even domestic law was held to have little impact because of a culture of impunity and a lack of implementation. In light of this, UNHCR was focusing in particular on getting cases to lawyers and paying judges' salaries.

CONCLUSIONS

The international law of *internal* conflict was developed through analogy to the international law of *international* armed conflict (Sivakumaran 2011). In other words, the legal and normative framework on which the ICRC bases its approach to protecting civilians in internal conflict was originally designed to regulate international conflict. Furthermore, in different contexts in which the ICRC operates, different parts of IHL apply or IHL does not apply at all, but the ICRC will not necessarily undertake different activities (Bugnion 2003: 306).

There is a single institutional protection methodology which applies in all situations of violence, including those in which IHL does not apply. Very often the ICRC invokes the whole body of humanitarian rules and seeks their application by analogy, even in those contexts where they are not directly applicable (Bugnion 2003: 306; Forsythe 1978: 275). In short, a particular notion of protection became institutionalized in the ICRC in its early years and has continued to impact on subsequent treaties and practice.

However, the task of protecting civilians in internal armed conflict is different from prior tasks in the ICRC mandate, most notably because internal armed conflicts by definition involve non-state armed groups. Although the IHL relating to internal armed conflict purports to bind these groups in the same way that it binds states, their relationship to this body of law is quite distinct from that of states. Only states can sign IHL treaties, and state practice is privileged in the development of customary IHL. Unsurprisingly, then, armed non-state actors often deny that IHL applies to them. In response to such denial, the ICRC has adopted a flexible and pragmatic approach to engaging with such actors. While there is an institutional preference for using legal argumentation, on a case-by-case basis this may be supplemented or substituted with non-legal argumentation if that is expected to generate better results. The problem with such substitution is that, all other things being equal, rules-based argumentation is expected to be more effective. If legal argumentation is more effective in general, and argumentation based on existing laws is found to be counterproductive with some armed non-state actors, it calls into question the adequacy of existing laws for maximizing the compliance of such actors (Bradley 2013).

UNHCR has also carried across a particular understanding of protection from IRL and its refugee protection work to its IDP protection work. Specifically, across both issue-areas UNHCR understands protection as being about getting states to come good on their legal responsibilities. However, there is no international hard law framework for IDP protection, which means the tools at UNHCR's disposal for IDP protection are very different from those available for refugee protection. UNHCR has sought to adapt to this difference by drawing on domestic legislation and on the Guiding Principles for Internal Displacement in lieu of a hard law framework. Such an approach remains limited, however, because in many settings there is little relevant domestic law, and the Guiding Principles are not expected to carry much persuasive power.

Furthermore, the emphasis on legal argumentation directed at the state may be inappropriate for IDP protection. Originally, UNHCR took a legalistic approach to refugee protection and focused on asylum. UNHCR worked with actual and potential host states, negotiating with them to protect the citizens of other states as per IRL. It did not attempt to make states more willing or able to protect their *own* citizens. However, with the expansion into IDP protection, UNHCR has maintained a legalistic approach and a modus operandi that favours negotiating with states for the protection of individuals on their territory despite the substantive difference between refugees and IDPs, namely that the latter have fled insecurity on the territory of the very same state and that they are threatened by armed conflict and the associated violence, and not by the lack of a legal status to be on the territory in which they reside.

In sum, the legal and normative frameworks on which the ICRC and UNHCR base their in-country protection efforts may not be fully appropriate for the tasks at hand. That said, these frameworks do play an important role in shaping their mandates, both in general and in specific contexts. Although the ICRC and UNHCR seek to address other issues too, they are both more confident working on those issues that fall squarely within their respective legal mandates. Thus, while the international legal frameworks from which they derive these mandates are not essential to their work, they do strengthen it. This raises questions about the effectiveness of their work on issues that fall outside their mandates in international law. The mandate of the ICRC is weaker in contexts where IHL does not apply, and despite many years' experience working in 'other situations of violence' and an institutional methodology for doing so, it appears that for many delegates in the field the lack of a legal framework and a correspondingly clear mandate weakens their confidence as to whether and how they can address the perpetrators. Similarly, UNHCR has a weaker sense of its own competence and mandate with respect to IDPs in comparison with refugees. The lack of an international framework also seems to engender a less consistent approach across different IDP contexts and allows for the governments of the affected states to set the parameters of UNHCR's work in those contexts.

Given the relevance (although not the pre-eminence) of their respective mandates in international law in determining the issues that the ICRC and UNHCR seek to address, it is not surprising that the legal frameworks they oversee are broadly consistent with the specific objectives pursued by each organization. In Chapter 4, we will see that the prioritization of the objective of threat reduction that characterizes both IHL and the prior mandate of the ICRC also characterizes its efforts to protect civilians in internal armed conflicts. Likewise, we see that the emphasis in IRL and UNHCR refugee protection work on reducing the exposure of refugees to violent threats and coercion, and on reducing the consequences they suffer as a result of such violence and coercion, is carried over into UNHCR IDP protection efforts.

4

Objectives and Strategies of Protection

This chapter analyses what the ICRC and UNHCR set out to achieve in their protection work, and how they aim to achieve it. The ICRC aims first and foremost to reduce the threat posed by armed actors to civilians, while UNHCR aims mainly to reduce the extent to which IDPs and those at risk of displacement are exposed to, and suffer from, such threats. Furthermore, the ICRC defines its objectives closer to the violence that is the central protection problem, taking a direct and actor-centred approach to threat reduction, while UNHCR tends to pursue objectives that are at least one level removed from violence, with an emphasis on achieving changes in public policy. The rest of this chapter proceeds in six main parts. The first briefly sets out a conceptual framework with which to classify and specify the protection objectives and strategies of humanitarian organizations. Each of the next four sections examines one type of protection objective (namely violence reduction, threat reduction, vulnerability reduction, and mitigating the consequences of violence), explaining the kinds of strategies that can contribute to the achievement of that objective, and analysing whether and how the ICRC and UNHCR employ such strategies. The sixth section analyses some of the means to protection that are commonly misconceptualized as ends in themselves, and their relationships with the different types of protection objective already discussed.

CLASSIFYING PROTECTION OBJECTIVES

Protection is generally not clearly conceptualized by humanitarian agencies, and the objectives of protection tend to be underspecified. The most widely agreed-upon definition came out of a series of workshops organized by the ICRC between 1996 and 2000, and attended by representatives of humanitarian and human rights agencies, according to which protection encompasses 'all activities aimed at ensuring full respect for the rights of the individual in accordance with the letter and the spirit of the relevant bodies of law, i.e. human rights law, international humanitarian law and refugee law' (Giossi Caverzasio 2001: 19). Instead of defining protection in terms of the overlap between different approaches, consensus was achieved through an all-inclusive definition. This is problematic because it includes an enormous range of objectives, without providing any kind of framework for prioritizing between them. Indeed the overall objective encapsulated in the definition encompasses such an expansive range of rights that it allows a wide range of humanitarian activities to be reframed as protection without identifying core and shared protection concerns, and thus without developing coherent strategies to address those concerns (Bonwick 2006: 271). Moreover, the expansiveness of the definition allows humanitarian agencies to go for the low-hanging fruit, focusing on those activities in which they have experience or those that are relatively easy, rather than addressing the priority issues which tend to be the more difficult tasks associated with achieving physical safety.

Specifying the objectives of protection, then, is both a more complex task than it may first appear, and an extremely important one, as it has consequences for how agencies practise protection and—ultimately—for the protection outcomes of IDPs and other civilians. We can start with two basic questions: who is to be protected, and what are they to be protected from? Different agencies have different populations of concern, and the question of who is to be protected was discussed in the section on impartiality in Chapter 2. But what are they to be protected from? If protection is fundamentally about violence, then it follows that they are to be protected from violence, but what does it mean to protect people from violence? This chapter develops a typology of protection objectives based on what humanitarian organizations do in the name of protection, and an analysis of how what they do relates to the violence that is the central protection problem. Expanding on models elsewhere that incorporate notions of threat and vulnerability (Jaspars and O'Callaghan 2010; Slim and Bonwick 2005), it identifies four main types of objective: (a) reducing the overall level of violence; (b) reducing the threat such violence poses to civilians; (c) reducing the vulnerability of civilians to the threats posed by violence; and (d) reducing or mitigating the consequences of violence for civilians.

The overall level of organized violence relates to the onset, spread, and intensity of armed conflict. It is theoretically possible, but highly implausible in practice, that organized violence can exist without posing a direct threat to civilians (as in the ideal type of conventional conflict, where the battle lines are far from the civilian population). The level of threat is the extent of violence or coercion against civilians, including both deliberate targeting and other forms of physical violence, and actions or measures which create fear of violence. The vulnerability of civilians refers to their exposure to such threats, and their propensity to suffer from them. Very often, when we think about the level of threat, we are thinking about threats to civilians in general, whereas when we think about the level of vulnerability, we are thinking about particular civilians or groups of civilians. Finally, efforts to mitigate the consequences accept that civilians will sometimes be the victims of violence, and seek to reduce how much they suffer as a result. This could include, for example, medical or psychosocial care provided to a rape victim.

These can be seen as ordinal categories in the sense that if the overall level of violence can be reduced to zero, there is no need to concern ourselves with reducing the threats posed by (non-existent) violence, or the exposure of civilians to those threats. Likewise, if the level of threat can be reduced to zero, there is no need to concern ourselves with civilian exposure to (non-existent) threats. Finally, if civilians are not exposed to threats, there is no need to mitigate the consequences of (non-existent) exposure. This means that, all other things being equal, violence reduction should be prioritized over threat reduction, which should, in turn, be prioritized over vulnerability reduction, which likewise should be prioritized over mitigating the consequences of violence. However, as we shall see in the remaining sections of this chapter, all other things are not equal. Higher-order objectives are often more difficult to achieve, so focusing on lower order objectives may be more effective. Furthermore, institutional characteristics and preferences may be at least as much a determinant of ICRC and UNHCR objectives as are strategic protection priorities.

In addition to these four categories, analysis of what humanitarian agencies do in the name of protection identifies three main classifications that cut across the four different types of objective. First, what are referred to here as maximalist approaches actively seek to reduce violence, threats, or vulnerability, while minimalist approaches aim only to *avoid increasing* the level of violence, threat, or vulnerability. For example, in the oft-cited example of a situation in which sexual abuse against women occurs as they walk long distances to collect water or firewood, the provision of assistance (water or fuel supplies) in a more safely accessible location (for example, close to the refugee camp) represents an active effort to reduce their vulnerability (a maximalist approach). By contrast, simply viewing assistance activities through a 'protection lens' so as, at a minimum, to avoid generating side effects from the provision of assistance that impact negatively on protection outcomes (for example, considering lighting around latrines) is a minimalist approach. This is sometimes called protection mainstreaming, and arguably such a minimalist approach is simply good assistance programming, and should not be labelled as protection.

Second, different approaches also vary in terms of whether the strategies adopted in pursuit of these different types of objectives are actor-centred or structural, and direct or indirect. For example, do they seek to reduce threats directly by addressing the violent actors who pose a threat, or do they instead work to promote changes to incentive structures and normative frameworks, with the aim of encouraging behavioural change indirectly? This is connected to the level of removal any such interventions are from the violence that humanitarian actors seek to protect against, and from the civilians they seek to protect. The further removed a strategy is, the harder it is to assess its impact.

Third, different organizations have different thematic priorities. Both the ICRC and UNHCR focus on protecting their respective populations of concern from specific types of violence or coercion. These include thematic priorities at the global level, as well as various priority issues in different field settings. In 2010, for example, there were five institutional protection priorities for the ICRC globally: mines/weapon contamination; medical missions; minors; women in war; and missing persons. More recently, the ICRC launched a major four-year global campaign on healthcare in danger (2012–15), and a four-year plan on sexual violence (2013–16). While UNHCR does not have such clearly defined global priorities, it is clear that issues such as sexual and gender-based violence (SGBV) and the recruitment of child soldiers often feature high on the UNHCR agenda. Sexual violence is a key priority for UNHCR because different phases of the displacement cycle make people particularly vulnerable. During the displacement phase (that is, in a camp or a host community), UNHCR seeks both to prevent sexual violence (threat and vulnerability reduction) and to respond to victims (mitigating the consequences). For both organizations, the particular threats they focus on also vary with the particular contexts they are working in. In the DRC, for example, both are particularly concerned with child recruitment, sexual violence, and restrictions on movement (as a result of control barriers and checkpoints operated by armed groups and the army, as well as of general insecurity hampering travel to fields, market, and other livelihoods activities).

On the basis of this typology, we can identify certain key differences that help to characterize the institutional approaches to protection of the ICRC and UNHCR. The ICRC emphasizes threat reduction through strategies that are mainly actor-centred and direct, while UNHCR is much more focused on structural change in the form of developing public policy with the aim of reducing vulnerability. The ICRC seeks to induce change at the local level where civilians experience violence, and at the level of global public policy, while UNHCR emphasizes change at the level of domestic public policy.

VIOLENCE REDUCTION

The overall level of organized violence depends on the onset and continuation of conflict or other mass organized violence, and the intensity of the ensuing violence. Accordingly, violence reduction efforts by a third party are either aimed at reducing the number of combatants or parties to conflict (through violent or non-violent means), preventing or resolving conflict, or building or maintaining peace. Correspondingly, such efforts can be directed at reducing one or more of capabilities, opportunities, incentives, or motivations for violence (Human Security Report Project 2011: 68; Nicolaïdis 1996).

Efforts to reduce the overall level of violence are deemed to fall outside the mandates of many humanitarian agencies, in particular those agencies that are committed to the principle of neutrality. However, some so-called multi-mandate agencies do pursue peace-building aims and other transformative goals (Slim and Bradley 2013). In addition, at the global level, rather than in relation to specific conflicts, humanitarian agencies have sometimes participated in efforts to develop normative frameworks to ban particular weapons, thereby seeking to reduce the capabilities or incentives for violence (Carpenter 2011; Petrova 2010). Conflict-resolution and peace-building activities are generally considered to be beyond the mandates—legal and de facto—of the ICRC and UNHCR. Mostly, they would not, for example, seek to address the grievances that may cause or contribute to conflict, to reduce the economic incentives for individuals and groups to engage in violence, or to prevent weapons being delivered to armed parties. All such efforts would be seen to contradict the principle of neutrality. Nonetheless, closer examination shows that both organizations can and do involve themselves in efforts to reduce the overall level of violence, albeit in limited ways.

The IHL framework, which is so closely linked to the identity of the ICRC, is not concerned with the justice of any given war (*jus ad bellum*), or the objectives of either side, only with regulating the conduct of war (*jus in bello*). Likewise, the work of the ICRC in armed conflict and in other situations of violence is not concerned with the rightness or wrongness of the resort to violence in pursuit of particular ends, but rather with the way in which violence is employed and, crucially, with the humanitarian consequences of that violence. The ICRC sees itself as fostering a 'spirit of peace' while avoiding involvement in the politics that are an essential constituent of any transition from conflict to peace (Sandoz 1987). However, the ICRC may contribute to violence-reduction efforts in two particular ways. First, while the ICRC started out with a focus on victims of war, it progressively got involved in weapons questions. In this regard, the organization has played a role in developing international legislation to prohibit particular weapons, including, for example, the Ottawa Treaty,[1] which bans landmines. ICRC support for banning a particular weapon depends on the ICRC legal division determining that use of the weapon necessarily contradicts IHL principles.

Second, as a neutral intermediary, the ICRC can provide a diplomacy service and even a physical space for negotiations between armed parties. In

[1] Convention on the Prohibition of the Use, Stockpiling, Production and Transfer of Anti-Personnel Mines and on their Destruction, 18 September 1997.

this way it may facilitate conflict resolution, albeit indirectly and through enabling, rather than engaging in, political discussions. For example, in 1962 the ICRC offered to help with the Cuban missile crisis by inspecting ships sailing to Cuba to check for missile parts (Forsythe 1977: 101). It also played a role in mediation in El Salvador in 1984, assisting the Catholic Church and the El Salvador Red Cross to escort representatives of the Farabundo Martí National Liberation Front (FMLN) to negotiations with the government (Forsythe 2005: 199). At the time of writing, the ICRC was similarly working as a neutral intermediary in support of the peace negotiations between the FARC and the government, specifically 'facilitating safe passage for some of their representatives and providing advice on IHL-related issues' (ICRC 2014a: 419).

UNHCR sees a reduction in organized violence—in the form of conflict prevention or resolution—as the only way to protect refugees and IDPs in conflict settings, insisting that the 'restoration of peace and the protection of human rights are the best ways to provide truly effective protection to the internally displaced' (UNHCR 2007b, para. 58). However, UNHCR sees this as the domain of states, and the activities that UNHCR undertakes in the name of protection are not directed at reducing overall violence. Numerous notes on international protection by UNHCR emphasize the responsibility of states in conflict resolution and prevention. In this, therefore, the role of UNHCR itself is limited to advocating for states to prevent and resolve conflicts. This includes not only the affected states, but also those in the broader international community. Most such statements made by UNHCR are in general terms, and do not relate to specific conflicts.

That said, UNHCR has at times actively sought to support peace processes. A key example concerns the role of UNHCR in the International Conference on Central American Refugees (CIREFCA—Conferencia Internacional sobre los Refugiados Centroamericanos), a process which ran from 1987 to 1995 and was specifically conceptualized as linking protection and solutions for Central American refugees to ongoing peace processes (Betts 2009: 78–111). In conflicts that generate large refugee flows, UNHCR may also support peace processes by getting the refugees accepted at the negotiation table to ensure they can participate in shaping any settlement, as in Guatemala in 1997–9, or by facilitating their participation in elections, as in Cambodia in 1993 (Brookings-Bern Project on Internal Displacement 2007; Long 2010). In some conflict contexts, including Colombia and the DRC, UNHCR has also worked on land issues, lobbying for public policy change, legal reform, or the application of existing laws, in particular to protect or restore the land and property of the displaced. While UNHCR's primary aim in such activities may be related to the displacement and return of individuals and communities, and not conflict resolution or violence reduction, it is inevitable that they may have an impact (positive or negative) on conflict and violence in contexts where land issues are one of the structural causes of conflict.

In sum, both the ICRC and UNHCR advocate measures to reduce violence and prevent and resolve conflicts in general, but they are unlikely to make recommendations in respect of particular contexts. However, both organizations have sometimes supported and enabled the political process towards peace in particular contexts. Such support has been closely linked to their legal mandates, and has involved facilitating the involvement of particular national stakeholders in peace processes. Neither organization has actively engaged in the processes itself.

THREAT REDUCTION

As with the overall level of organized violence, the threats that violence poses to civilians are directly determined by the behaviour of its perpetrators. In internal conflicts, the perpetrators of organized violence include national military forces and non-state armed groups, and their motivations and capabilities both play a role in determining the level of threat. Threat reduction therefore entails changing the behaviour of armed actors, and this can undoubtedly be a difficult task. Unsurprisingly, then, many humanitarian agencies do not emphasize threat reduction, preferring instead to focus on efforts to reduce vulnerability or to mitigate the consequences of violence. Nonetheless, there are a number of strategies that international humanitarian agencies can undertake with the aim of threat reduction. This section explains the logic underpinning different types of strategy, and shows how the ICRC and UNHCR can and do employ some such strategies.

In contexts where IHL is applicable, the ICRC sees threat reduction as broadly equivalent to increasing compliance with IHL. The institutional protection policy of the ICRC states that 'Protection relates firstly to the causes of, or the circumstances that lead to, violations—mainly by addressing those responsible for the violations and those who may have influence over the latter—and secondly to their consequences' (ICRC 2008b: 752). The ICRC approach is thus proactive, seeking primarily to prevent harm and only secondarily to remedy it after the event. The primary objectives are about changing the behaviour of armed actors, both state and non-state. This approach is direct and actor-centred, and the primary means is bilateral, confidential dialogue with weapons-bearers.

While threat reduction is a central objective for the ICRC, in most contexts it is considered to be either less important or less feasible for UNHCR. An exception to this is in the DRC, where UNHCR has adopted a modus operandi more akin to that of the ICRC. With respect to sexual violence in particular, UNHCR deems rape prevention to be a fundamental priority in the DRC, and adopts both direct and indirect strategies to reduce the threat of sexual violence. Direct strategies include dialogue with potential perpetrators (both military and civilian), and indirect strategies include work to improve the justice system and reduce impunity. Moreover, the following analysis shows that UNHCR also engages in some threat-reduction strategies elsewhere, even if it does not conceptualize them that way or engage in them as systematically as the ICRC.

Rationalist perspectives suggest armed actors will pose a threat to civilians when such behaviour is in their strategic interests—in other words, when it increases the security, power, or resources of that armed actor (Snyder 2011: 37). Targeting civilians may be a rational strategy for combatants who seek to win a war, as well as for combatants who are pursuing other goals, such as economic advantage or personal power (Keen and Lee 2009: 17–18). Conversely, abstention from attacking civilians and abiding by IHL may also be in the rational interests of combatants, for reasons of reciprocity, engendering international or local public support, economy, military advantage, or planning for after the conflict (Bangerter 2011: 360–7; Keen and Lee 2009: 18; Veuthey 1983: 89–90). Similar arguments can work in opposing directions, depending on the dynamics of the specific context, the aims of the armed groups in question, and their relationships with local communities and with international actors.

Such rationalist perspectives, then, suggest that third parties can reduce the level of threat by creating rational incentives for armed actors to behave in a particular way. Humanitarian agencies often consider that they themselves are not in a position to create rational incentives. Certainly, they do not tend to offer material inducements for armed actors to change their behaviour. However, they may undertake strategies which are indirectly aimed at changing the incentives that armed actors face. For example, the ICRC, UNHCR, and many other organizations seek to provide some kind of passive protection through presence. Presence alone is thought to have a deterrent effect on some armed parties. The underlying logic is that armed actors are less likely to threaten civilians where their behaviour is witnessed, because witnessed bad behaviour affects the legitimacy of the armed party, and reduced legitimacy can impose costs. Even the bilateral confidential dialogue of the ICRC ultimately carries with it the possibility of public denunciation.

While not necessarily conceptualized by UNHCR itself as a means to threat reduction, work by UNHCR on land rights does have the potential to serve that purpose. For example, in Colombia, it has been shown that informality of property rights increases the likelihood that an armed group will attack (Velásquez Guijo 2008). In this sense, by working on land rights in Colombia UNHCR may have been able to reduce the threat posed by armed non-state actors indirectly, through work with the state itself. On the other hand, land reform may just displace the threats elsewhere as armed groups employ violence to secure other sources of finance. In the DRC, efforts by UNHCR to strengthen the judiciary aimed to reduce impunity, and hence to alter the incentive structure to make the perpetration of rape, sexual violence, and other threats more costly (i.e. more likely to be punished).

Thus, there are several examples of the ICRC and UNHCR exploring means to alter incentive structures with the aim of reducing the threats posed to civilians. These efforts are indirect in that they seek to alter incentive structures rather than to offer concrete incentives or inducements directly to the actors whose behaviour they seek to change. In addition to altering incentives to encourage more positive behaviour, humanitarian agencies may also take a more minimalist approach, to work in such a way as to *avoid* creating incentives for armed actors to behave in such a way that *increases* the threat faced by civilians.

Beyond rational incentives, a constructivist perspective in international relations suggests that norms and identity also shape behaviour at the international level in the absence of a common sovereign. Corresponding with this idea, in the context of conflict, 'anti-civilian ideologies' may exist among armed groups and provide a normative motivation or explanation for threats against civilians (Slim 2008). Identity and moral convictions can also encourage protective behaviour towards civilians (Bangerter 2011: 358–60). In the long run, humanitarian agencies may be able to work to change the ideological and normative frameworks, in other words to change shared understandings of what constitutes appropriate standards of behaviour. In so doing, they may also contribute to a change in the incentive structure, because inappropriate behaviour may be more costly than appropriate behaviour.

In this way, the work of the ICRC goes beyond efforts to change the immediate behaviour of combatants in line with the standards set out in IHL. It also seeks to change the attitudes of armed groups *towards* IHL, specifically to change their understanding of what constitutes appropriate behaviour, and their will to behave appropriately. Further, in working for the development and expansion of IHL, the ICRC seeks to change global understandings of what constitutes appropriate behaviour for armed parties to conflict. The development of international laws and norms is an indirect strategy aimed nonetheless at changing the behaviour of armed actors. UNHCR also works to develop legal frameworks, but these frameworks are not mainly concerned with violent threats to civilians.

In addition to creating or altering incentives to promote behaviour change, or developing new norms, humanitarian agencies can call attention to existing incentives, standards, and norms, and they can make moral arguments. This kind of dialogue is the bread and butter of ICRC protection work, and a less central but nonetheless important feature of UNHCR work. All such dialogue is usually labelled 'persuasion' in the humanitarian policy literature (Slim and Bonwick 2005: 81), but we can usefully distinguish a number of key logics underpinning such dialogue. Specifically, we can distinguish between dialogue based on a 'logic of consequences' which draws attention to the rational incentives to behave a particular way, and dialogue based on a 'logic of appropriateness' which draws attention to the moral arguments for particular behaviour (March and Olsen 1998). Furthermore, we can distinguish between legal argumentation and non-legal argumentation (Ratner 2011). Drawing attention to international laws and norms can comprise part of a rational argument (because failure to comply with those laws and norms can be costly) or part of a moral argument (because compliance with the law is the right thing to do). Conversely, both rational and moral arguments can be made without reference to international laws and norms. This is illustrated in Table 4.1.

Depending on the context, and on the delegates involved, the ICRC may use any or all of the four logics of dialogue set out in Table 4.1. In situations like Afghanistan, IHL is common sense, and there are strategic arguments (mainly related to reciprocity) to persuade weapons-bearers to respect it, but in a context where violence is largely one-sided and is viewed as an end in itself, delegates struggle to identify strategic arguments against the use of violence. In such a context, the catchphrase 'even war has a limit', which captures the essence of IHL and of the protection methodology of the ICRC, does not make sense. Interviewees in the DRC reported that some interlocutors understand the rules as helping them to do better, and accept the ICRC explanation that if they respect IHL, they will do a better job (militarily speaking), and be better respected by the civilian population. By contrast, other interlocutors listen to the ICRC because they do not want to be seen as bad guys, but do not see a strategic argument for adherence to IHL. In both cases the interlocutors engage in the dialogue, but in the second case they are less likely to change their behaviour accordingly.

The question of whether they make interest-based arguments (logic of consequences) or moral arguments (logic of appropriateness) elicited a rare example of inconsistency across the responses of different ICRC interviewees. It would appear that there is no institutional preference here, and delegates adopt whichever approach they deem more effective, or whichever balance of the two they deem most effective. A purely moral argument would emphasize the negative humanitarian consequences of particular conduct in the hope of

Table 4.1. Examples of different techniques or logics of dialogue

	Logic of consequences	Logic of appropriateness
Legal argumentation	Reciprocity arguments	Reminder of international law, domestic law, and the internal rules of armed groups
Non-legal argumentation	Arguments about the military inefficiency of certain behaviour, e.g. use of child soldiers	Explanation of the humanitarian consequences of particular behaviours

getting the relevant actor to change that conduct. One interviewee reported asking interlocutors to 'think about what you believe is the right thing to do'. However, such an argument may also be supplemented with a reminder that the armed actor needs the trust of the people and should change their conduct accordingly. At the other end of the spectrum, interest-based arguments can be used in an effort to change the perception of interlocutors of the military benefit of particular conduct. For example, an argument can be made that the short-term benefits of landmine use do not outweigh the long-term disadvantages, or that in the long run child soldiers are more of a liability than a military advantage.

UNHCR is anyway less focused on threat reduction than the ICRC, but to the extent that it does aim to induce actors to change their behaviour, it has a strong preference for legal argumentation. That said, where there are no relevant laws, UNHCR staff will use non-legal argumentation based on a logic of consequences. This kind of argumentation may be in the form of a dialogue or it may be a more practical demonstration of the consequences of particular actions. In many cases it is about drawing attention to the benefits of particular behaviour, but it can also entail demonstrating that the costs are lower than the actor might have thought or expected. In Rakhine state in Myanmar, for example, UNHCR was engaged in dialogue trying to convince the government to take incremental concrete steps—increasing freedom of movement, negotiating cheaper fishing permits, more regular fishing access, etc. One interviewee described the logic underpinning this dialogue as 'how to make it less scary for the government to take the next step'. In other words, a form of argumentation was in play, one which instead of highlighting the benefits of a particular course of action, sought to argue that the cost of that action was not so high as perceived.

In addition to these different logics of dialogue, ICRC or UNHCR staff can adopt different styles or approaches in their dialogue with different actors. Specifically, interventions can be written or verbal, and they can be more or less formal. Both organizations adopt different styles, depending on the interlocutor and the nature of the discussion. In Colombia, the ICRC was using a more formal, top-down approach with the national military, which ranged from providing overviews of violations and annual trends at the level of the defence minister to less formal, but nonetheless regular meetings at the level of the department and local commanders. With the non-state armed groups contact was generally less formal and less regular. In the DRC, the ICRC was combining both official and non-official dialogue with the authorities, and UNHCR was engaging in verbal dialogue for most interventions, but would write to higher-level officials in the case of more serious violations by the FARDC.

In Rakhine state, the ICRC had an emerging dialogue which, at the time of interviews, remained mainly verbal. Furthermore, as is normal in the early stages of a relationship and dialogue, delegates preferred to focus on humanitarian consequences and to avoid discussion of specific rules or norms (that is, they employed non-legal argumentation). They reported that when they got to the point of using written interventions, they would use the same approach they always use in other situations of violence, which may include reference to human rights obligations. While in some contexts ICRC delegates are very cautious about which legal norms they refer to, this was not expected to be an issue in Rakhine. ICRC delegates thought that in Rakhine specifically and in Myanmar more broadly, oral interventions were better accepted, because written interventions can create fear around a particular department, which may be counterproductive for the dialogue. This is indicative of the delicate balance ICRC delegates seek in their dialogue; the aim is to change behaviour, and the ICRC perspective is that this is best achieved through a kind of constructive criticism which should not make interlocutors feel uncomfortable.

Likewise, for UNHCR, dialogue with the local authorities in Rakhine state was generally verbal, and when staff heard of or feared an incident, they would first try to discuss it with local government interlocutors. However, UNHCR interviewees suggested they needed to use written interventions in a more systematic manner, explaining that when they raised issues verbally, the dialogue would seem positive, but then nothing would happen. Given the highly bureaucratic nature of the state, the expectation was that local officials would have to record all letters received, and that this might force their hand to address these concerns. However, UNHCR staff also acknowledged that they did not generally receive a reply when they did make written interventions. They explained that it was nonetheless important for UNHCR to write (especially in light of the 'human rights up front' initiative within the UN[2]) to prove they had tried. In a sense, then, making written interventions may reflect a concern about covering backs more than about outcomes.

Strategies to reduce threats must ultimately seek to change the behaviour of state and non-state armed groups and the individuals within them. They may do so directly or indirectly, and on an ad hoc or systemic basis, but they must in some way seek to change the behaviour of armed actors, both state and non-state. Changing behaviour is always likely to be a relatively long term endeavour. Judging the effectiveness of any intervention aimed at behaviour change is complicated by the fact that causality is likely to be complex, and effects are unlikely to occur immediately. The further removed the intervention is from the actor or behaviour it seeks to change, the more difficult it is to evaluate effectiveness, and the greater the danger the means come to define the ends (or become ends in themselves). On the one hand, measuring the impact of indirect methods, such as changing incentive structures, may be more difficult

[2] See <http://www.un.org/sg/rightsupfront/> for more information.

than for more direct interventions with the actors themselves. Furthermore, having an impact on their behaviour may be less likely—or at least less immediate—with such indirect methods. On the other hand, high-level law and policy changes may have the *potential* to affect the behaviour of a larger number of actors. In other words, while having an effect may be more likely with more direct, local-level interventions aimed at reducing immediate threats, indirect interventions—*if effective*—may have an effect of greater magnitude.

If threats could be reduced to zero, then there would, of course, be no threats for civilians to be vulnerable to. However, threats are never reduced to zero, and vulnerability reduction is the mainstay of many humanitarian agency approaches to protecting civilians.

VULNERABILITY REDUCTION

Despite its emphasis on working to change the behaviour of weapons-bearers and thus to reduce the threat they pose to civilians, the ICRC also seeks to work directly with civilians to reduce their vulnerability. This is a secondary aim in acknowledgement of the fact that the ICRC will not always be able to reduce the threats posed to civilians, and even where threat reduction is effective, threats will not be reduced to zero (ICRC 2008b: 752). In Colombia, for example, the focus is on threat reduction, but in Myanmar and at least certain parts of the DRC, the ICRC was devoting more effort to activities aimed at reducing vulnerability. In most contexts, UNHCR activities more often have a vulnerability-reduction element than a threat-reduction element, although in many cases the relationship between these activities and the level of vulnerability of IDPs and others of concern to UNHCR is not well conceptualized.

While a range of literature seeks to explain what factors determine the threats posed to civilians, the factors that determine vulnerability are much less well researched. Deductive reasoning suggests that they will vary depending on the nature of the threat, both in terms of the means of violence employed and in terms of whether the threat is intentional or unintentional, direct or indirect, and selective or collective. Consideration of the different types of threat set out in Table 4.2 illustrates this argument.

Vulnerability to all kinds of threat depends in part on location. Armed violence is by its nature physical; therefore, vulnerability to such violence depends on proximity to the scene of violence (though in modern warfare the technology exists for the scene of violence to be far from the *perpetrators*). The importance of location as a determinant of vulnerability is reflected in the importance of displacement as a protective strategy, and one that may be

Table 4.2. Examples of threats to civilians

	Intentional	Unintentional
Direct	Selective: assassination—shooting Collective: massacre	Crossfire
Indirect	Selective: assassination—drone attack Collective: bus bomb	Landmine (if targeted at combatants)

effective in reducing vulnerability to multiple threats. Displacement may involve crossing an international border (as in the case of refugees), or it may be internal displacement, it may be permanent, or it may be short term displacement as in the case of daily or nightly 'commuting' away from sites of danger where insecurity varies according to the time of day. We know that the granting of asylum has historically been one of the most effective means to physical protection for those fleeing conflict, and we also know that the ability to flee very quickly when a threat arrives or occurs can be life-saving. Location, then, plays a key role in determining civilian vulnerability.

Where civilians have the option to relocate away from threats, this can reduce their vulnerability significantly. Thus, encouraging or facilitating mobility is one way third parties can seek to reduce civilian vulnerability. With no specific focus on refugees or IDPs, the ICRC cannot be said to have a general policy encouraging or even concerning mobility. However, implicit in its more general policies is a concern for refugees and IDPs. After World War I the ICRC lobbied the League of Nations to set up a refugee agency, and there have been many instances of the ICRC playing a key role in the provision of assistance to refugees and IDPs (Krill 2001). On occasion, the ICRC may also engage in direct efforts to facilitate the movement of civilians away from threats.

In exceptional cases, the ICRC in Colombia would pay for individual civilians to relocate elsewhere in the country. This relocation programme was specific to Colombia, and would not be applicable in most contexts. Such a policy made particular sense in the Colombian context, where violence was individualized and the conflict dynamics varied greatly from region to region, such that individuals who were threatened in one place may be safe in another. The ICRC Colombia policy of relocating individuals in grave danger was not referred to as a programme and was not publicized, and the ICRC tried to minimize this activity. However, in response to very immediate threats which appeared credible, the ICRC may help a threatened person to move elsewhere in the country. The ICRC assisted 362 people in this way in 2009, and 609 in 2013 (ICRC 2010b: 21, 2014b: 14). The ICRC is not a state and as such could not offer asylum but might pay for travel to another area of Colombia. In cases where bus travel was not a risk (in many cases community leaders have been assassinated on bus journeys, so this was often not an appropriate mode of transport), the ICRC could pay for a bus ticket; otherwise they might buy a plane ticket. They would never transport a threatened individual in an ICRC vehicle because of the impact it could have on the perceived neutrality of the organization. Historically the ICRC also had an arrangement with the Canadian embassy to expedite applications for asylum and resettlement in Canada. Occasionally in extreme cases, the municipal government would also pay for a flight or transport for people to leave. UNHCR would liaise with the state and the ICRC, but would not relocate someone itself.

More often, the ICRC provides assistance to refugees and IDPs. Such assistance can be seen as indirectly facilitating mobility in that it removes some of the economic barriers to displacement (which very often entails leaving behind livelihoods and relocating to an area without livelihoods opportunities). Thus, in Colombia, for example, the ICRC was providing a package of assistance to IDPs who were unable to receive assistance from the state, and in the DRC, the ICRC sought to provide livelihoods programming for IDPs.

Likewise, UNHCR's work with IDPs—which encompasses not only protection but also shelter and camp management, and may entail the provision of other forms of material assistance—facilitates displacement, so that people can move away from the threats they face in one location to somewhere safer. This reflects the origins of UNHCR in refugee protection—facilitating displacement by providing international protection to those who have fled from the source of their insecurity in their country of origin. However, UNHCR does not always seek to facilitate displacement. For UNHCR in Colombia, for example, IDP protection is virtually synonymous with the *prevention* of displacement, and the two terms are often used interchangeably by UNHCR staff. At the very least, the prevention of displacement is seen to be a primary protection objective in Colombia. The notion of 'preventive protection' is problematic precisely because the prevention of refugee flows is often not in the interests of refugee protection (Barutciski 1996; Chimni 1993; Frelick 1992). In the same way, emphasizing the prevention of internal displacement is problematic because displacement is often a vulnerability-reduction strategy undertaken by civilians, and thus the objective of preventing displacement may be in direct conflict with the objective of protection (Zapater 2010). Despite this, UNHCR focused its work in Colombia on the prevention of displacement.

In Colombia at least, UNHCR was more cautious about supporting the return of IDPs. Thus, despite the Colombian government's preference for return as the solution to displacement, as at 2010 the official UNHCR position in Colombia was that the conditions necessary for return were mostly not in place. UNHCR would not support returns, because the required minimum security conditions were not present. For example, even if there was state presence, mines in rural areas made them unsafe. Thus, UNHCR was observing—but not supporting—some returns in Colombia. Often people were trying to return out of desperation and because of a lack of opportunities in the zones they had displaced to, but in the zones they returned to there were no health centres, secondary and tertiary roads had been destroyed, there was no economic activity or livelihoods opportunities, and the area was still heavily mined. UNHCR sought to push for the needs and agendas of the communities to be taken into account in return plans, to bring attention to the returns in order to increase security, and to get institutional attention to ensure socio-economic needs were met. This highlights a more general dilemma as to whether UNHCR should support (and potentially entice) returns to unsafe areas, or leave people unsupported. In Kachin state in Myanmar, for example, UNHCR interviewees explained that if they saw spontaneous return, they would offer low-key tailored assistance but that they did not want to create a pull factor. Forced return and recruitment were also occurring, whereby people returned to farm their land (sometimes under threat of losing that land) and were forced by the army into sentry duty as 'village volunteers'. Viewing this as forced return, UNHCR was not dismantling the shelters from which people were returning.

In addition to location, other factors may affect the vulnerability of individuals to particular types of threat. Selective violence may be used to punish individuals suspected of supporting rival armed groups, or of engaging in activities which run counter to the interests of combatants. In Colombia, for example, individuals have been threatened and killed in response to activism on land and indigenous issues. Therefore, vulnerability to selective targeting depends on the activities, associations, and behaviour of the civilians concerned—or, more accurately, the beliefs and perceptions of armed actors about the activities, associations, and behaviour of those civilians. Collective violence occurs when groups of civilians are targeted on the basis of a shared characteristic such as ethnicity, neighbourhood, or an other group-level identifier: civilians 'who fit the profile of a rival sympathizer' (Steele 2009: 422). Where information is incomplete, an armed group may use collective targeting to punish suspected defectors or rivals, or to push rivals to defect. Vulnerability to collective targeting thus depends on being part of a particular group (which may simply be a neighbourhood) and/or being in the location that the massacre (or other incident of collective violence) takes place.

In many of these cases, civilians have some (albeit often limited) information about the differing levels of risk of different locations and behaviour. For instance, even if the precise location of landmines is unknown, civilians in a mined area will often know which paths are high-risk. In general, reliable information about threats is necessary for civilians to be able to devise effective self-protection strategies (Baines and Paddon 2012). However, the ability of civilians to use this information to undertake protective strategies to reduce their own vulnerability will depend on the choices open to them in particular in pursuing their livelihoods strategies (Jaspars, O'Callaghan, and Stites 2007).

Thus if a farmer has to travel along a particular path to get to his fields and has no alternative income-generating opportunities, he has limited options for reducing his vulnerability to landmines, even with the knowledge that the path is mined. It follows that the more choices open to civilians in pursuing their own protection strategies, the less vulnerable they will be. While poverty does not always increase vulnerability (the reverse may be true, for example, where the threat comes from kidnapping for ransom), poverty and limited livelihoods options will restrict the choices available to civilians, and in many cases they will thus increase vulnerability. In short, vulnerability depends primarily on: (1) location; and (2) activities and associations—or perceptions thereof. These in turn depend on: (3) information; and (4) the choices and opportunities open to the civilians in question. With perfect information, and infinite choices, an individual would have no *need* to participate in activities or maintain associations or be in locations that make them vulnerable. However, there are two important caveats to be made here.

First, information is never perfect. The future is uncertain because conflict dynamics and even civilian strategies themselves affect the level, nature, and location of threats. If a civilian takes up arms (albeit losing his claim to civilian status in the process) in order to reduce his vulnerability or that of his family, his action may have the effect of increasing overall levels of violence and the threats posed by that violence. Furthermore, even the act of fleeing to a more secure zone can impact on the security of other civilians. Forced migration may be not only the result of violent strategies to clear land, but may also result in the violent redistribution of land ownership (Engel and Ibáñez 2007: 336). Internal displacement may alter the composition of different areas or regions, thus giving one side or other an advantage and so affecting the course of conflict and the threats faced by different individuals and groups (Steele 2009). There may also be a perverse effect of internal displacement such that hiding among others with similar characteristics reduces an individual's or a household's likelihood of being targeted selectively but as more individuals and households with similar characteristics cluster together, the community's likelihood of being collectively targeted may increase if it is perceived to be affiliated with one side or another (Steele 2009). In the Rwandan genocide, for example, potential victims who did not follow the crowd (and thus did not seek shelter in supposedly safe places such as schools and churches) had a higher survival rate (Verwimp 2004).

Second, even with very good information and a range of choices, choices remain just that—and civilians may choose to follow a strategy known to be more risky (or in other words to make them more vulnerable) than other options available to them, because physical security is not their only objective. For example, civilians engaged in land activism or the defence of human rights may choose to maintain such engagement in spite of the knowledge that it increases their vulnerability. More generally, they may choose to confront threats through active resistance and public advocacy instead of prioritizing their own vulnerability reduction (South 2012: 187).

The implications of this for humanitarian agencies are that efforts to reduce civilian vulnerability can be directed at supporting the strategies of civilians to protect themselves. In concrete terms, this could include the provision of information, the expansion of choices and opportunities, or both. When humanitarian agencies adopt a maximalist approach to vulnerability reduction, they actively seek to expand the options available to IDPs and other civilians. They may do so, for example, by providing shelter in a safer place to make relocation an option, or by creating livelihoods activities to enable people to choose to avoid more dangerous livelihoods strategies. A minimalist approach to vulnerability reduction seeks only to ensure that the pursuit of other objectives by humanitarian agencies, such as the provision of assistance and livelihoods for their own sakes, does not increase vulnerability by unintentionally exposing civilians to threats.

While the ICRC places primary emphasis on threat reduction, it also aims to reduce individuals' 'vulnerability and/or their exposure to risks, particularly those arising from armed hostilities or acts of violence' (ICRC 2008b: 752). It does so primarily through strategies aimed directly at increasing the range of choices open to those individuals, and hence supporting their own self-protection strategies. Livelihoods programming is a key component of this in many contexts. The ICRC also does so through direct strategies to improve certain kinds of information available to civilians, enabling them to develop better-informed self-protection strategies. For example, through landmine awareness training and light weapons awareness training, the ICRC seeks to educate or inform people of ways to reduce their own vulnerability. While the ICRC provides this kind of information about the threats from specific weapons that enable people to reduce their exposure to those threats, it would not provide information about the threats from particular actors. In some cases, providing such information may compromise neutrality. In all cases, there would be a risk of misinformation that could increase rather than decrease exposure. Thus, instead of providing information directly, the ICRC may negotiate with an armed actor to get them to provide information to civilians (on, for example, the location of landmines).

Much of the vulnerability-reduction work of UNHCR is related to facilitating displacement. However, IDP protection is primarily about protecting those who are already displaced, who very often continue to face threats of violence or coercion during displacement. Sometimes those threats or people's exposure to them can be aggravated by displacement. Like the ICRC, UNHCR undertakes some livelihoods programming, though in many cases this is relatively low-scale. UNHCR also adopts a number of more indirect strategies for vulnerability reduction, notably lobbying for legal developments and public policy change to get states to provide information or expand choices.

MITIGATING THE CONSEQUENCES OF VIOLENCE

Finally, protection work may be aimed not at reducing the risk of being affected by violence, but on mitigating the effects when they occur, being reactive rather than proactive, responsive rather than preventive. Here we see that the humanitarian usage of the term 'protection' implies a much more expansive set of objectives and activities than everyday use would suggest. For example, the provision of medical or psychosocial support to a rape victim is not protection in the everyday sense of the term, because it does not prevent the victim from being raped. For humanitarian actors, however, such an activity is very much a part of protection, and prevention of threats is very often distinguished from protection, or understood as a subset of protection. This is not simply a bureaucratic point on definitions; some very real dangers emanate from the way humanitarian actors define protection differently from how the rest of the world understands the concept. If protection aims only or mainly to mitigate the consequence of violence, but is interpreted by other actors as preventing that violence or the associated threats, it risks undermining civilians' own protection strategies and serving as a justification for political inaction and restrictive asylum policies.

In spite of these risks, many humanitarian agencies do include, emphasize, or even exclusively focus on reducing or mitigating the consequences of violence as part of their protection work. Much of what both the ICRC and UNHCR do has this as an aim, including through the provision of material assistance, water, health and infrastructure programming, and livelihoods activities. However, there are two key differences between the two organizations here. First, the ICRC emphasizes mitigating the consequences of *violence* and always makes the link back to conflict and violence, while UNHCR tends to focus on mitigating the consequences of displacement. Second, for both organizations, these kinds of activities can also impact on the level of violence, threat, or vulnerability, but only the ICRC consistently conceptualizes the links to these higher-order objectives.

While working to ensure that rape victims in the DRC have access to post-exposure prophylaxis, and to psychosocial care (an activity undertaken by both the ICRC and UNHCR), is about mitigating the very immediate consequences of violence, rebuilding infrastructure damaged by violence, or providing food to those who can no longer afford to buy it because conflict has inflated prices, is somewhat further removed. Including the mitigation of the consequences of violence as a protection objective becomes increasingly problematic the further removed strategies are from the violent incidents. Taken to its logical conclusion, it allows for almost every humanitarian activity undertaken in contexts of conflict or violence to be reformulated as a protection activity.

ENDS AND MEANS

As we have seen, when it comes to reducing violence, threat, or vulnerability, there are both direct, actor-centred strategies, and indirect strategies that seek to provoke or contribute to structural or policy change. Indirect strategies involve process goals which may or may not be valuable in themselves, but which do not in and of themselves increase the physical safety and security of civilians. For example, providing food aid to people in need of food is of intrinsic value, and may or may not also be instrumental to vulnerability reduction. Developing public policy is unlikely to be of any intrinsic value, but it may or may not be instrumental to one or more types of protection objective. In short, these process goals are *means* to the ultimate *ends* of violence, threat, or vulnerability reduction. The further these process goals are removed from these ultimate ends, the less we can be sure about the causal chain through which the means are supposed to be linked to the ends. Given the frequently poor conceptualizations of protection and the associated objectives and activities, sometimes the link between process goals (or means) and the ultimate objectives (ends) is not even conceptualized. This is much more of an issue for UNHCR than for the ICRC for two reasons. First, the ICRC is more actor-centred and immediate in its objectives. Second, the ICRC does a much better job of defining what protection means for the organization, and of conceptualizing how the different strands of its work fit together.

Michael Barnett and Martha Finnemore identify five mechanisms through which international bureaucracies may create pathologies, the first of which is the 'irrationality of rationalization' through which 'means (rules and procedures) may become so embedded and powerful that they determine ends and the way the organization defines its goals' (Barnett and Finnemore 2004: 8). Means may even come to be seen as ends in themselves. This appears to be much more likely in an organization like UNHCR, where internal communication and information-sharing is relatively weak, and the rationale for policies is not widely shared or well communicated. In such organizations, staff do not necessarily know what the ultimate objectives of some activities are, or through what mechanisms those activities are expected to translate into the desired outcomes. Instead, they implement policies, procedures, and activities without knowing or keeping in mind the rationale for those policies, procedures, and activities. Implementation of activities (the means) inevitably then comes to be seen as an end in itself.

As an extreme example of this, several of the achievements cited by UNHCR interviewees in Myanmar related not to outcomes for IDPs, but to UNHCR (or cluster or sector) processes. For example, they talked about the coordination and functioning of the protection sector rather than successes for the intended beneficiaries. The gradual expansion of the operation was highlighted as a major success. This is problematic, because a well-coordinated protection sector and an expanding operation are of no use if the operation does not consist of activities that translate into positive protection outcomes for IDPs. The further removed process goals are from the people who are to be protected, and the violence they are to be protected from, the more tenuous the link between means and ends, and the greater the danger that reaching the process goals does not yield better protection outcomes.

This section examines two of the most common kinds of process goals, legal protection or public policy change, and material assistance or other practical projects.

Law and Public Policy

For the ICRC, law is a means to an end rather than an end in itself. The ICRC is primarily concerned with the level of compliance with underlying principles, and while IHL is usually a key tool, delegates sometimes draws on tools other than IHL in seeking to persuade armed parties to adhere to those principles. The way that the ICRC understands the relationship between legal protection and physical protection underpins several of the issue-areas within the ICRC mandate (specifically, all those that are covered by IHL) and reflects the process by which policy has developed within the ICRC. Practical action has preceded legal codification, and that legal codification was always intended to support rather than supersede the practical activities.

Analysis of relevant policy documents from the 1990s suggests that UNHCR conceptualized legal protection as one among multiple means to protection. UNHCR took the view that 'meeting the protection needs of the internally displaced and those at risk of displacement and promoting solutions is not only, and often not even primarily, a question of legal norms and remedies' (UNHCR 1994b, para. 26). At that stage, UNHCR was averse to committing itself to ongoing involvement with IDPs. It is notable that as UNHCR has expanded its IDP protection role with reference to the similarities between refugee protection and IDP protection, judicial protection has become the main focus of its IDP projects. What was described as only one, and often not the primary, means to protection has come to be seen as an end in itself. Since UNHCR became the lead UN agency for IDPs in 2006, policy documents emphasize 'protecting the *rights* of the internally displaced' (UNHCR 2007g, para. 20, emphasis added) and 'the establishment of national laws, institutions and mechanisms that safeguard the rights of IDPs' (UNHCR 2007g, para. 28). There is a great deal of reference to the realization of rights, the protection of rights, and the safeguarding of rights. The particular rights with which UNHCR is concerned are not specified, but the Guiding Principles, IHRL, and IHL are all invoked (UNHCR 2007g, para. 27). Thus, legal protection is prioritized often without any clear conceptualization of how, if at all, it may contribute to physical safety.

The emphasis that UNHCR places on legal protection in its IDP protection work can be seen as a replication of the institutional approach to refugee protection. Refugee protection is primarily seen as a legal concept, albeit one with political dimensions, and can be understood through analogy to the national protection that states are expected to provide to their citizens (Goodwin-Gill 1989: 6; Helton 2003: 20). For refugees in a non-conflict setting, physical protection is implicit in legal protection, because the legal protection means that the host state accepts responsibility for physical protection in the same way that the state is responsible for the physical security of its own citizens. Legal status and some quasi-citizenship rights are exactly what refugees need in order to be able to live without harassment in a host state. However, legal protection may not be of much importance to IDPs if it does not translate into physical protection. In spite of this, in many contexts UNHCR understands IDP protection in terms of judicial protection rather than the provision of physical security. The focus is on the legal entitlements of IDPs and those at risk of displacement, rather than the threats they actually face, and it is not made clear whether or how such judicial protection is expected to translate into physical protection.

A related issue concerns the question of how high-level policy interventions are translated into protection outcomes on the ground. Andrew Bonwick has argued that in Colombia, for example, protection 'analysis does not seem to translate into appropriate objectives. When these are set, they seem to be at least one step removed from the people at risk. Many organizations, particularly those based in Bogotá, set objectives based around changes in public policy, without a serious analysis of how these changes would affect people on the ground' (Bonwick 2006: 19). The protection activities with the most immediate success are often on a smaller scale and at a local level, but UNHCR frequently focuses its efforts on the public policy level. As with legalistic approaches, changes in public policy are ultimately only valuable in so far as they have a positive impact on the lives of civilians.

Material Assistance and Other Practical Projects

Much if not most of the work of most humanitarian agencies focuses on providing material assistance and undertaking practical projects such as installing water points, building schools, and providing medical care. Meeting material needs for food and shelter can be expressed as protection from hunger and as protection from the elements, material assistance can be life-saving, and safety and security are of no use to someone who dies from starvation or disease (Forsythe 2013: 72). In other words, other objectives may be just as important as physical safety and security. In addition, the provision of material assistance can very often *contribute to* physical safety and security. However, the provision of medical care and material aid is not *equivalent to* physical safety and security. This section, therefore, examines the main mechanisms through which these kinds of activities can reduce threats or vulnerability, and the ways in which the ICRC and UNHCR conceptualize the relationship between such activities and the objectives of protection.

Within the ICRC, protection and assistance are seen as inextricably linked. Protection for the ICRC is about saving lives and diminishing the humanitarian consequences of armed conflict. Assistance projects aim to contribute towards these objectives either directly or indirectly, and the provision of aid and services aimed at reducing exposure to risk is common to all issue-areas addressed by the ICRC. Practical projects relating to health, education, and water, for example, may contribute to threat and vulnerability reduction through a number of different mechanisms, as explored below. The provision of assistance and practical projects enables the ICRC to gain access to communities, to understand the local conflict dynamics, to develop relationships with the various armed groups in a given region, and to generate information from the civilian population on specific protection cases. The access, understanding, relationships, and information are not ends in themselves, but are valuable in so far as they contribute towards greater security for the civilian population. The access is seen to be instrumental to the other three, while the information and the understanding are used in documenting protection cases. Finally, the understanding and the relationships are necessary to increase the impact of the cases when presented to the alleged perpetrators of IHL violations, with the desired impact being a positive change in the behaviour of the relevant actor.

The provision of material assistance and the undertaking of practical projects by the ICRC may also mitigate the consequences of violence experienced by those the ICRC seeks to protect. The ICRC likes to emphasize its multidisciplinarity, and the connections between different aspects of ICRC work. Various interviewees for this book highlighted how the ICRC response in any given context is put together for the concrete needs of the victims, taking a holistic view of their needs: one victim can have several needs and the ICRC may not be able to address all of them, but they would try to offer a multidimensional response, and may also refer the victim to other actors for additional support. Given the focus of this book on protection, most of the ICRC delegates and headquarters staff interviewed in the course of the research had a particular responsibility for, or focus on, protection. They invariably saw the provision of assistance and practical projects as valuable in and of themselves, but also designed to maximize their protective potential, and often focused on particular areas according to a protection rationale. By contrast, the (admittedly much smaller number of) non-protection-focused delegates interviewed for this book tended to see practical projects mainly as ends in themselves and not influenced by protection needs.

On the other hand, most UNHCR interviewees labelled a wide range of practical projects as protection activities, but without a clear conceptualization of how they might relate to physical safety and security. Thus in the south-east of Myanmar, for example, the construction of schools, clinics, and water points was cited as the main protection activity with no explanation of how or why this was expected to contribute to protection objectives.

In many cases, the main protection element of these kinds of practical activity may be that of passive protection through presence. It is one of the ways in which the ICRC, UNHCR, and other humanitarian agencies can create rational incentives for armed actors to change their behaviour. Seeing ICRC or UNHCR vehicles is understood to reduce violations. This kind of passive protection by presence is aimed at threat reduction, and while it may have proven ineffective in many contexts (such as the former Yugoslavia), it was deemed reasonably effective in Colombia, for example.[3] While the success of prevention is notoriously difficult to measure, the reactions of the civilian population in Colombia to the presence of the ICRC and UNHCR (and other international actors) suggested that this kind of passive protection did have a positive impact in these communities, at least for the duration of the presence. Presence was also deemed to be one of the main protection elements of ICRC water projects in Myanmar, and on this same logic UNHCR sought to visit each IDP site around Sittwe at least once every other week, and also operated a hotline that the IDPs could call in the event of a violent incident. Whether or not this kind of passive protection through presence simply displaces violence to other communities or to a later date is less clear. There is also a danger that such presence could increase the threat of violence within the communities, because international presence draws greater attention to those communities.

Practical projects also provide an apolitical reason for the ICRC and UNHCR to be present in zones where they may otherwise be unwelcome, which facilitates more proactive protection activities. For the ICRC, this is primarily about getting access to the civilian population, and also to armed actors in areas identified as high-risk. Access to the civilian population occurs, as they are the intended beneficiaries of these projects, and are thus automatically involved on some level. Additionally, the projects bring the ICRC into the centre of the communities as a whole and thus facilitate contact with those communities. Access to the armed groups is facilitated, because once the ICRC starts implementing one of these projects, the armed groups tend to arrive on the scene to find out what is going on. Once the armed groups are there, the

[3] NGOs also engage in protection by presence in Colombia, most notably Peace Brigades International.

ICRC can initiate a dialogue with them. Gaining access to both the civilian population and the armed groups is seen as a crucial, 'pre-protection' activity.

This is deemed especially important when the ICRC is new to an area, or in areas where relations with armed actors are not deemed strong enough for a classic protection dialogue. In Myanmar, for example, the newness of operations was a pervasive and defining characteristic of ICRC work at the time of interviews, and much of what the ICRC was doing there was either pre-protection work, or what might be termed protection by stealth. In other words, the ICRC was preparing the ground for its classic protection work and additionally engaging in activities that were ostensibly focused on health, livelihoods, and water and sanitation, but also included a protection element. Such practical activities are thus expected to have a protective impact either in the immediate term, or in the longer term, as they enable delegates to gather information and build understanding of protection needs, and to develop the relationships necessary for the documentation and presentation of protection cases. For example, work on access to healthcare is often accompanied with a dialogue on protection and healthcare, and is seen as protection in and of itself, as well as a way in for 'standard' ICRC work.

For UNHCR, the basic rationale is the same but the main objectives are slightly different. In Colombia, for example, UNHCR undertakes practical protection projects (PPPs). These include the building of schools, the canalization of water, and the restoration of health centres. The underlying logic is that a PPP provides an apolitical excuse to be in an at-risk community more regularly, talking to people (not necessarily about sensitive issues), and also to increase the presence of the state. PPPs facilitate UNHCR presence in zones where there is high risk of displacement, particularly where territory is contested by competing armed groups, and where armed groups would not accept UNHCR presence without a concrete project (UNHCR 2008a: 12). PPPs are seen as a means to 'buy a way in'; assistance is provided to facilitate UNHCR presence. PPPs are thought to contribute to protection through three mechanisms: UNHCR presence is expected to provide direct protection; they provide contact with communities through which to deepen UNHCR understanding of particular contexts and risks of displacement; and they often involve bringing the social services of the state to the communities. In respect of this third point, the project may comprise part of a direct deal with the state to share responsibility. For example, UNHCR might offer to furnish a school if the government brings in teachers. In other cases, the projects may not be directly conditional on specific involvement from state agencies but more generally they may seek to make the situation of a particular zone or community more visible and to get the administration to pay attention to the zone.

While the provision of assistance and the implementation of various practical projects may be used as an apolitical excuse for the ICRC and UNHCR to be present and to undertake other activities, they also serve more direct ends.

In some cases, these ends include protection. By providing assistance or other services to IDPs and other civilians, these kinds of activity may serve to reduce vulnerability or to mitigate the consequences of violence, and they are often designed with this specifically in mind. For example, both organizations undertake livelihoods programming in Myanmar with the aim of reducing vulnerability, and both provide psychosocial support to rape victims in the DRC with the aim of mitigating the consequences of violence.

The activity of providing material assistance or other practical programming may thus be a protection activity, in the sense that it may be undertaken with the intention and effect of increasing the physical security of its recipients. On the other hand, it may have no effect on their physical security (as in the case of the well-fed dead) or it may actually reduce their physical security by, for example, making them the target of attacks. Thus, while improving nutrition, curing disease, and supporting livelihoods may all be important and laudable objectives in a humanitarian response, and may also offer a means to physical safety and security, they should not be conflated with it. The increased concern for protection came about through recognition that meeting people's needs for food, shelter, and other material commodities was insufficient to save their lives, instead resulting in the 'well-fed dead'. It therefore stands to reason that meeting such needs cannot be an *objective* of protection even if, under certain conditions, meeting those needs may be a means to protection.

CONCLUSIONS

In both international and internal conflicts, the contemporary ICRC approach to civilian protection centres on regulating the conduct of hostilities as well as on the entitlement of civilians to humanitarian assistance (and the corresponding duty of armed parties either to provide or to facilitate such assistance). This understanding of the objectives of protection runs through all of the issue-areas the ICRC addresses, and issues relating to conflict and violence are core to the identity of the ICRC, and also key to how they define their aims. The main protection objectives of the ICRC can be classified as threat reduction, but vulnerability reduction and mitigating the consequences of violence are also seen as important.

UNHCR is much less focused on threat reduction than is the ICRC, seeing threat reduction as an important component of protection, but not necessarily an important part of its own work. UNHCR documentation suggests that the organization agrees that protection in the context of armed conflict is primarily about physical safety and security. For example, the note of a 2007 informal consultative meeting with Excom stipulates that IDP '[p]rotection activities should first and foremost be designed to protect against threats to life, prevent torture or discrimination, and promote respect for dignity and the preservation of family unity' (UNHCR 2007c, para. 20). However, the objectives that UNHCR sets for its own work in conflict contexts do not match up with these primary aims, and they do not for the most part focus on reducing threats from violence. That said, in some contexts—and in relation to some particular kinds of threat—UNHCR does engage in efforts to reduce the threats faced by IDPs and those at risk of displacement. While the ICRC favours a direct and actor-centred approach to threat reduction, where UNHCR adopts threat-reduction strategies, they tend to focus on structural changes.

The ICRC was inspired by the witnessing of a battle, and, from the time it became operational, the idea of working in the midst of conflict has been an important part of its identity. For the ICRC, even activities that are not labelled as part of protection must be linked to conflict and violence. Instead of conflict and violence per se, the notion of forced displacement is central to defining who is of concern to UNHCR, and also to the institutional understanding of what those people are to be protected against. The note of a May 2007 consultative meeting between UNHCR and Excom sums this up: 'The overall goals of UNHCR's protection activities are to assist governments to ensure that IDPs are not discriminated against for reasons related to their displacement, have access to the same rights as other citizens, and that their specific displacement related protection needs are met' (UNHCR 2007f, para. 31). While this notion is rarely stated so explicitly, implicit in UNHCR doctrine as a whole is the idea that IDPs and those at risk of displacement are to be protected from forced displacement and the impact of forced displacement.

It is not the impact of violence or conflict per se, but the impact of displacement with which UNHCR is primarily concerned. The underlying idea here is that those affected by displacement should not be adversely affected by that displacement, and should be able to enjoy the same rights as those unaffected by displacement. The analogy with refugee protection is obvious in that the content of protection laid out in the 1951 Refugee Convention and its 1967 Protocol is largely defined by analogy to the rights and benefits accorded either to nationals or to other aliens in the country of refuge. Essentially these treaties provide for a refugee to reside legally in the country of refuge, and not to be discriminated against in terms of economic and social rights. However, for IDPs it may not be displacement per se that is the primary problem.

Sometimes, some of the concrete objectives pursued by humanitarian organizations are so far removed from the violence, threats, and victims that it is not even clear which, if any, of violence, threat, vulnerability, and consequences they are ultimately aimed at reducing. As we have seen, compared with UNHCR, the ICRC tends to work closer to the conflict and violence that are the fundamental protection problem, and with a clearer conceptualization of how its protection activities are expected to contribute to either threat reduction or vulnerability reduction. UNHCR engages in IDP protection because IDPs suffer from conflict, violence, and physical insecurity, but the institutional response very often focuses on high-level legal and public policy changes rather than physical protection, without a clear conceptualization of how it should contribute to physical security. In other words, legal protection and public policy changes have come to be seen as ends in and of themselves, rather than as means to physical safety and security.

In Chapters 5 and 6, we will see how the different objectives pursued by the ICRC and UNHCR translate into particular roles for other actors and a range of concrete activities.

5

Protection Roles and Responsibilities of Other Actors

In accordance with the legal frameworks emphasized by each organization, and the specific objectives that characterize their respective approaches to protection, the ICRC and UNHCR each ascribe particular protection roles to different actors. The ICRC emphasizes the importance of armed parties to conflict in its threat-reduction efforts in the midst of armed conflict, of states in the development of the IHL framework, and of civilians in vulnerability reduction. By contrast, UNHCR focuses on the state, and specifically the civilian agencies of the state. This chapter argues that the importance attributed to particular actors, and the ways in which the ICRC and UNHCR interact with them, can be largely explained by institutional factors. Moreover, their respective interpretations of the roles of different actors, and their styles of interaction with them, inevitably impose some limits on what the ICRC and UNHCR can achieve in terms of their protection work. This chapter proceeds in three main sections, each of which examines a different type of actor. The first section focuses on states, the second on armed non-state actors, and the third on the civilian population as a whole, including affected communities, civil (and uncivil) society. Each section discusses the protective potential of each actor type, the challenges associated with engaging with them, the roles the ICRC and UNHCR envisage for them, and the ways in which each organization relates to, and interacts with, them.

In international law, the state has primary responsibility for the protection of those within its jurisdiction, and all armed parties to conflict also have responsibilities under IHL. Where the state in question is unwilling or unable to meet its protection responsibilities, member states of the UN and signatories to the Geneva Conventions bear protection duties, and finally the mandated protection agencies (including the ICRC and UNHCR) bear their own particular responsibilities (ICRC 2009: 29–33). However, this hierarchy of legal responsibilities contrasts with the hierarchy of factors determining civilian safety set out by Sorcha O'Callaghan and Sara Pantuliano, who argue that the most critical factor is the actions of parties to the conflict, second is the actions that civilians take to protect themselves, and third is the interventions of third-party protection actors, including humanitarian agencies (O'Callaghan and Pantuliano 2007: 3). Furthermore, the responsibilities of the ICRC and UNHCR kick in precisely *because* those with primary and secondary responsibility have failed to ensure protection. This failure contributes to a tension in the work of humanitarian agencies engaged in protecting civilians—and the international community more broadly—between holding those actors to their responsibilities, and accepting their failure and seeking alternative means of protection. This tension in turn generates a number of dilemmas for humanitarian agencies in terms of how best to relate to the various actors that may have responsibility for, and/or a practical impact on, the protection of IDPs and other civilians.

STATES

Nowhere is the disjuncture between responsibility and reality more evident than in the role of affected states in protecting their own people. States are supposed to ensure the physical safety of their citizens. This is the essence of the social contract. Yet in the context of civil war, the state in question is either unwilling or unable to protect its people from violence, and in many cases the state itself perpetrates violence against its own people. According to the norm of 'conditional sovereignty' or 'sovereignty as responsibility', external sovereignty—with its associated freedom from outside interference—is supposed to be conditional on internal sovereignty, including the protection of the population internally (Cohen and Deng 1998; Deng et al. 1996). International humanitarian agencies undertake protection work precisely because the state in question has failed the test of internal sovereignty, and yet many such agencies maintain a normative commitment to external sovereignty.

State Sovereignty

In general, the ICRC and UNHCR will not undertake activities in any given country without permission from the state. Only on very rare occasions has the ICRC conducted cross-border operations without the consent of the state concerned. In respect of UNHCR, UN General Assembly Resolution 53/125 makes it clear that protection and assistance to IDPs must be 'with the consent of the State concerned'. In part this can be explained by practical or security considerations rather than ideological ones. Going against the wishes of a state in which an organization is operating can be difficult or dangerous. However, respect for external sovereignty also seems to run deeper. The debate in 2013 and

2014 over cross-border humanitarian action into non-government-controlled areas in Syria is instructive. While some NGOs and legal scholars argued in favour of providing humanitarian assistance into non-government-controlled areas (without the need to cross government-controlled areas for access), both the ICRC and UNHCR initially refused to do so, on the basis that such action would violate Syrian sovereignty (see, for example, *The Guardian*, 28 April 2014). After UN Security Council Resolution 2165 authorized such action on 14 July 2014, UNHCR engaged in cross-border activities, but the ICRC did not.

While a complete denial of access to non-government-controlled areas represents an extreme end of the spectrum, the Syrian context is by no means unique in this respect. Moreover, ICRC and UNHCR commitments to state sovereignty also play out in more subtle ways in other contexts, affecting the way that each organization relates to the governments of the countries in which they are working, and the nature and extent of the work they can carry out in different parts of those countries. Despite taking state sovereignty very seriously (rhetorically at least), and taking state interests into account in developing the legal and normative framework on which its practical work is based, the independence of the ICRC can be seen in the way that the organization sets conditions for engagement in any state. While the ICRC will not normally operate in a country without the consent of the state concerned, neither will it negotiate on a number of criteria it sees as essential to its operations. In this sense, the ICRC is comfortable asserting its authority in relation to states (particularly regarding issues which fall squarely within its legal mandate). By contrast, UNHCR's terms of engagement in each country in which it operates are set very much by the government in question, often constraining the mandate and work of UNHCR. A few comparisons are illustrative.

In Colombia, the Memorandum of Intent agreed by UNHCR and the government in 1999, and more general rules for international cooperation agencies set by the government in 2005, impose clear restrictions on the mandate of UNHCR in that context (*El Tiempo*, 15 June 2005; UNHCR 1999). The terms of UNHCR engagement were framed in terms of assisting the state to prevent displacement, and UNHCR was prohibited from having contact with the non-state armed groups. The focus on the prevention of displacement is problematic for the reasons set out in Chapter 4, and the limits of not engaging with armed non-state actors are discussed in the next section of this chapter. The ICRC was the only international humanitarian agency that was permitted to engage with the Colombian non-state armed groups.

In Myanmar both organizations sought to work within areas that were not controlled by the government, but they faced greater difficulties accessing non-government-controlled territory than government areas. Their commitment to respecting state sovereignty prevented them from operating in areas without state consent, even when those areas were controlled by non-state actors, and when they could access them from across the border in Thailand.

Both organizations acquiesced to government restrictions on movement in the name of security concerns, even if they were sometimes being manipulated by the government in this way. However, the precise nature of government restrictions was not uniform, and the ICRC and UNHCR responded somewhat differently to them. As we have seen in the Introduction, in 2007 the ICRC suspended operations in Myanmar rather than acquiesce to the restrictions then being imposed by the government. This is not to say that the ICRC does not compromise, only that its tolerance for government-imposed restrictions on its work appears to be lower than that of UNHCR. In general, the rhetoric and practice of UNHCR has been limited to issues acknowledged and accepted by the Myanmar government. After nearly ten years of working in the south-east of the country, it was only in 2013 that the letter of understanding between UNHCR and the government mentioned refugees, IDPs, and protection for the first time. By 2014, UNHCR continued to be required to liaise with the government over the detail of project plans, including negotiating in which villages UNHCR would install water points, and providing information on how much rice would be delivered and where. Interviewees reported the need for a constant dialogue to get these kinds of projects done.

In sum, deference to the state imposes constraints on where these organizations can work, and the kind of work they can undertake. In part, such deference can be explained by practical considerations, but the different ways in which different organizations relate to the state suggest there is also something else at play here. The evidence from Colombia and Myanmar suggests that the ICRC defers less to states than does UNHCR. It is not clear whether the differing levels of deference are cause or consequence of the different roles and importance each organization attaches to states in protection, but there does appear to be a correlation between the level of deference and the level of importance attached to states as protection actors.

Protection Roles of Affected States

Coming from an IHL perspective, the ICRC emphasizes the responsibility of both state and non-state authorities. Thus, a document outlining the ICRC protection methodology explains that 'protection is primarily the responsibility of the authorities and organized armed groups' (ICRC 2012b: 10). Coming from a human rights perspective, UNHCR continually emphasizes that the state in question has primary responsibility for the protection of all those on its territory. All UNHCR documents on the protection of IDPs highlight the responsibility of the state (UNHCR 2007c, para. 6; 2007e, para. 19; 2007f, para. 27; 2007g, para. 19), and Excom conclusions No.75 (1993), No.80 (1996), No.105 (2006) and No.108 (2008) all note that the primary responsibility for the welfare and protection of IDPs lies with the state concerned. Thus, both the ICRC and UNHCR see the state as having a significant responsibility for protection. However, each organization ascribes different roles and levels of importance to the state in its practical protection work.

For UNHCR, the fact that the state has primary responsibility for those who are internally displaced within its territory means that the state is the primary actor in protection, ignoring the fact that a mandate or duty to protect is no guarantor of protective action. The ICRC also sees states as key actors in protection, in particular the military agencies of the state, and increasingly also the police. The role ascribed to the military is very much based on IHL. In other words, it is about the military avoiding posing a threat to civilians, or minimizing the threat it poses, by conducting hostilities in line with IHL. In order to encourage the military to fulfil this kind of protective role, the ICRC envisages constant interaction between delegates and all levels of the armed forces.

Whereas the ICRC is primarily concerned with the behaviour of the armed forces, UNHCR directs most of its efforts towards working with the civilian agencies of the state. These are not exclusive focuses. On the one hand, ICRC delegates also meet with local civilian officials to negotiate access and discuss protection issues, all the more so in contexts that fall short of armed conflict. In such cases, the work of the ICRC may also focus on the police, with the dual aim of reducing any threat they may pose to the civilian population and of increasing their will and ability to protect that same population from threats posed by others. In addition, the ICRC implements projects in the spheres of health and education, usually in liaison with the relevant civilian agencies for these issues. In many cases, such projects have a protection element, as we see in Chapter 6. On the other hand, there are exceptions to the civilian focus of UNHCR. Indeed, UNHCR does view the police and military apparatus of the state as a potential threat to civilians (through forced displacement or abuse of human rights), and also as a potential actor to protect against threats from others (Global Protection Cluster Working Group 2010: 70). UNHCR thus envisaged some form of interaction with state military actors, and indeed in some parts of the DRC, UNHCR—together with OCHA—was trying to engage the FARDC on protection issues, in particular to discuss allegations of sexual violence and extortion by FARDC soldiers. In North Kivu, for example, UNHCR was holding weekly meetings with both the military and police.

However, the DRC is the exception rather than the rule. For the most part, UNHCR views the national military and police as having an impact—positive or negative, depending on the specific context—on the security of UNHCR staff rather than the protection of IDPs (UNHCR 2007e, para. 13). Missing from most UNHCR discourse is consideration of the protective role national forces may play by abstaining from threatening civilians. For example, the note of a 2007 meeting between UNHCR and Excom lists a range of national actors with whom UNHCR establishes working relationships in its IDP protection: 'central government structures and local authorities, human rights institutions, parliamentarians, the judiciary, NGOs, religious bodies and other members of civil society' (UNHCR 2007g, para. 21). No mention is made of any kind of armed forces. Whereas the ICRC works with armed actors precisely *because* they are perpetrators of violence against civilians, one UNHCR interviewee in the DRC suggested that the fact that the FARDC was a perpetrator *limited* the extent UNHCR could or should engage with them.

In keeping with this general approach, UNHCR was only interacting with the military in limited ways in Colombia. Where individuals were faced with an immediate physical threat, UNHCR would request the intervention of the Colombian military; but for most of its work, UNHCR focused on the social agencies of the state. The two state agencies UNHCR worked most closely with in Colombia were the Defensoría del Pueblo (Office of the Human Rights Ombudsman) and Acción Social. Even in the DRC, where UNHCR was engaging with the FARDC—and indeed with some non-state armed groups—in some parts of the country, much of its work focused on affected communities and on the civilian branches of the state. For example, UNHCR was working a lot with the National Commission for Refugees (Commission Nationale pour les Réfugiés—CNR) within the Ministry of the Interior, assisting the government to enact IDP legislation, and trying to support the justice system at the local level by, for example, paying the salaries of some judges.

Myanmar presents an interesting case, because the country was run by a military junta until 2011, and at the time of interviews, the military continued to hold significant influence over the nominally civilian government. Nonetheless, in keeping with its general approach, UNHCR saw the Myanmar army mainly as a facilitator of (or a hindrance to) the work of UNHCR, rather than as an interlocutor in substantive protection dialogue. For example, travel authorizations for non-government-controlled areas could not be granted by state-level officials, but had to be referred to the central government, which in turn had to check with the military. None of the interviewees mentioned direct dialogue between UNHCR and the military. By contrast, UNHCR had little choice but to meet with various civilian state officials in order to be allowed to operate and to implement projects. In addition, in Rakhine state in particular, UNHCR had at least weekly government contact at the state level to discuss concrete protection issues.

In keeping with these differences in emphasis by the ICRC and UNHCR, each organization uses different methods to encourage the state to respond in particular ways. It is not by any means clear how humanitarian organizations should relate to states in order to maximize protection outcomes in either the short term or the long term. It is because the state is unwilling or unable to protect its citizens that the ICRC and UNHCR see the need for their own involvement. This yields a dilemma as to how best to responsibilize unwilling or unable states. Essentially, international humanitarian agencies have three options open to them. They can seek to hold the state to account, they can support the state, or they can substitute for it. Logically, the best course of action would be to hold an able but unwilling state to account, and to support a willing but unable state, perhaps substituting for it until it is more able. However, very often states are both unwilling and unable, or unwilling in some areas and unable in others. In addition, in any given situation, it is not always possible for humanitarians to identify whether the main problem is ill-will or inability. Moreover, the activities undertaken by humanitarian agencies do not always fit neatly into these categories—indeed, given the fact that states often exhibit both ill-will and inability, those interventions that overlap these different categories may be the most effective.

Supporting the State

In a sense, supporting a willing but unable state is the ideal kind of work for humanitarian agencies. However, where the state lacks capacity to protect, the support of a civilian humanitarian agency may not be expected to have much effect either. In general—though not always—states have far greater resources at their disposal than do humanitarian agencies. Furthermore, there may not be too many examples of states that have the best of intentions but a lack of capacity.

Where the state is unwilling to protect its own people, it often also poses a threat to them (or to some of them) itself. Where the state is a cause of violent threats and displacement, international humanitarian agencies seeking to protect IDPs and other civilians face a particularly difficult task (Orchard 2010). Providing support to a state that itself poses a threat can have hugely damaging consequences for civilians, as seen in the civil war in Sri Lanka, where the UN as a whole was strongly criticized for its failure to stand up to and speak out against the actions of the government (Internal Review Panel 2012). UNHCR in particular was accused by one aid worker of being 'in bed with the government' (cited in Keen 2009: 81). In essence, a blind focus on the state as the solution meant UNHCR supported the Sri Lankan government, thereby indirectly facilitating further abuses by the state itself. The Sri Lanka example may be extreme, but there are plenty of other cases in which a state poses a threat to its own people, or to some subset of them.

The role of UNHCR in relation to IDPs is seen as one of promoting or reinforcing protection to be provided by their own government, and the work of UNHCR is largely about supporting the state. This includes financing positions and units or departments. In the DRC, for example, UNHCR was covering the vast majority of the CNR budget. In Colombia, UNHCR was subsidizing posts for 'gestores comunitarios', people to work for the Human Rights Ombudsman in critical zones in order to increase the presence of the state (UNHCR 2008a, para. 49). Their role was to help the displaced population and specifically to provide a link between the communities and the apparatus of the state, to get IDP issues onto the agenda and into the budget of local government, and also to provide eyes in the field in order to monitor the situation. UNHCR was additionally financing units dedicated to working on displacement-related issues in both the Ombudsman's Office and the Procuraduría (Office of the Inspector General). The rationale was that if UNHCR paid for services that the government did not value, it would be able to demonstrate their worth, and over time it could negotiate for the government share of funding to increase until the state took full responsibility. At work here is a form of 'argumentation' that highlights the benefits to the state of acting a particular way. However, this argumentation is not based on dialogue, but on a more practical demonstration of the underlying arguments that the provision of such services is valuable.

UNHCR likes to see itself as a partner of the state, facilitating the work of the state through, for example, the provision of information and technical assistance. However, providing such assistance may be problematic if the goals of the government are different from those of UNHCR, and particularly when they *conflict with* those of UNHCR. The ICRC also supports the state, but in more limited ways, such as by providing advice on incorporating IHL into domestic legislation, and by assisting the state in the provision of specific services to the population. For example, the ICRC was supporting local authorities in water provision in the DRC, and health authorities in Colombia and Myanmar.

At the other end of the spectrum of strategies for engaging with the affected state, international humanitarian organizations can seek to hold the state accountable when it fails to live up to its responsibilities.

Holding the State to Account

Holding a state to account might involve naming and shaming, support for international prosecutions, or the provision of information to other states through advocacy to diplomatic representatives, or to other actors who can put pressure on the affected state, such as human rights organizations like Amnesty International and Human Rights Watch. However, it is not clear whether or not—or under what conditions—naming and shaming has much effect on the conduct of the state (Franklin 2008; Hafner-Burton and Ron 2009; Hendrix and Wong 2013; Krain 2012; Murdie and Davis 2012). Moreover, public criticism of the state can lead to expulsion from the country in question. Likewise, collaboration—or perceived collaboration—with international criminal proceedings can lead to expulsion. In March 2009, thirteen international NGOs were expelled from Darfur, and three national NGOs had their licences revoked by the government of Sudan immediately following the issuance of an arrest warrant by the International Criminal Court (ICC) for Sudanese president Omar al-Bashir (IRIN News 2009). Although these agencies had taken care not even to appear to be providing information to the ICC, the government had long suspected they were providing evidence to prosecutors (Addario and Polgreen 2009).

Neither the ICRC nor UNHCR seeks to hold governments to account in the sense of strict legal accountability, and it is rare for either of them to criticize a state publicly. However, if we define accountability more generally, as a principle which requires public authorities to be subject to public scrutiny and to account for their actions, then we can see that both the ICRC and UNHCR do take some steps to hold particular branches or agencies of the state accountable for certain of their actions. The ICRC (privately) scrutinizes the way that the state conducts hostilities, and through direct dialogue, seeks to get national militaries to account (privately) for their misconduct. UNHCR tends to take a less direct approach, but with the aim of more public accountability, supporting other actors to hold the state, or specific parts of the state apparatus, accountable.

Indeed it could be said that the ICRC works on the cusp of supporting the state and holding it to account, as it does with non-state armed groups. As David Forsythe has described it, the ICRC 'has tried to be a "friendly legal adviser" rather than policeman' (Forsythe 1976: 613). Delegates encourage compliance with IHL, but they do not enforce it. The ICRC sees the enforcement of IHL—through such judicial proceedings as those of the ICC—as complementary to its own work (Forsythe 2005: 275; La Rosa 2009). However, such enforcement is distinct from the work of the ICRC, and staff members do not participate or testify in specific judicial investigations, believing that any such activity would compromise ICRC neutrality and confidentiality, and might endanger those civilians who provided the ICRC with information about violations of IHL. Certainly, the ICRC does act as a 'friendly legal adviser', but it also goes somewhat beyond this. Delegates present allegations of IHL violations to the military (and to non-state armed groups), with the expectation that the allegations will be investigated, and that their interlocutors will report back to the ICRC after having carried out an investigation. While this approach, centred as it is on bilateral confidential dialogue, does not come close to holding the state legally or publicly accountable for violations of IHL perpetrated by its agents, it does go beyond simply providing legal advice.

While UNHCR favours supporting the state, in some contexts the organization also supports programmes and mechanisms that enable other actors to hold the state (or a particular branch or agency of the state) legally accountable when it fails to meet its obligations. For example, in Colombia, UNHCR has worked closely with the Constitutional Court on IDP issues, seeing support for the Court as a way of maximizing leverage over national policy and practice (UNHCR 2008a, para. 22). The Colombian Constitutional Court is independent and activist, often holding the government to account on human rights issues in general, and in relations to IDP rights specifically (Nunes 2010). UNHCR was both feeding the court with information on how relevant decrees were (or were not) being implemented on the ground, and communicating new decisions by the court relating to IDPs to local authorities on the ground. In addition, UNHCR Colombia was providing financial support to the Procuraduría, which has responsibility for evaluating the compliance of state agencies with their obligations to the displaced population, and can take disciplinary action in cases of non-compliance.

In order to help IDPs access their citizenship rights, and those rights relating to displacement specifically, UNHCR may also provide legal aid to IDPs to inform them what those rights are, and training for IDP and community organizations to show them the official channels through which to claim their entitlements (UNHCR 2007f, paras. 37–8). For example, UNHCR and the Norwegian Refugee Council funded consultorios jurídicos (legal aid clinics) in eleven universities throughout Colombia, to train law students in IDP law so that the students could provide legal aid to individuals, with the aim of helping them to access rights and state programmes (UNHCR 2008a, paras. 52–3). This project was not unique to Colombia, or to IDPs. It is something both UNHCR and the Norwegian Refugee Council have also done elsewhere for refugees and returnees.

In Rakhine state in Myanmar, UNHCR staff considered that they were challenging the state on all the issues the state did not want to be challenged on. There was understood to be a bias against UNHCR, and some national staff were arrested and detained for up to six months, apparently for no reason other than that they were UNHCR staff. Within the UN, parallels have been made between Sri Lanka and Rakhine, and it is clear that UNHCR is concerned not to repeat the same mistakes it made in Sri Lanka. However, it is less clear whether this results in UNHCR taking the best approach, or whether it is more a concern about institutional reputation. For example, one UNHCR staff member in Rakhine state said they were trying to use written interventions more with the local government, despite the fact they did not generally receive replies to them. The rationale for this was that it was important for UNHCR to be able to demonstrate it had tried, particularly in light of the 'Human Rights up Front' initiative. Tellingly, one UNHCR interviewee explained that in the DRC they have space to raise matters with the government and the FARDC without the threat of being silenced or declared *persona non grata*. On the other hand, UNHCR interviewees in Myanmar noted that UNHCR presence in Kachin state was welcome, providing they do not did anything against the interests of the Northern Command. The implication of this is that, somewhat paradoxically, UNHCR will make efforts to hold a state to account if and only if the state allows them to do so.

Efforts to hold the state to account may or may not be effective in inducing the desired behaviour change, and the level of effectiveness is likely to depend in part on the nature and strength of the relationship between the organization and the state in question.

ICRC and UNHCR Relationships with the Affected State

On the one hand, it is understood that the ICRC and UNHCR need good relationships with affected states in order to get those states to change their behaviour. On the other hand, too close a relationship can make it somewhat difficult to see what the state is doing wrong, and to put effective pressure on it to change this.

Most of the work carried out by UNHCR in Colombia revolved around technical assistance to the state, lobbying for the state to meet its obligations, and capacity-building in communities so that civilians know their rights in national law and how to go about claiming those rights. The idea was that where the state was not responding appropriately, UNHCR sought to show them how, and where the state did not have the will to respond, UNHCR offered concrete inducements or assistance through joint projects, or provided public information and judicial assistance so that individuals could take their cases to the state. While these two roles are not intrinsically incompatible, in practice it can cause a difficulty when the same individual staff members of UNHCR who are so often supporting the state and working together with state agencies are then required to put pressure on the state to change.

The ICRC places great emphasis on building strong relationships with its interlocutors, and these relationships are deemed to depend on the ICRC demonstrating its trustworthiness, reliability, and confidentiality. All of this takes time to demonstrate. In Colombia and the DRC, it was easy for the ICRC to meet with the army, in order to disseminate IHL and present protection cases. By contrast, relationships with the national military in Myanmar were much less developed, at least in part because the ICRC was relatively new there. However, it is interesting to note that the ICRC was able to develop constructive dialogue with the police in the space of a few months, whereas more than a year after the ICRC restarted operations in Myanmar, the same kind of relationship still seemed a long way off with the army.

Other States

To a greater or lesser extent, depending on the context, both the ICRC and UNHCR engage with other states. As we have seen, the ICRC emphasizes the development of IHL as a key dimension of its protection work, and views states as the main actors for this aspect of protection.

In any operational context, the ICRC maintains regular contact with donor countries and institutions, and also with other countries that can have an impact on the situation there. Each delegation briefs diplomatic visitors on ICRC humanitarian concerns and on ICRC activities. Beyond these kinds of general briefings, the ICRC is not very open about its interactions with third parties. This is not surprising, given the institutional preference for bilateral, confidential dialogue, and given the assurances it gives to armed parties about the confidential nature of its engagement with them. However, where bilateral, confidential dialogue does not yield results, the ICRC may make 'discreet representations to third parties', including states that may have some influence over the armed parties in question (ICRC 2005, 2008b). From WikiLeaks we know that the ICRC has sometimes shared information with the US, some of the time with the apparent motive of getting help from the US to put pressure on a particular government. We also have indications that, prior to the ICRC's public denunciation of the Myanmar government in 2007, the organization sought the diplomatic intervention of a number of Asia-Pacific states (WikiLeaks 2007, para. 3).

Similarly, UNHCR may maintain relationships and dialogue with the diplomatic community in the countries in which it is working. In relation to Myanmar, UNHCR had an especially strong relationship with the diplomatic community, both within Myanmar and in Bangkok, in particular with the Swiss, German, French, EU, UK, US, Canadian, Australian, and Turkish missions. However, interviewees noticed that this was something specific to Myanmar, and that the impact of these diplomatic relations may have been limited by their Western-centricity. Although there was a good relationship with the Japanese (at the time of interviews, the head of UNHCR in Myanmar was Japanese), this was perhaps less focused on advocacy than were the relationships UNHCR had with some Western diplomats. In general, neither the ICRC nor UNHCR appears to have the same kinds of relationships with non-Western states as it does with its major donors. In countries such as Myanmar, this may limit the effectiveness of diplomatic interventions made by such states.

NON-STATE ARMED PARTIES TO CONFLICT

In internal conflicts, the perpetrators of organized violence include national military forces and non-state armed groups. Civilians are affected by violence in conflict either because violence from a clash between two or more armed groups spills over to affect them, or because they are deliberately targeted by armed actors. In internal armed conflict, clashes between armed groups necessarily involve at least one non-state armed group. Moreover, since the end of the Cold War, there has been an upward trend in the proportion of one-sided violence (the use of lethal force by governments or non-state armed groups against civilians that causes twenty-five or more deaths in a calendar year) perpetrated by non-state actors from 25 per cent in 1989 to 80 per cent in 2008 (Human Security Report Project 2011). While the Syrian conflict is a major exception, long-term trends suggest that worldwide armed non-state actors are responsible for a greater proportion of civilian fatalities from deliberate targeting than are government forces (Eck and Hultman 2007; UCDP 2012). Therefore, changing their behaviour should be a central focus of efforts to generate better protection outcomes for civilians.

Thus humanitarian policy analysts consistently argue that greater engagement with armed non-state actors is a necessary (if insufficient) condition for improved protection outcomes (ADH 2011; HPCR 2011; Jackson 2012; Zeender 2005). Such perspectives are also heard within the UN; both the Office for the Coordination of Humanitarian Affairs and the UN Secretary-General have emphasized engagement with non-state armed groups as necessary for improved civilian protection outcomes (UN OCHA 2006; UN Security Council 2009, para. 40). However, respect for state sovereignty and, in some cases, uncertainty over the political, legal, and ethical implications of engagement limit the extent and effectiveness of interaction between international humanitarian agencies on the one hand, and non-state armed groups on the other. The ICRC views armed non-state actors as important protection actors in all contexts, and seeks to build relationships with them in order to influence their behaviour for the better. UNHCR also sees non-state armed groups as a cause of displacement and of threats to IDPs and other civilians, but generally does not see them as central to protection, and does not seek to engage them anywhere near as systematically as does the ICRC.

ICRC and UNHCR Engagement with Non-State Armed Groups

The ICRC seeks to treat state armed forces and non-state armed groups equally as parties to conflict (as per the principle of equality of belligerents, and in keeping with the ICRC interpretation of the principle of neutrality). For the ICRC, the application (or non-application) of IHL is seen to depend on the combatants and the ICRC role is perceived to be about encouraging the armed parties to apply IHL (Bugnion 2003: 443). Thus, for the ICRC, just as states have an important role to play in protection through compliance with IHL, so too do non-state armed groups in the context of armed conflict (ICRC 2010a). In addition, in other situations of violence that fall short of the armed conflict threshold, the ICRC views all weapons-bearers as having a role to play in protection through limiting or reducing their use of violence. As the ICRC role has expanded to encompass internal armed conflict, non-state armed parties to conflict have been treated as akin to states in their capacity as armed parties to conflict, and are bound by the same rules and norms. The targets of ICRC bilateral dialogue in internal conflicts have accordingly been extended to include armed non-state actors. This adaptation has occurred over time, with specific interventions on violations of IHL taking place with armed non-state actors ever since the ICRC started working with an IHL framework for internal conflict, and with IHL training for non-state armed groups following later (Ratner 2011: 468).

However, the ICRC does not provide advisory services to non-state armed groups on the implementation of IHL in the same systematic way it has done for states since 1996 (Berman 1996; Sassòli 2007: 65). Moreover, armed non-state actors have remained largely excluded from the development of the international law that binds them. The IHL treaties were negotiated by states and in general only states have the option to sign up to them.[1] The ICRC does not negotiate agreements with non-state armed groups as such—delegates can provide expertise to help bring internal regulations up to IHL standards, but they do not want to validate or condone the internal regulations of any armed group. The customary IHL which the ICRC has played a role in developing is based primarily on state practice (Henckaerts 2005: 179–80; Kellenberger 2005: xvi). In the early days of the ICRC, states were the parties to conflict with which the organization was concerned, as only international conflicts came within its mandate. Although the ICRC is now also concerned with internal armed conflicts and non-state armed groups, it does not ascribe much importance to them in the development of the legal framework with which the ICRC seeks to regulate their behaviour, and this may reduce the effectiveness of ICRC interventions with armed non-state actors.

[1] There are some exceptions to this, notably cases of provisional or unrecognized governments depositing instruments of accession. For example, the Provisional Government of Algeria deposited an instrument of accession to the four Geneva Conventions of 1949 on 20 June 1960, more than two years prior to independence on 3 July 1962 (Roberts and Guelff 2000: 356, note 3). The Provisional Revolutionary Government of the Republic of South Vietnam acceded to the 1949 Geneva Conventions on 3 December 1973 (Roberts and Guelff 2000: 361, note 15). The UN Council for Namibia deposited instruments of accession for the four Geneva Conventions of 1949 and the two Additional Protocols of 1977 on 18 October 1983, prior to independence in 1990 (Roberts and Guelff 2000: 359, note 12). These accessions were accepted by the depositary. Additionally, the Palestine Liberation Organization has attempted to accede to the 1949 Conventions and their 1977 Additional Protocols. However, the depositary declined to decide whether or not such accession was valid because of uncertainty over the existence of the state of Palestine (Roberts and Guelff 2000: 362).

Moreover, even in its work in the field, where the ICRC does seek to treat state and non-state parties to conflict equally, interventions are not always as effective with armed non-state actors as with state forces. The effectiveness of protection interventions with a particular group is seen to be closely correlated with the level of contact with that group. Very often, the ICRC has less contact with armed non-state actors than with national militaries. In Colombia and the DRC, for example, the ICRC could easily meet with the army to disseminate IHL and present protection cases. By contrast, as we shall see in the next three sections, contacts with non-state armed groups in Colombia, the DRC, and Myanmar were limited by a number of factors. Furthermore, the ICRC often—though not always—has longer-standing and stronger relationships with national militaries than with non-state armed groups. In addition, where groups lack hierarchy or organization, the will to adhere to particular standards may be present among some elements of the group but those elements may be unable to control or punish the behaviour of other elements. Even among non-state armed groups that are well-structured and disciplined and where there is the will to behave 'appropriately', the work of the ICRC in the short run will depend on shared understandings of appropriateness.

Despite the fact that UNHCR is concerned with internal armed conflicts, and that such conflicts necessarily involve non-state armed groups, such groups are rarely mentioned in UNHCR documents regarding IDP protection. Analysis of institutional policy documents on the protection of IDPs and refugees in conflict contexts, and in respect of armed attacks on refugee camps, reveals two kinds of reference to non-state armed groups. First, there are those that affirm the applicability of IHL and the relevant provisions of the Guiding Principles to such groups. For example, UNHCR asserts that 'International humanitarian law is binding on both States and organized armed groups' (UNHCR 2007b, para. 17). The Guiding Principles are intended to apply not only to states but also to '[a]ll other authorities, groups and persons in their relations with internally displaced persons' (UN Commission on Human Rights 1998: 5, para. 3(c)). There is no effort to justify the claim that these legal and normative frameworks apply to non-state actors, simply the assertion that they do. Second, there are references that claim that successful protection from armed attacks can only occur when all parties to a conflict pursue policies based entirely on humanitarian principles (UNHCR 1988, para. 34; 1989, para. 45). Beyond such statements, however, there is no suggestion of how the protection work undertaken by UNHCR might encourage non-state actors to comply with humanitarian principles. UNHCR does not set out any strategy to increase the compliance of armed non-state actors with the existing legal and normative framework, and 'there is no universal policy on how to engage [armed non-state actors], nor has there historically been a standard method for connecting with rebels, guerrillas or insurgents' (Keogh and Ruijters 2012: 2).

UNHCR does envisage some interaction with armed non-state parties to conflict. However, this is not with the direct aim of protecting refugees and IDPs, but with institutional neutrality and staff security in mind. For example, UNHCR recognizes

> that IDP situations will more typically than refugee operations involve UNHCR and other agencies working in tenuous environments including those not controlled fully by the national authorities. The dynamics of interventions will thus have to take into account interaction with armed groups and/or *de facto* authorities. Working with parties to a conflict and ensuring the neutrality of the Office are thus vital, and staff security is often times among the foremost issues of concern.
>
> (UNHCR 2007c, para. 39)

There is no suggestion that UNHCR works to increase compliance by armed non-state actors with the relevant rules and norms as a means of protecting IDPs. In practice, in some contexts UNHCR does seek to engage non-state armed groups on substantive protection issues. However, this is the exception rather than the rule. Moreover, even where such engagement does occur, it is a secondary aim of any contact with such groups, which is first and foremost concerned with access and staff security (Keogh and Ruijters 2012: 11). Both the ICRC and UNHCR consider the establishment of trust and a strong relationship with an armed group to be a prerequisite of substantive protection dialogue with that group. However, whereas the ICRC actively seeks to establish such relationships in order to be able to engage in such dialogue, for UNHCR, any such dialogue seems to be more of an afterthought—something which staff may or may not engage in if the organization happens to have a good relationship with the armed group in question. Moreover, despite its own institutional protection mandate, UNHCR tends to see other parts of the UN—such as OCHA or MONUSCO—as responsible for establishing and developing contact with non-state armed groups.

Colombia

In Colombia, ICRC field delegates could meet with members of the national military every day and thus had plenty of opportunity to try to convince them to change their behaviour when it was in violation of IHL. However, when a delegate could only see one of the other armed groups every six months, the protection work was necessarily limited. At the field level in some parts of Colombia, the lower ranks of all the armed groups were visible to the ICRC, but delegates found it could be harder to establish and maintain contact at the higher ranks. When the guerrilla groups were stronger it was much easier to access them at both lower and higher levels, and to develop dialogue. However, by the time of interviews, they were more hidden and on the move. Both the FARC and the ELN had suffered major military losses over the previous ten years and the sizes of their forces had greatly diminished. They had conceded a good deal of territory to the army, and in 2009, then FARC commander Alfonso Cano declared the FARC was shifting from a war of territory to a guerrilla war. Given that the group was more on the defensive than previously, and less able to hold on to territory, it increasingly employed classic guerrilla hit-and-run style tactics (Ávila Martínez 2010). As a consequence of their more defensive, mobile strategies the ICRC had less contact with the guerrilla groups. Furthermore, at the time of interviews in 2010, the ICRC had little or no contact with the so-called new or emerging groups in much of Colombia. These groups were smaller and more disparate than their AUC predecessors (and than the national military, FARC, and ELN), which made it more difficult to build contact and relationships. The lack of hierarchy and clear structure made it more difficult to exercise leverage over the behaviour of such groups as a whole.

The relationship between the ICRC and the FARC in Colombia also illustrates how the strength of relationships and dialogue can vary even across a given armed group. The ICRC tended to have a better relationship with the FARC in areas which were under full control of the FARC. Given that civilians are in any case usually more secure in such contexts (where one armed actor has control), this highlights how protection work is often most difficult in the places or at the times it is most needed. A further problem with the FARC in some areas of the country was a lack of trust and confidence in the ICRC, particularly following Operation Jaque.[2]

Armed non-state actors were rarely mentioned by UNHCR Colombia staff members except where interviewees were specifically asked about them. Where they were mentioned, it was more likely to be about the FARC preventing UNHCR from carrying out its normal activities (for example a joint project with the state) than as a cause of civilian insecurity or as an actor whose behaviour UNHCR might seek to change. Essentially their activity was taken as exogenously determined. The situation in Colombia was slightly different from elsewhere in that there was a government ban on talking to non-state armed groups. However, most UNHCR staff members interviewed for this research were in favour of the ban, as they viewed it as being in their own personal security interests. Few had given any thought to how it might impact on their protection work per se, reflecting the wider institutional

[2] Operation Jaque was a military operation undertaken by the Colombian forces in the department of Guaviare on 2 July 2008 to free fifteen hostages (the former presidential candidate Ingrid Betancourt, three Americans, and eleven Colombia military and police personnel) held by the FARC. The operation reportedly involved the misuse of the Red Cross emblem, and the Colombian authorities have since investigated and found that one officer had individually decided to make unauthorized use of the emblem.

approach that largely ignores armed non-state actors. Non-state armed groups were deemed relevant to staff security and to access to territory and populations in need, but were not deemed to have much bearing on the protection of IDPs.

DRC

As in Colombia, ICRC relations with the armed non-state actors in the DRC appeared to be less developed than with the FARDC. The multiplicity of armed groups in the DRC makes it more difficult to generalize, but with respect to some non-state armed groups at least, interviewees reported that it was not so easy to set up meetings, that contact was mainly about making sure they knew who the ICRC is and what the ICRC does, and about getting security guarantees. In some regions, delegates felt they did not yet have the contacts for an IHL discussion with the relevant armed non-state actors. The nature of engagement depends in part on how long delegates have been in contact with a given armed group or particular interlocutors within it. Thus, work on child recruitment in some parts of the DRC was more about explaining ICRC child reunification routes, rather than persuading the relevant armed group to stop using child soldiers. Where non-state armed groups were very mobile, delegates may not see them for six months and so they did not have the kind of relationship deemed necessary to present allegations of IHL violations, and they could not simply call to arrange a first-aid course or other kind of training. However, in other regions, delegates were collecting and presenting allegations of IHL violations by at least some of the armed non-state actors.

The UNHCR perspective in Kinshasa was that it was not the responsibility of UNHCR, but rather of MONUSCO, to engage with armed non-state actors. In the UNHCR field offices elsewhere in the DRC, perspectives were a bit different. In North Kivu, for example, UNHCR did have relationships with some armed groups and in fact did undertake some work more akin to ICRC efforts at persuading state and non-state armed actors to change their behaviour. One interviewee noted that there was ample space and needs that went beyond ICRC capacities, and that the protection cluster should reach out to any perpetrator. UNHCR was doing more advocacy with the FARDC than with the non-state armed groups, and had better access to the FARDC, but in North Kivu UNHCR could and would also call non-state armed groups directly. In addition, UNHCR could contact armed non-state actors indirectly via OCHA. OCHA was responsible for negotiating access with armed groups, and UNHCR could ask OCHA to raise protection concerns. In the absence of any other channel, UNHCR could also take its concerns to the ICRC, although in Goma it did not do (or need to do) this systematically. It seemed to be the case that specific individual staff members in the UNHCR office in Goma were extremely open to direct contacts with armed non-state actors. However, this is the exception rather than the rule, and general UNHCR policy does not allow for much of this kind of work. In many contexts such engagement would be extremely sensitive, but in the DRC the government did not have a problem with UNHCR engaging with non-state armed groups. This appeared to be a key factor in UNHCR being so proactive in liaising with armed non-state actors in North Kivu.

Myanmar

In contrast with Colombia and the DRC, at the time of interviews, ICRC dialogue with non-state armed groups in Myanmar was in many ways more advanced than the dialogue with the army and the police, at least as far as the armed groups present in Thailand were concerned. It was more difficult to see armed non-state actors inside Myanmar, but the ICRC had some contact with the KIA and was working towards contact with the UWSA and the Shan State Army South. With the KIA, it was deemed to be early days, but delegates reported good contacts, and a general discussion focused primarily on explaining the ICRC and its mandate. The ICRC was also interested in making contact with the other armed groups within Myanmar, but as they were mainly in ceasefire mode and not involved in active conflict, this was not a major concern or high priority. Interaction with the non-state armed groups in the east of Myanmar was mainly from the Thai side, where dialogue largely consisted of a general discussion on IHL and on the issues of child soldiers, landmines, and respect for the wounded and for medical missions. Interestingly, although the dialogue was further advanced with the non-state armed groups than with the army, on particular issues—notably landmines—delegates felt they were even further away with the armed groups. There was some optimism that the army would agree to demining, while some of the armed groups were not expected to be willing to give up their use of that weapon.

In Myanmar, as elsewhere, the ICRC was committed to working within areas that were not controlled by the government, and to building relationships with armed non-state actors. UNHCR also aimed to work in non-government-controlled areas, in particular in the south-east of the country and in Kachin state. In both these regions, many or most of the IDPs were in non-government-controlled areas. Additionally, as a main donor to UNHCR, the UK Department for International Development had been very insistent that UNHCR should undertake protection activities in non-government-controlled areas in Kachin state. However, in practice both the ICRC and UNHCR faced greater difficulties accessing non-government-controlled territory. The government sought to restrict access to these areas, and while this affected both the ICRC and UNHCR, it did not affect them both equally. For example, the ICRC was able to establish a permanent expatriate presence in KIO/A-controlled territory in 2014, whereas UNHCR was only able to undertake occasional 'cross-line missions' of around one month each.

Because UNHCR was not present in the non-government-controlled areas, the organization worked more with the civilian wings of the non-state armed groups than it normally would. Even then, however, it seemed that UNHCR was cautious about developing official relationships with armed non-state actors. For example, the KIO humanitarian department was running IDP camps in non-government-controlled areas of Kachin state. UNHCR had implementing-partner agreements with various church organizations, and these organizations themselves were working with the KIO. However, for UNHCR it was important that, on paper at least, its own agreements were with the church groups and not with the KIO. One interviewee noted that being Kachins, the KIO/A was supported by the population in general, but that they were abusing the population (through child recruitment, for example). In spite of this, UNHCR had only very nascent contact with the KIO regarding protection. Interviewees noted that they were relying on OCHA to help build relationships, and that OCHA had not done so.

In the south-east of Myanmar, UNHCR similarly had very limited access to non-state areas. When they wanted to go into a non-state-controlled area, they had to make a request to the border agency (NATALA—Ministry for the Progress of Border Areas and National Races and Development Affairs), and NATALA would then make the request to the relevant non-state armed group. Generally the relevant armed group would accept, and at the time of interviews UNHCR was getting more and more contact with non-state actors, but that contact was always mediated by NATALA. Interviewees acknowledged that the government was using UNHCR to get access itself, but also believed there was no way they could go into these areas without armed government escort. Thus, while other international agencies, such as the Norwegian Refugee Council, had wider access than UNHCR in the south-east, UNHCR accepted the government requirement that access was with armed government escort, which obviously imposed limits on the kinds of relationship they could develop with the non-state armed groups.

Engagement with International Peacekeeping Forces

In the DRC, the ICRC was engaging MONUSCO on different issues, much as it would engage a regular party to a conflict, albeit a relatively well-trusted one. Delegates discussed concrete concerns, especially, but not exclusively, in relation to MONUSCO's joint operations with the FARDC. They would remind MONUSCO troops that they had a responsibility to ensure the FARDC complied with IHL, or at least to remind the FARDC of their obligations. UNHCR was working much more closely with MONUSCO, despite concerns about this compromising institutional neutrality and the humanitarian mandate of UNHCR. There was a coordination body involving the highest levels of MONUSCO, OCHA, UNICEF, and UNHCR at both central and provincial level. Because the intervention brigade had an offensive mandate, UNHCR had major concerns about coordination, which it regularly discussed with MONUSCO.

AFFECTED COMMUNITIES, CIVIL (AND UNCIVIL) SOCIETY

In addition to state agencies and non-state armed groups, there are a number of civilian non-state actors who can have an impact on the security and protection of IDPs and other civilians. First, there are affected individuals and communities themselves. Second, there are local and international NGOs and civil society groups. Third, in many contexts, there is what we might describe as uncivil society: civilians who pose a violent threat to other civilians. This last category includes, for example, urban gangs in Colombia, perpetrators of communal violence in Rakhine state in Myanmar, and the many civilian perpetrators of sexual violence in the DRC. Both the ICRC and UNHCR do, at times, seek to involve all of these different actors in their protection work. However, their engagement with them is mostly less systematic than is ICRC engagement with armed parties to conflict, or UNHCR engagement with the civilian agencies of the state.

The ICRC seeks to distinguish itself from other humanitarian actors by, among other things, its 'field presence and proximity to affected persons' (Aeschlimann 2005: 25). It aims to stand 'resolutely by the victims. It works closely with people affected by violence and armed conflict, listens to and respects them, empathizes with their plight and is determined to act for their benefit' (ICRC 2007b: 2). Further, the ICRC acknowledges and seeks to support the existing capacities of civilians to protect themselves (ICRC 2008b: 762). The role ascribed to civilians by the ICRC is essentially twofold. First, with respect to vulnerability reduction, the ICRC aims to increase the choices available to civilians, thus giving them greater option to pursue their own protection strategies. Second, with respect to threat reduction, the ICRC sees civilians as a key source of information in terms of reporting IHL violations, and as the key decision-makers in what the ICRC may do with that information. Thus, while threat reduction is ultimately seen to depend on the perpetrators of violence, the ICRC ascribes more agency to the civilians affected by violence than do many other humanitarian organizations.

UNHCR maintains a rhetorical commitment to participation by those whom the organization seeks to protect, at least in the design of protection policies, if not in the implementation of those policies. Specifically, UNHCR claims to be 'committed to the principle of participation, believing that refugees and others who benefit from the organization's activities should be consulted over decisions which affect their lives', and has developed an operational tool for the participation of intended beneficiaries in the definition of the problems facing them and the design of solutions to those problems (UNHCR 2007a). However, the extent to which the UNHCR approach to protection involves meaningful participation in practice is questionable. The hierarchical culture and top-down decision-making processes in UNHCR impede meaningful participation from intended beneficiaries. Senior staffer Martin Gottwald explains that 'One of the biggest obstacles is that the same UNHCR staff who are called to involve persons of UNHCR concern at all stages of decision-making do not enjoy the same right within UNHCR's own internal decision-making processes' (Gottwald 2010: 31).

ICRC doctrine is less clear and its practice weaker when the perpetrators of violence are not organized groups but civilians. In Medellín in Colombia, for example, ICRC delegates explained that dialogue with the gangs required a pragmatic step-by-step approach: first getting agreement from the gangs that the ICRC could work on their territory on issues of urban violence, and then asking them if they were interested in having a dialogue with the ICRC. Working in schools was expected to facilitate proximity to the victims and potentially to provide access to gang members, and the ICRC could further draw on its core competency of working with detainees, with prisons providing a second entry point to meet and establish relations with leaders of criminal gangs. Nonetheless, the lack of a clear legal mandate appears to reduce the speed and confidence with which the ICRC is able to build such trust and dialogue.

In Rakhine state in Myanmar, most of the violence was not perpetrated by recognized authorities—or even necessarily by organized groups, and the humanitarian community as a whole was quite weak at engaging with local (un)civil society. The fact that the perpetrators of violence were not authorities or organized groups distinguished Rakhine from many of the contexts in which the ICRC and UNHCR work, and posed particular challenges to their protection approaches. Whereas ICRC doctrine on dealing with organized armed groups is quite clear, there was some uncertainty as to how to address the Rakhine communities. Initially the core activities undertaken by the ICRC in Rakhine were about access to healthcare. Muslims had to pass communal lines to access Sittwe hospital, and the Rakhine population also faced restricted access because of curfew at night. Undertaken together with the MRCS, whose support for medical referrals in this context was seen as crucial, initial activities included direct transportation to the hospital, and the negotiation of passage for such transportation. Interviewees reported that when the *authorities* prevented access to health, the ICRC could negotiate with them, but that they could not do much when the communities prevented individuals from getting to hospital, or when they intimidated health staff.

In relation to classic ICRC protection work, there was a sense among some delegates that they could not simply go, for example, to a shopkeeper to address misbehaviour. In this context, the security forces and government were seen more as a stabilizing force than anything else. A particular challenge identified by delegates in Rakhine was the need to build a network with leaders of civil society. In addition, for some delegates, the mandate of the ICRC was seen to restrict the kind of dialogue they could engage in with individuals in the community, in that with this kind of violence, entering into a dialogue with perpetrators would essentially be peace-building. All of this highlights the limitations of an authority-centric approach when the authorities are not the main source of threat. Such limitations are not unique to Rakhine state or to Myanmar. Where sexual violence was perpetrated by civilians in the DRC, for example, the ICRC was not making interventions with perpetrators, and was limited to working with the communities to help them to protect themselves.

UNHCR had very limited contact with either Rakhine or Rohingya community leaders in Rakhine state. Interviewees reported that with the Rohingya it was difficult to find leaders who represented the whole population, and that on the Rakhine side, the challenge was to find moderates. It was apparent that UNHCR did not consider it to be its own responsibility to deal with this core issue, but that it was in the hands of OCHA. Interviewees mentioned several times that UNHCR was not used to talking with non-state elements, and that they themselves did not have much contact with the extremist groups, but that OCHA was trying to reach out to affected communities, including extremist elements. On the other hand, UNHCR does engage with civil society. In Kachin state, for example, there were fewer international actors but a strong national NGO scene, and at the time of interviews, UNHCR was working with nine national NGOs there. UNHCR was doing a lot of capacity-building of these nine NGOs, especially training on SGBV prevention and on psychosocial interventions. They were mainly faith-based organizations of various Christian denominations, and they had come together to develop their own advocacy strategies. UNHCR was fortifying links between them.

In many contexts, the ICRC works closely with the national Red Cross or Red Crescent society. For example, the DRC Red Cross society has an impressive network, and the ICRC was working closely with them on restoring family links. In addition, the ICRC was collaborating with them to train National Society volunteers in livelihoods programming, and was financing some small projects to reinforce structures in the national society. The ICRC was also working with the Myanmar Red Cross society for the provision of healthcare, and to expand ICRC access in government-controlled areas.

For UNHCR, a community-based protection approach focuses on the victims and local NGOs, and only rarely addresses the perpetrators. Once again, of the three country cases that are the focus of this book, the DRC provides the exception, where, for example, UNHCR was trying to change attitudes among (potential) civilian perpetrators of sexual violence through sensitization with youth groups and working with traditional and religious leaders. In addition, UNHCR was working with communities to try to prevent forced or child marriages. As an example of success in such endeavours, one interviewee explained how in one area, the whole community agreed that no one would attend the wedding of anyone under twelve years of age. With nobody at a wedding, it is not socially a wedding, and so such an approach seemed to be effective in reducing the number of child weddings. In some places in the DRC, a lot of women were being raped on their way to market. In one such place, the market started at 6 a.m. so the women had to walk through the night to get there, which made them more vulnerable to attack. In liaison with local communities, UNHCR got the start time changed to 8 a.m., which reduced vulnerability. In other places, men began to accompany the women, and in some cases, the women got dogs. In another area, the community agreed to stop selling alcohol earlier in the evening to reduce alcohol-related sexual violence.

Depending on the context, UNHCR views other UN agencies as having a role in protection and international NGOs as (not always equal) partners in protection. UNHCR works closely with other UN agencies, with implementing partners and with the rest of protection cluster. The ICRC also sees many of these organizations as having important roles to play in protection, but its commitment to confidentiality and independence prevents it from working very closely with any of them. Thus, the ICRC is not part of the protection cluster, and does not participate in formal coordination mechanisms, except as an observer.

CONCLUSIONS

In terms of immediate protection in the context of conflict and violence, the ICRC views combatants—or, more generally, weapons-bearers—as the primary determinants of threats to civilians, and correspondingly as the most important actors in protection. This reflects the approach taken by the ICRC to the protection of prisoners of war and the protection of civilians in international conflict in that it is authority-centric. However, the authorities in the two prior issue-areas are states, and in internal conflict the ICRC has extended its understanding of who is an authority to include armed non-state actors. This extension serves an important purpose in adapting the approach to the political realities of internal conflict, and has been driven by field-level experience. At the level of the development of IHL, however, the ICRC ascribes importance only to states. Treaty-based IHL is negotiated and signed by states, and the ICRC documentation and interpretation of customary IHL privilege state practice. Further, the content of IHL applicable to internal conflict (a body of law which the ICRC has played a significant role in developing) does not take into account the difference in capabilities, opportunities, and threats experienced by non-state armed groups as opposed to states. In short, the IHL applicable to non-international armed conflict has been developed through analogy to the IHL of international conflict, and has not been sufficiently adapted to the political context of internal conflict.

Just as the objectives of UNHCR are often at least one step removed from some of the most pressing protection concerns that relate specifically to conflict and violence, so the actors deemed to be most important in protection are not necessarily those with most control over the conduct of conflict and violence. Given that UNHCR emphasizes international human rights law, domestic legislation, and the development of public policy, it is unsurprising that the UNHCR approach to protection is state-centric. In this sense, UNHCR IDP protection efforts look a lot like its refugee protection efforts, which are similarly based on the idea that states provide protection. However, the 'IDP problem' is fundamentally different from the 'refugee problem'. In the case of refugees, where one state fails to protect a citizen and that citizen is able to flee, another state takes on responsibility for the protection of that individual. In the case of an IDP, one state has failed in its responsibility to protect that person, and UNHCR works to get that same state to resume its protection responsibility. This is a very different task, and the distance between the understanding of protection carried through from refugee protection and the actual requirements of in-country protection limits the scope of protection by UNHCR.

The lack of any serious consideration of non-state armed groups is in keeping with the traditional understanding of refugee protection, where attention to non-state armed groups was unnecessary. UNHCR developed its understanding of refugee protection at a time when refugees were arriving in peaceful countries. Granted, in many cases since then refugees have fled to a country characterized by armed conflict and in which refugees face threats from armed non-state actors. Indeed these are the very contexts in which both refugees and IDPs tend to be found, and in which the arguments that IDP protection and refugee protection are similar tasks that require the same competencies carry most weight. In such contexts, attention to non-state armed groups is as relevant for refugee protection as it is for IDP protection. However, these are also the contexts in which UNHCR is arguably least effective in its refugee protection efforts.

Beyond the question of *who* the ICRC and UNHCR engage with, and to *what* ends, is that of *how* they engage with them. The ICRC views states in two distinct but related roles: as the parties to IHL treaties (and makers of customary law) and as parties to conflict. The roles are related in that the ICRC has sought to get states to become parties to those treaties in order to influence their subsequent behaviour as parties to conflict. However, the different roles elicit a different kind of interaction between the ICRC and the relevant states. With respect to the first role, the ICRC defers to and supports the system of states, acknowledging states as the primary actors in international relations and as those with the capacity to make international law. With respect to the second role, the ICRC relates to states individually rather than collectively and asserts its own authority in order to change the behaviour of states. In general, UNHCR defers to states more than the ICRC does. Furthermore, in contrast to the ICRC, UNHCR is more likely to demand action from states as the collective international community than it is to make demands on the individual states in which it is operational.

It is not at all clear how humanitarian agencies should relate to the states in which they are working. However, the dilemmas they face as to whether to support the state, hold it to account, or bypass it may well be amplified the more transformative and wider ranging their goals or projects. Thus, the ICRC has an easier time treading a line between the three modes of action with its more limited focus on the military and police, and on the conduct of hostilities, than does UNHCR with its own work, which is more akin to a partial state-building project. By focusing on the immediate manifestations of threats and violence against civilians, the potentially grave risks of supporting an unwilling state are minimized, and the potential tensions between supporting a state and holding it to account may also be minimized. On armed non-state actors, the message is perhaps clearer. Both the ICRC and UNHCR have the possibility of extending the scope of their protection work through more and better engagement with non-state armed groups, UNHCR at all levels of its protection work, and the ICRC in the development of IHL.

6

Protection Activities

This chapter turns to the activities that constitute the protection policy and practice of the ICRC and UNHCR, examining seven broad areas of activity. For each of these, it explains the activities envisaged in headquarters-level policy, and those implemented in practice in Colombia, Myanmar, and the DRC. Moreover, the rationale for these activities is critically analysed vis-à-vis the objectives discussed in Chapter 4, and the challenges associated with implementing them are highlighted.

The ICRC protection policy lists twelve activities, and every protection strategy should be based on a selection of these activities, depending on which are appropriate in any given context: (1) bilateral and confidential representations; (2) discreet representations to third parties; (3) public denunciation; (4) development of the law; (5) promotion of the law; (6) structural support for implementation of the law; (7) activities as neutral intermediary; (8) registration/monitoring of individuals; (9) presence and accompaniment; (10) self-protection capacity building; (11) risk education; and (12) assistance aimed at reducing risk exposure (ICRC 2008b: 766). This is a list of generic activities applicable across the different issue-areas that the ICRC works on. Thus, the activities undertaken by the ICRC for the protection of civilians during internal armed conflict are broadly the same as those undertaken for the protection of civilians and those *hors de combat* in international armed conflict, as well as in internal disturbances and other situations of violence falling short of armed conflict, and also for those deprived of their liberty. However, a disjuncture exists between the formal policy which includes these twelve activities, and the more widely held institutional understanding and practice, which often focuses overwhelmingly on dialogue-related activities.

UNHCR emphasizes that the activities it will undertake depend on the situation, the needs of IDPs, the relationships between IDPs and authorities and between UNHCR and authorities, and the will and ability of the affected state (UNHCR 1994b, para. 27; 2007c, para. 24). Certainly, in UNHCR, there is nowhere near the consistency of approach that there is in the ICRC, and there are pluses and minuses to this flexibility. On the one hand, it enables UNHCR to adapt its approach to the different contexts in which it works. On the other, it can contribute to uncertainty over what UNHCR should be doing in a given context, and a corresponding lack of confidence on the part of some UNHCR staff. In the course of the research for this book, for example, there were times when UNHCR interviewees asked me what their colleagues in other offices were doing. In various places UNHCR sets out or evaluates what it has done in a given situation, but nowhere does it provide an exhaustive list of potential activities. Nonetheless, by drawing out the main protection activities documented by UNHCR in different places, and recounted by UNHCR interviewees in Colombia, the DRC, and Myanmar, the main protection activities undertaken by UNHCR in contexts of armed conflict can be identified. In keeping with the focus on the state as the primary protection actor, the activities undertaken by UNHCR focus on the provision of support to the state, individuals, and communities, to bring the state closer to the population of concern. Activities include monitoring the situations and protection environments within which UNHCR operates, developing the national legal framework or persuading the state to adhere to its obligations as set out in various legal frameworks, providing legal documentation to those of concern to UNHCR, direct provision—or support to state provision—of social services, promotion of land and property rights, provision of legal advice to IDPs and those at risk of displacement, provision of humanitarian assistance, and management and coordination of refugee and IDP camps.

The rest of this chapter is structured around seven different types of activity undertaken in different forms by both the ICRC and UNHCR. In practice, there may be some overlap between these different activity types, and they are separated for the sake of presentational clarity, and not to derive any analytical traction from distinguishing between them.

MONITORING AND ANALYSIS

Both the ICRC and UNHCR undertake a range of monitoring and analysis activities. There is some possibility that state and non-state actors will behave differently if they know their activities are being observed by international actors. However, for the most part, monitoring and analysis activities in and of themselves are unlikely to reduce violence, threats, or vulnerability, or to mitigate the consequences of violence. Nonetheless, monitoring and profiling activities can serve an important purpose if they are used to inform efforts to change the behaviour of armed actors (to reduce overall levels of violence or to reduce threats to civilians) or to increase the choices available to civilians in reducing their own vulnerability. That said, there is a danger that such monitoring activities come to be seen as an end in themselves rather than as a means to develop effective practical activities. Again, then, we see the importance of always keeping in mind well-specified objectives and a clear conceptualization of how different activities relate to those objectives.

In their monitoring and analysis, the ICRC and UNHCR each emphasize different sources of information, and each has somewhat different objectives. Both organizations undertake monitoring and analysis in order to understand conflict and displacement dynamics, assess needs, decide where to focus, and devise appropriate responses. In Colombia, for example, the ICRC was operating a priority-zone approach according to which it focused its presence and activities on areas in which there were greatest needs or risks, and where the ICRC could have greatest impact. Political analysis was also used for planning and budgeting. For example, if the analysis showed that manual eradication of coca crops led to increased use of landmines, and that manual eradication was expected to increase in a particular region, then the ICRC would increase the budget for its operations in that region. Furthermore, as the ICRC explains:

> Understanding the causes and circumstances behind violations is essential in order to identify the most effective means of addressing them—addressing only the symptoms can sometimes do more harm than good . . . Different contexts call for different protection responses, and an analysis specific to the context is key to determining both an initial course of action—and to informing its adjustment over time.
>
> (ICRC 2009: 21)

Likewise, UNHCR was permanently analysing where there were expulsions in Colombia, and asking why the population was being displaced. This kind of analysis impacts on policy and focus, and the Buenaventura office opened as a result of reflections by UNHCR on the dynamics of the conflict. UNHCR interviewees in the DRC similarly reported that they changed policies in response to active monitoring, and in Rakhine state in Myanmar, UNHCR was going to a lot of effort to do the mapping in order to understand the politics of the situation better.

To monitor trends and assess needs, reliable information is needed. However, there are often gaps in information that limit its usefulness. Examples from UNHCR monitoring and analysis efforts in the DRC and Myanmar are illustrative. First, the capacity of UNHCR and its partners to collect data is limited. In the DRC, UNHCR was funding NGOs to undertake protection monitoring in an ambitious and costly exercise. By 2014, they had conducted 25,000 individual interviews in North Kivu alone. The NGO was monitoring incidents, and UNHCR was producing weekly reports based on the data collected by the NGO. However, because of access restrictions and staff capacity, the monitors were unable to document everything. For example, of 200 rape victims going for treatment in clinics supported by UNHCR, monitors may only have reported twenty cases because they lacked sufficient staff to verify the information received. As a consequence, the number reported depended less on the level of sexual violence, and more on the capacity of the monitors. In Myanmar, UNHCR was very unsure about the numbers of IDPs in different locations, because agencies were not collecting information on displacement, in part because of objections from the government to such monitoring. Second, the data gathered in monitoring exercises is not always used properly, either because agencies do not coordinate or share information effectively, or because there is not the capacity to analyse the data or to follow up on the analysis. UNHCR interviewees in the DRC reported that each agency had a multitude of surveys and information, but that they were not shared, and that there may have been overlaps and inconsistencies. Moreover, the information from the protection monitors was, despite the limits of the information itself, deemed to be overwhelming in terms of quantity. The main aim was to analyse trends and identify hotspots, and monitors were also supposed to provide orientation, referring victims to the nearest service available for them, especially in sexual violence cases. However, beyond the initial referral, there were too many cases to follow up.

In addition to the general protection context, the ICRC monitors violations of IHL specifically, and here primary sources are essential, and the information is used in ICRC threat-reduction efforts. Individual testimonies are used to identify trends and also as evidence with which the ICRC seeks to change the behaviour of perpetrators. Confidential dialogue and persuasion are the ICRC trademark, and in many contexts this is the bread and butter of ICRC protection work. It involves the documenting of protection cases, detailing alleged events or incidents that represent a violation of IHL. These are based on information provided by the civilian population regarding violations of IHL by armed groups (including both the national military and non-state armed groups). Once the information is verified, and if the victim (or the victim's family in cases where the victim has been killed) agrees, the ICRC presents the case to the armed group accused of perpetrating the violation. Delegates see the presentation of concrete cases as most effective, but the ICRC wants to avoid endangering a victim (or his or her family). Thus, for the ICRC to present a particular protection case to the alleged perpetrators, even when the victim consents to the case being transmitted, the ICRC does its own risk analysis to assess the potential danger. Delegates also seek to identify trends in order to focus on a particular armed group or battalion, or on particular violations. Therefore, even when they are not transmittable, the individual testimonies of victims contribute to understanding trends and patterns in violations.

To some extent, UNHCR also uses these kinds of primary sources as evidence with which to make representations to different actors with a bearing on protection—in the case of UNHCR, such representations are mainly to the civilian agencies of the state. In Rakhine state in Myanmar, for example, UNHCR officials were visiting the IDP sites once or twice a week and collecting information on issues such as forced labour and arbitrary arrest and detention. The information was used to map violations, and staff might pay a courtesy visit to the relevant authorities/commander, as well as using the information for wider advocacy with the diplomatic community in Yangon. In the DRC, the information gathered by the NGOs that UNHCR was contracting to do protection monitoring could also be used in this way. However, just as the ICRC will not present allegations if it believes doing so would put the victim or victim's family at risk, so UNHCR can be somewhat cautious in its use of information gathered this way. Interviewees reported that in some cases, accusing the government of something could endanger the monitors, and hence they were careful about how they used the material.

UNHCR also places great emphasis on analysis of the public policy response to displacement. In the IDP contexts in which it is operational, UNHCR monitors the 'protection environment, including laws, access to justice, living conditions, and access to basic services' (UNHCR 2007f, para. 32). In Colombia, for example, UNHCR was conducting analysis of structural issues at the national level, specifically gaps in public policy and in the coverage of state services. At the local level, from its field offices, UNHCR sought to identify protection gaps and risks by understanding what was happening in different communities, and how different sub-populations were affected. In Kachin state in Myanmar, where land-grabbing was a big issue, UNHCR was mapping land issues and looking at legislation. With the information from this political, legal, and needs analysis, UNHCR seeks to help develop public policy in such a way as to minimize the identified gaps. All of this is aimed at understanding what public policy is, where it is lacking, how it plays out in practice, and how it could be improved.

In part because of the different uses and objectives of their monitoring and analysis, each organization emphasizes different sources. The ICRC places great emphasis on collecting testimony from individual victims, and from other direct contacts between delegates and affected communities. Only where such direct contacts are restricted is the ICRC likely to rely heavily on secondary sources. By contrast, UNHCR depends more on secondary sources, triangulating between government information, other humanitarian agencies, and affected communities.

In Colombia, for example, UNHCR risk analysis drew on various sources, primarily the risk reports of the Human Rights Ombudsman and forced displacement figures produced by Acción Social, which were analysed to determine the areas of highest expulsion in order to focus prevention efforts. Additionally, UNHCR was collating homicide figures from Medicina Legal (the forensic body in Colombia which has an obligation to carry out autopsies on all victims of violent deaths), getting information from inter-institutional communication, information from the Comisión Nacional de Reparación y Reconciliación (National Commission for Reparation and

Reconciliation) which does a lot of community work, and maintaining ongoing discussions with local communities and Pastoral Social (the charitable arm of the Catholic Church in Colombia, which provides social care and assistance, including to the displaced). All of this was used to help understand conflict dynamics. Similarly, in order to analyse the risks and needs of IDPs in Rakhine state in Myanmar, UNHCR was triangulating between a number of sources: IDP leaders and women's groups; the IDP community as a whole; and government sources. It was seen as necessary to triangulate, because risks and incidents were underplayed by the government and overplayed by the IDPs.

The ICRC collects much more of its information first-hand. For example, although political analysis in Colombia did not necessarily involve talking to the victims, it was based on field-trip reports, and it was seen as a significant advantage that the ICRC had access to the whole country so that it could receive first-hand information with which to build this analysis. In addition, ICRC delegates were spending a lot of time in the field (often three weeks in every four), and felt that they were respected and that people knew and understood their confidential approach to their work, and were comfortable sharing information with them. Despite the emphasis placed on first-hand information, the ICRC sought to cross-check this information by talking to the armed groups, the police, civilian leaders, the church, hospitals, and other humanitarian organizations. In the DRC, the ICRC was similarly emphasizing first-hand information, and it was seen to be important to have a small team in every area of the Kivus, for example, in order to collect allegations. ICRC protection teams were regularly visiting the *maisons d'écoute*,[1] because even if they could not collect concrete protection cases, the general information contributed to analysis to decide priority areas. By contrast, in Myanmar, where the ICRC had not established its presence in a great deal of the country, delegates placed significant weight on information from the government for its needs analysis.

REGISTRATION AND DOCUMENTATION

The registration of individuals and/or the provision of documentation to those individuals may lead to a reduction in threats, or it may provide or prove entitlement to particular services which may in turn reduce the vulnerability of those individuals to violence, or mitigate the consequences of violence they have experienced. On the other hand, registration can also be an instrument of

[1] *Maisons d'écoute* are locally run 'listening houses' in the DRC, which offer counselling and referrals to other health facilities, and seek to raise awareness of the problem of sexual violence, the availability of health services, and the importance of seeking treatment within seventy-two hours.

control. Both the ICRC and UNHCR include some kinds of registration activity in their work. However, as with their monitoring and analysis activities, each organization has a somewhat distinct focus and aim.

In some cases, the ICRC registers individuals at high risk of violence as a means of threat reduction. The registration and follow-up of individual civilians mirrors the ICRC approach to the protection of prisoners of war, and is based on the rationale that if authorities (in places of detention) or armed parties (in the context of conflict) are aware that individuals are known to the ICRC, and that the ICRC will ask questions about their welfare and whereabouts, those individuals are less likely to be mistreated, killed, or disappeared. Effectively, this kind of registration seeks to make mistreating or disappearing the registered individuals more costly (i.e. altering incentives). In addition, the ICRC works to trace missing persons and restore family links. This replicates the modus operandi of prisoner-tracing, and may contribute to vulnerability reduction, because people are often less vulnerable when they are with their families or other support networks.

UNHCR attaches great importance to the registration and documentation of IDPs. These activities are broadly aimed at the realization of citizenship rights and the prevention of discrimination against IDPs on the basis of their displacement. For example, legal documentation is provided with the aim of enabling IDPs to access social services and education, and to participate in elections (UNHCR 2007f, para. 33). This mirrors activities UNHCR undertakes with refugees, which include the provision of identity documents and the negotiation of refugee status to ensure refugees can access social services and education in their host country. In Colombia, UNHCR was supporting state-run campaigns to register individuals and provide them with identity cards. This is seen as protection, because, without registration, people do not exist in the eyes of the administration, and administrative non-existence is seen to present an enormous protection problem. This underscores how protection is seen as something provided by the state apparatus, and something abstracted from the context of armed conflict and the armed actors that pose violent threats to civilians. Such activities may reduce vulnerability by facilitating travel and access to state services, which may in turn increase the choices and opportunities open to civilians, enabling them to pursue their own protective strategies. It is, however, an indirect strategy, and it is difficult to assess its impact on vulnerability in any given context.

Myanmar offers an example in which UNHCR considered working on citizenship issues and documentation to be of paramount importance. This was partly due to high numbers of stateless people, and also because in Rakhine state in particular, there were significant restrictions of movement imposed on segments of the population, primarily the Rohingya Muslims. However, it is not always entirely clear what UNHCR hopes to achieve through its registration and documentation efforts. Some staff members reported that citizenship or residence status meant everything in Rakhine, because without some kind of formal status, individuals could be deported to Bangladesh or disappeared. In other words, documentation was expected to reduce the threat posed by the state. Others questioned the value of documentation and status in practice, because even if Muslims in Rakhine had documents, they could not live the lives of normal citizens.

For UNHCR, registration often goes hand in hand with profiling, to contribute to needs and context assessment. In the DRC, UNHCR wanted to make IDP registration and documentation a major activity in 2014–15, but this was underfunded, so they had to cut back. Interviewees acknowledged that in the DRC context registration and documentation was less important for IDPs in terms of having identification, and that it was mainly about the tracking of population movement and dynamics, as a means of monitoring, and of allocating assistance delivery.

DIALOGUE AND ADVOCACY

Dialogue-related protection activities come in many forms, and comprise much of the protection work of both the ICRC and UNHCR. In keeping with the differing levels of importance each organization places on different actors in protection, the main interlocutors for the ICRC are weapons-bearers, while UNHCR dialogue centres on civilian officials of affected states and, in some cases, the wider diplomatic community. Both organizations also engage in some kinds of dialogue with affected individuals and communities. Moreover, in line with their respective emphases on different types of objectives, ICRC dialogue is mainly aimed at threat reduction, while UNHCR dialogue is primarily aimed at changing government policy and practice, and it is not always clear how such changes are expected to affect IDPs and other civilians.

Dialogue with the Perpetrators of Violence

For the ICRC, direct dialogue with the perpetrators of violence is standard and essential practice, aimed primarily at threat reduction. While the formal policy includes a range of other activities, the understanding of many within the ICRC is that dialogue is the main protection activity at the field level. Indeed, the core ICRC protection activity is the documentation of violations of IHL and the presentation of those allegations to armed groups with the aim that the violations will be investigated by the group, and individual violators punished. Confidential dialogue and persuasion are trademark ICRC activities, and derive from the institutional interpretation of neutrality. Though not 'fundamental principles' of the Red Cross, dialogue and confidentiality are seen as underpinning ICRC protection work as means to generate access (ICRC 2008b: 758).

The preference for bilateral and confidential dialogue replicates the ICRC approach to all other issue-areas, but it has now also become central to the identity of the organization. As Steven Ratner has put it, 'were the ICRC to choose a radically new set of tactics, e.g., through frequent public condemnations, or consideration of *jus ad bellum* in its assessments, it would, in essence, no longer be the ICRC' (Ratner 2011). Confidential dialogue with weapons-bearers can entail interventions regarding specific cases of violations of IHL, thematic interventions regarding multiple cases of the same type of IHL violation or other abuses of the civilian population, and informal day-to-day contact with armed actors. Where a victim does not agree for his or her allegation to be transmitted to the alleged perpetrator, or where delegates think naming names would put someone at risk, they can make thematic interventions in which they do not present specific cases but discuss a trend with alleged perpetrators.

In-country protection activities by UNHCR may also include advocacy with parties to the conflict (UNHCR 2007c, para. 27). In practice, however, such advocacy is more often about securing access for UNHCR staff and activities than about substantive protection issues. For example, UNHCR may 'negotiate safe passage for relief supplies' (UNHCR 2007c: 7). While this is likely to involve attempting to change the behaviour of armed actors, it is with the aim of protecting relief supplies and those transporting them rather than the intended beneficiaries of the relief. The aim of such relief may be reducing vulnerability or mitigating the consequences of violence, but this is not necessarily the case, and the relief will not necessarily have a protective impact. Where UNHCR dialogue does raise concrete protection concerns with the aim of threat reduction, it does not often extend beyond advocacy with the state. An exception is found in the Kivus in the DRC, where UNHCR was engaging in dialogue with both the FARDC and armed non-state actors in a manner akin to that of the ICRC.

The nature, strength, and effectiveness of any dialogue depends on the armed actor in question, the relationship the organization has with that actor, and the issues the dialogue deals with. For this reason, in 2013 the ICRC 'maintained relations with the armed forces of 163 countries and engaged in dialogue with armed groups in more than 40 countries' (ICRC, 2014a: 96). In addition, delegates constantly seek to build trust and goodwill with national militaries and non-state armed groups through, for example, ICRC activities with detainees or with wounded combatants, as well as through the provision of effective assistance to civilian populations to demonstrate the worth of the organization. Like the ICRC, UNHCR sees protection dialogue as dependent on a good relationship with the relevant interlocutor. However, unlike the ICRC, UNHCR does not place emphasis on building such relationships *in order to* engage in a protection dialogue.

At the time of interviews in both Colombia and the DRC, the ICRC generally had stronger relationships with the army than with the non-state armed groups, and hence a deeper dialogue on protection issues. In the Kivus, for example, the ICRC had a well-established dialogue with the FARDC, delegates knew which battalions were more problematic, and they met with the higher levels of the FARDC every three months as well as maintaining a direct dialogue at the field level with the perpetrators of specific violations. With the non-state armed groups in the same area, contact was less routinized and dialogue was weaker, but delegates sought to collect as many allegations as possible, and to present them to those responsible. In Myanmar, relationships between the ICRC and both the army and the non-state armed groups were nascent, but in general stronger relations could be observed with the armed non-state actors. Delegates were still very much at the stage of building contacts and relations, which was seen as essential before they could present the potential cases they envisaged they would find. Furthermore, the ICRC cannot document protection cases without contact with victims, which was still quite limited at the time of interviews in Myanmar. ICRC dialogue with armed non-state actors from Myanmar was much more advanced across the border in Thailand, and included dissemination of IHL and humanitarian principles in general, as well as discussion of particular themes, such as the presence of landmines, child recruitment by armed groups, and medical care for those wounded by violence (ICRC 2014a: 317).

In Rakhine state in particular, ICRC protection dialogue was similarly constrained by the general challenge of being a new actor, and delegates emphasized it was still a struggle to gain acceptance for assistance work, before even thinking about protection. In addition to the state authorities, which have the duty to bring order, the ICRC sought to develop a dialogue with community leaders in Rakhine state—from Buddhist groups, women's groups, or youth groups—whom the ICRC saw as influential. However, delegates were spending a lot more time convincing these community groups that the ICRC had to work on both sides, and the dialogue was much more focused on explaining the mandate and work of the organization, and aimed at getting acceptance for practical projects, and for activities such as restoring family links, rather than dealing with protection issues directly. Furthermore, a fundamental difference with traditional conflict contexts is that these community leaders were not necessarily the organizers of violence. Delegates reported good understanding with their interlocutors, but that understanding was not getting down to the street level. In sum, at the time of interviews, the ICRC was not for the most part presenting protection cases as such. In part, this was linked to the relative newness of the ICRC in this context, and the associated limits to ICRC presence and relationships with victims and weapons-bearers. In part, it was because the perpetrators of violence were not authorities or even necessarily organized groups, and this poses a particular challenge to the ICRC, highlighting the limits of an authority-centric approach to protection in contexts such as Rakhine state.

At the time of interviews, UNHCR had occasional contacts but not a relationship as such with armed non-state actors in Colombia and only a minimal relationship with the army. It was not engaged in substantive protection dialogue with either. In Myanmar, dialogue with the military was mainly about access and permission to work. However, in Kachin state, UNHCR together with OCHA was supposed to be making interventions to the government on IHL violations, and also had very nascent contact with the KIO/A regarding protection. Interviewees suggested that they had recently started to build some trust with the KIO/A, who were asking what protection meant, and were concerned the spotlight might fall on them. In this dialogue, local NGOs were seen as a huge asset, because they were closely linked to the KIO/A. In the DRC, UNHCR had a stronger relationship with the FARDC than with non-state armed groups, but in both cases weaker than the ICRC's relationship with the same actors. Nonetheless, UNHCR was engaged in disseminating the law and protection messages to both state and non-state armed parties (although much of this work was done by other organizations in the protection cluster, such as the NGO Search for Common Ground). UNHCR staff felt able to raise sensitive issues with the government and the FARDC without fear of being silenced or expelled from the country. Whereas for the ICRC, the relationship and the acceptance of dialogue are something the organization actively seeks to build with different interlocutors, for UNHCR the acceptance of such dialogue seems to be understood as something more exogenous.

The extent and effectiveness of dialogue depend not only on the strength of the relationship between the ICRC or UNHCR and the perpetrator in question, but also on the substantive protection issue under discussion. With any given actor, for example, the ICRC especially might choose to discuss some issues and avoid others. As we have seen, at the time of interviews, ICRC delegates in Myanmar did not feel that their relationship with the national military was generally strong enough to present protection cases. However, the issue of child soldiers was an exception to this general rule. Focused on the Eastern conflict zones, this work was ongoing even during the period in which the ICRC had closed most of its Myanmar operations. Although there was no dialogue with the government at this time, the authorities still dealt with cases presented by the ICRC, and released child soldiers. Families came to the ICRC to report the recruitment of their children, and while the ICRC had no direct contact with the armed forces, it sent written interventions to the Myanmar Ministry of Defence. In general, no direct response would be received but the ICRC would hear back indirectly in the form of public statements from the

Ministry of Foreign Affairs listing children released, and stating who had submitted the release request.

Conversely, ICRC delegates have often seen landmines as too sensitive an issue to discuss with non-state armed groups in Colombia and Myanmar, believing that the groups would not give up their use, and that pushing them to do so could undermine their relationship—and hence their dialogue on other issues. Likewise in Colombia, while hostage-taking is against IHL, it was a common practice of some armed groups, and one the ICRC did not expect to be able to change. Where the ICRC does not expect to be able to reduce particular threats, it often pursues lower-order objectives instead. In the case of landmines in Colombia, for example, the ICRC would seek to negotiate with the armed group to encourage them to inform civilians of the locations of mines. In other words, in acknowledgement of its inability to reduce a particular threat, the ICRC sought to reduce the vulnerability of civilians to that threat. Similarly, where Colombian armed groups took hostages, the ICRC would negotiate to bring medicine to the hostage and transmit news to the family of the hostage, seeking to mitigate the consequences of the coercion it was unable to prevent.

Moreover, both organizations report that with some actors dialogue on particular issues yields more results than dialogue on other issues. In the Kivus, for example, UNHCR reported positive responses from the FARDC on checkpoints and extortion, and significant results following UNHCR interventions on these issues. However, on other issues, results were felt to be much more limited. On the issue of sexual violence, in particular, it seemed that ICRC and UNHCR dialogue was well received by a number of different interlocutors, but had little or no effect on their behaviour in practice, and hence little or no effect on the incidence of rape.

Where the ICRC and UNHCR engage in dialogue with the perpetrators of violence in an effort to get those perpetrators to change their behaviour in order to reduce the threat they pose to IDPs and other civilians, the intervention is direct and actor-centric. Thus, it is reasonable to think the ICRC and UNHCR staff members undertaking these kinds of intervention are in a position to make some kind of assessment of their impact. The further removed activities are from those who perpetrate violence and from those who suffer from it, the more difficult it is to assess their effectiveness.

Dialogue with Police and Civilian Agencies of Government

Dialogue with the civilian agencies of government in the affected state is a mainstay of UNHCR work. Such dialogue is also somewhat important, but not a priority focus, for the ICRC. Both organizations additionally sometimes engage with the police. They maintain a dialogue with these state agents in particular to negotiate access for their programming and, where relevant, to reduce restrictions on the movement of affected communities. Furthermore, in some cases they use such dialogue to discuss concrete protection policies and incidents.

In some contexts, the police are an important interlocutor. In the cases under study in this book, this was most evident in Rakhine state in Myanmar, where both the ICRC and UNHCR maintained a dialogue with the police. The first concern of the ICRC after opening its Sittwe office in 2013 was to see that the main security actor was the police and not the army—and to develop constructive dialogue with the police at all levels. When the police were involved in a protection case—notably in cases of arbitrary arrest and detention—then the ICRC could undertake its normal dialogue-focused activities. However, for the most part, the dialogue with the police was more general and focused on issues such as excessive use of force by the police, restriction of movement, and access to basic services, rather than specific cases. The ICRC was also liaising with the police in relation to medical evacuations, because they had to pass through police checkpoints (although they did not use police escorts). In addition, delegates worked to ensure the safe return home of released prisoners, facilitating travel particularly in Rakhine state, where Muslims may have to cross communal lines between where they were released and home.

Like the ICRC, UNHCR was concerned that in Rakhine state, there was a tendency to resort to military solutions, and interviewees regarded the de facto segregation of the population as essentially a military solution based on the premise that if the two populations could be kept apart, order could be maintained. One interviewee explained that for the police, order and security, not humanitarian interests, were primary concerns, and so UNHCR was trying to make the case that particular activities or behaviour by the police were in the interests of security and public order (in other words, non-legal argumentation based on a logic of consequences). For example, in a clash between some Rohingya farmers and some Rakhine Buddhists, someone was killed, and people felt aggrieved because the police did not arrest the alleged perpetrator(s). UNHCR called the police chief in command and argued that if the police were seen as biased, things would get out of control.

In all contexts, UNHCR engages with the civilian agencies of government, very often with the aim of pushing or promoting public policy change for the benefit of the displaced. For the ICRC, much of this kind of work would be considered a breach of neutrality, because it involves working too closely with the government, and because most public policy issues are too far removed from IHL and hence outside the range of ICRC competence.

In Colombia, UNHCR was engaged in constant dialogue with all levels of government and with several specialized state agencies. For example, UNHCR was lobbying Acción Social at the national level to recognize intra-urban displacement and provide assistance to those displaced within cities, and engaged in dialogue with local government officials to inform them of rulings from Bogotá and to push them to comply with their obligations under domestic law. Issues to do with land ownership, dispossession, and restitution were closely related to issues of protection and the prevention of displacement, and UNHCR was also engaging the government on these issues, but tended to adopt a low profile when doing so. Often there were land dispossessions and massive buying of land which appeared to be legal but the land had been sold under pressure, and UNHCR lobbied in some areas to get a freeze on selling land (with some success). With respect to megaprojects, UNHCR sought to make visible the risks that such projects presented to communities. The Santos government articulated a commitment to improving land tenure, and UNHCR was working with Acción Social on its Tierra project.

In Myanmar, UNHCR was undertaking advocacy directly with the civilian agencies of government at the local, state, district, and Naypyidaw levels. In Rakhine state, UNHCR was engaged in significant dialogue with local government. Although there were some cases of direct intervention where they would say exactly which incident they were referring to, UNHCR staff were not for the most part referring to specific events, but instead were raising general concerns. However, given that the government interlocutors always knew exactly where UNHCR had been and who they had seen, they generally knew exactly what UNHCR staff were referring to. The more general protection dialogue mainly concerned restriction of movement, arbitrary arrest and detention, and access to livelihoods and basic services (such as education and health). In addition, at the state and district level, UNHCR—as part of the Protection Working Group—was holding regular meetings bringing together several humanitarian agencies and various state representatives to present their humanitarian mandates to local authorities. This was considered to be a kind of advocacy, but one that was aimed at securing acceptance and access rather than substantive protection objectives.

Private Advocacy with the Diplomatic Community and the Wider International Community

Both the ICRC and UNHCR may also engage with other states and international actors on protection issues within a context in which they are operational. Certainly both organizations often provide general briefings on a context and on their concerns to donors and diplomatic contacts. In addition, they may engage in private advocacy about specific issues and specific actors. In the vocabulary of humanitarian protection, this is often referred to as 'mobilization'. Mobilization entails sharing information in a discreet way with selected actors—people, organizations, and states—who have the capacity to influence those actors whose behaviour a humanitarian agency seeks to change (ICRC 2005: 396–7; Slim and Bonwick 2005: 81).

The ICRC has a strong preference for, and a commitment to, bilateral, confidential dialogue. However, this preference and this commitment are not absolute, and under certain conditions, it will privately share information with third parties, usually states but potentially also other organizations or even individuals. This may include confidential information (ICRC 2005: 397). Given its commitment to bilateral, confidential dialogue, and given such mobilization is intended to be private advocacy, the ICRC would not discuss or even admit to specific cases in which it has shared information with third parties. However, leaked US embassy cables published on WikiLeaks provide us with examples of what kind of information the ICRC has shared with the US. In Colombia, for example, at different times ICRC delegates provided information to US officials on conflict dynamics (WikiLeaks 2004; 2008, para. 3), and on the conduct of the army (WikiLeaks 2009b, para. 4; 2009b, para. 6), the FARC (WikiLeaks 2005), the ELN (WikiLeaks 2005), and the AUC (WikiLeaks 2004, para. 3). These cables report meetings between US officials and ICRC delegates from the perspective of US embassy officials, and we do not necessarily see the ICRC rationale for sharing this kind of information. However, in the cited examples, it is not immediately obvious that the ICRC was trying to get the USA to put pressure on any actors to change their behaviour. Prior to the public denunciation of the Myanmar government in 2007, we see the ICRC sharing its concerns and frustrations about the government with US diplomats, but specifically requesting they do not intervene (WikiLeaks 2006b, para. 10; 2006a, para. 10), preferring to ask Asia-Pacific countries to use their influence on the Myanmar government (WikiLeaks 2007, para. 3).

UNHCR does not share such a strong commitment to confidentiality, and staff are more open about ongoing dialogue with diplomatic communities. In Rakhine state in Myanmar, UNHCR was producing reactive advocacy notes which document particular incidents and outline a number of recommendations in a one- or two-page document. The advocacy notes were produced by the protection working group (PWG), which was led by UNHCR, and were called 'PWG advocacy notes'. What an NGO can and will say in its statements is different from what the UN can and will say, so UNHCR was careful not to include anything the rest of the group would be uncomfortable with. The advocacy notes were not presented at the local level, but they did inform UNHCR discussions with local government. They were primarily for diplomats and were usually used at the Yangon level, where there were some strong voices supporting UNHCR politically. In particular, UNHCR was holding regular meetings with its main donors to the Myanmar operation (including Japan, the USA, the UK, and ECHO). The embassies and donors apparently valued the analysis provided in the advocacy notes and were using it bilaterally. Depending on the issue, the interlocutors from the Myanmar government might or might not have known the information or issue was coming from UNHCR. The way the notes were used by the diplomatic community depended on what line was expected to be most effective: 'the international community says/thinks . . .' or 'UNHCR says . . .' Often government interlocutors would be able to guess where the information was coming from anyway, and at the time of interviews UNHCR had not experienced any repercussions from being cited as the source of the information. In Kachin state, UNHCR was generally feeding information on the situation to UNHCR Yangon, which might then forward it on to the diplomatic community or to Nyapidaw. However, there was not such a formal system as in Rakhine.

Public Advocacy—Criticism and Denunciation

Finally, the ICRC and UNHCR may make public statements, although neither engages much in public criticism. Thus, they may make public statements about the kinds of threats facing civilians in a particular context, and about the needs of civilians, but they will only rarely make accusations against specific actors. ICRC policy is quite clear on this, explaining that the organization can 'express its humanitarian concerns through public communication, which means reporting humanitarian problems and the ICRC's responses to them or, in some instances, reporting the violations committed by all parties, but without publicly attributing responsibility for them' (ICRC 2012b: 48). UNHCR advocates at the international level for increased political commitment to solve the crises that cause displacement, seeing reduction of violence as the ultimate means to protection, and as the ultimate responsibility of governments.

In addition, in some circumstances, the ICRC and UNHCR may engage in public criticism. Where bilateral, confidential dialogue and mobilization have been tried and deemed ineffective, the ICRC will make a public declaration or—as in the case of Myanmar in 2007—a public denunciation. A public declaration comments on the quality of dialogue with a particular party to a conflict, or on the responses of that party to ICRC recommendations, but it does not detail the violations perpetrated by that party or the content of the recommendations made to the party by the ICRC (ICRC 2005: 397). A public denunciation enumerates IHL violations perpetrated by a named party to conflict. In essence, this is the 'naming and shaming' undertaken by human rights organizations such as Amnesty International and Human Rights Watch. In theory, the ICRC has clear criteria for when it will make these kinds of public statements (ICRC 2005: 397). In practice, however, there is sufficient ambiguity in the fourth condition, which stipulates that 'such publicity is in the interests of the persons or populations affected or threatened', that the decision to make a public denunciation will always be a judgement call and not a clear-cut decision. One seasoned observer of ICRC work commented to me that the decision to make a public denunciation of the Myanmar government in 2007 'was more testosterone than reflection', so there is certainly scope for divergent attitudes on the appropriateness of denunciation in any given case.

UNHCR also prefers to avoid denunciation. However, this preference is less entrenched for UNHCR and there is not a clear set of institutional criteria to determine when persuasion will be used or when other forms of advocacy may be employed. While UNHCR does not generally make dramatic proclamations, and does not always have access to the same kinds and levels of information as the ICRC, a review of UNHCR press releases demonstrates that it does engage in public criticism much more freely than does the ICRC (UNHCR undated). UNHCR does sometimes comment publicly on actions taken by armed non-state actors that cause displacement and pose a threat to IDPs (see, for example, UNHCR 2008b, 2014a). In addition, UNHCR sometimes identifies fighting between government forces and armed non-state actors as a source of displacement and threats to IDPs (see, for example, UNHCR 2003, 2007d). However, UNHCR mainly limits its criticisms of states to refugee-receiving countries, which it quite frequently criticizes for failing to meet obligations under refugee law and for what UNHCR deems to be overly restrictive asylum policies more generally (for just a small sample of recent examples, see UNHCR 2014e, 2014f, 2015). It does not for the most part identify states as a cause of displacement or of threats to IDPs.

EDUCATION, TRAINING, AND SENSITIZATION

Aside from using the relevant frameworks as a tool in their dialogue-based activities, both the ICRC and UNHCR go to significant efforts to make those frameworks better known and understood, undertaking a number of activities aimed at educating, training, or sensitizing different actors. The ICRC trains armed forces and non-state armed groups in IHL. Depending on the context, UNHCR may provide training and information in relevant domestic law to local governments and affected communities, and in the Guiding Principles and other international standards to governments (at national and local levels), and in some limited cases to non-state armed groups.

The ICRC places great emphasis on IHL dissemination and training. In 2013, for example, '32 specialized ICRC delegates conducted or took part in more than 150 courses, workshops, round-tables and exercises involving some 125,000 military, security and police personnel in more than 90 countries' (ICRC 2014a: 96). Such events can encompass general explanations of ICRC activities as well as training in IHL and in first aid. Whereas one-hour sessions provide an opportunity to establish contact and introduce the work of the ICRC to combatants, longer three- or four-day workshops are required to provide serious training in IHL. The rationale for IHL training is threat reduction, but its effectiveness depends on the right people being trained, and on their training driving improvements in their behaviour. Thus, in 2006, Andrew Bonwick explained that the ICRC had been working with the armed forces in Colombia and the 'level of understanding of international humanitarian law (IHL) in the senior ranks of the military is now high, although this has yet to be translated to the operational level' (Bonwick 2006: 9). Nonetheless, it remains a central feature of ICRC work.

Wherever possible, the ICRC runs multi-day workshops on IHL. With the Colombian army, for example, several ICRC offices reported organizing multi-day workshops with practical exercises to instruct the soldiers in IHL. It was very easy to maintain contact with the national military, and it was anyway part of their internal training plan to receive courses on human rights and IHL. Additionally, with the army, the ICRC was undertaking 'after-action reviews' in which delegates developed practical exercises based on real cases (without mentioning where in the country the cases occurred, or which units of the army were involved). The ICRC was also able to work at the highest levels of the Colombian military, up to the level of the Ministry of Defence. In the DRC, the ICRC was training trainers within both the FARDC and MONUSCO, as well as providing pre-deployment training on IHL and the ICRC to MONUSCO troops in a number of troop-contributing countries within Africa. MONUSCO troops also received a briefing from the ICRC on arrival in the DRC. In training the FARDC in IHL, delegates were trying to make links with the major protection issues in the relevant area, and sometimes sharing lessons learned from better battalions with those that most needed to improve.

In addition, in many contexts, the ICRC offers first-aid training. Given that wounded combatants are the original category of person that the ICRC sought to assist and protect, and that they continue to be a part of the ICRC mandate, such training is naturally deemed to be of intrinsic importance. However, first-aid training is also always linked to a discussion of the ICRC and IHL; it serves as a 'sugar cube' with which delegates are able to administer an explanation of who the ICRC is and what they do, and an introduction to IHL. In the DRC, first-aid training is mainly for the non-state armed groups, and courses last two to three days. Interviewees reported that the FARDC did not need first-aid training; otherwise they would be doing it for them too. With the non-state armed groups in Colombia, it was much more difficult to organize such training events. At the time of interviews, the guerrilla groups were very much on the defensive and not in control of much territory. As a consequence, they were increasingly mobile and would not take the risk of keeping a whole unit in one location for a few days. The ICRC was sometimes able to organize much shorter first-aid training sessions, but there was only very occasionally the opportunity for the longer workshops on IHL and humanitarian principles, and it was becoming increasingly difficult.

One of the first things the ICRC did on its return to Myanmar in 2012 was to run a one-day workshop on IHL for senior government officials, with the aim of fostering dialogue and interest in IHL (ICRC 2013a: 250). However, more than a year later this initiative had not progressed to IHL training for the armed forces. Although government officials and representatives from the army and police participated in IHL training courses run by the ICRC elsewhere in Asia, delegates did not know whether or when IHL dissemination to the army would begin within Myanmar. At the time of interviews, IHL training for the armed non-state actors in Myanmar was not yet happening either, but was on the horizon, and interviewees were confident that IHL workshops would happen in 2014 in the north of Myanmar, perhaps in Laiza, the headquarters of the KIO/A. Across the border in Thailand, the ICRC had longer-standing relationships with some of the opposition groups, and innovative methods for IHL dissemination, albeit more through regular informal contact than through formal, organized training sessions. There was every reason to assume that these same kinds of discussions could also take place in-country, but at the time of interviews, delegates in Myanmar had not established sufficient contacts and relationships.

Compared with both the army and the non-state armed groups, the ICRC was further ahead in training the Myanmar police force. In 2013, the ICRC conducted two high-level seminars with the police—one in Naypyidaw and one in Sittwe—and was also liaising with police at the officer level. Police training is a relatively new activity for the ICRC, with the first edition of 'To Serve and Protect', the ICRC manual for law-enforcement training published in 1997—and an updated edition published in 2014 (ICRC 2014d). Training is based on international policing standards, and the topics covered are at the fringe of IHL and human rights. ICRC seminars for the police in Myanmar focused in particular on crowd control—an area in which the ICRC had observed major deficiencies in Rakhine state, and which the police themselves had recognized as a weakness, and as something they needed help with.

In many contexts, UNHCR seeks to disseminate the Guiding Principles and/or any domestic laws with a bearing on IDP protection. The focus depends on the context in question. In Colombia, for example, UNHCR considered the domestic legal framework to be largely sufficient and the primary problem to be that laws made in Bogotá were not implemented in practice. Much of the work undertaken by UNHCR thus involved communicating the most up-to-date decrees, laws, and judgments to local government officials, and working with local institutions to make sure national legislation was understood and implemented at the departmental and municipal level.

Often the local government and Acción Social were not aware of new legislation and requirements, and UNHCR was the only organization to receive information on new laws and decrees, so it saw an important role for itself in informing local officials of the policies and decisions they were supposed to implement.

However, in many countries, domestic law is deemed to be insufficient, and sometimes it even includes clauses that are anti-protection. Naturally, in such cases it is only of limited use and effectiveness, and UNHCR often turns instead to international laws and standards. Thus, in Myanmar, where there is very little relevant domestic legislation, UNHCR was providing training for various actors in international laws and norms. At the national level, UNHCR was training government officials and MPs on international statelessness and citizenship standards, including the direct provision of in-country training and also sending some on courses overseas. Interviewees reported some positive responses, with middle-level officials hearing about international law and best practices, and starting to question their own domestic legislation in light of such international standards. In Kachin state, UNHCR was training the KIO/A and the state government on Guiding Principles. In the south-east of Myanmar, workshops on standards were held in 2013 with key documents—including the Guiding Principles, the IASC framework for durable solutions, and the 1951 Refugee Convention—translated into local languages and distributed. Again, these involved both government and non-state actors.

Both organizations also seek to educate individuals and communities, but each has a different focus. The ICRC primarily emphasizes risk reduction, through education or training in direct vulnerability-reduction strategies. UNHCR mainly seeks to inform people of their rights, and of the institutional routes for claiming them. In other words, it is a more indirect strategy, and it is not always clear what the ultimate objective is. In both these cases, we see the provision of information as a means to reduce vulnerability.

The ICRC has a number of initiatives that aim to provide people with information about how to reduce their vulnerability to different kinds of weapons. For example, in some areas of Colombia, the ICRC was providing landmine awareness training to civilians. In addition, in responding to urban violence in Colombia, the ICRC was offering light-weapons awareness training. In some communities in the Kivus in the DRC, the ICRC was promoting the return of child soldiers, and working to prevent re-recruitment through sensitization programmes with the communities, and also with the child soldiers before they return. More generally, delegates sought to raise awareness of the risk of child recruitment in the communities, in order to reduce the vulnerability of children to recruitment.

UNHCR is less concerned about these very direct vulnerability-reduction strategies, or at least it does not always see them as part of its own responsibility and mandate. In Kachin state, for example, UNHCR was pushing UNICEF hard to do mine risk education, because under the cluster approach, the landmine issue comes under UNICEF. In the DRC, UNHCR was engaged in training and capacity-building for the prevention of sexual and gender-based violence, including focus groups for men only which were aimed at the transformation of behaviour among IDP men, and hence at reducing the level of threat of sexual violence.

In many cases, however, UNHCR efforts to educate individuals and communities are not about directly reducing their exposure to violence and coercion, but about helping them claim their rights vis-à-vis the state. Thus, UNHCR provides legal aid to IDPs to inform them what those rights are, and training for IDP and community organizations to show them the official channels through which to claim their entitlements (UNHCR 2007f, paras. 37–8). For example, at the time of interviews, UNHCR was undertaking a number of projects throughout Colombia aimed at educating individuals, groups, and communities in their rights as well as providing them with the information and skills necessary to claim those rights from the state. Pamphlets and calendars setting out key laws or decisions of the Constitutional Court relevant to the local community were widely distributed among the Afro-Colombian communities in the department of Chocó, and legal-aid clinics run jointly with the Norwegian Refugee Council were educating law students in IDP law so that the students could provide legal aid to individuals, and thus help them to access rights and state programmes.

DEVELOPING LEGAL AND NORMATIVE FRAMEWORKS

In addition to engaging in advocacy to increase compliance with existing laws and norms, and educating a range of actors in the content of the same, the ICRC and UNHCR can also work to develop new laws and norms. The ICRC focuses primarily on developing IHL, and UNHCR places particular emphasis on developing domestic legislation in the IDP contexts in which it works.

The ICRC sees the development of IHL as a central part of its own role in protection (ICRC 2007b: 3, 2011a). This is based on the implicit assumption that if a legal framework can be approved, then protection will be wider-reaching and more systematic than would otherwise be the case (Forsythe 2005: 259). Such an assumption has underpinned ICRC activity from the very origins of the organization, as reflected in Dunant's *A memory of Solferino* and his proposal for the first Geneva Convention of 1864. The ICRC does not and cannot create IHL, which consists of treaties agreed by states and customary law based on the customary practice of states. However, the ICRC has been instrumental in the development of both. The development of IHL treaties has largely been characterized by the *ex post* codification of pragmatic ICRC action on the ground, with moral imperative (and practical response) leading the law, not the other way around (Baudendistel 2006: 16; Bugnion 2003; Durand 1984: 85; Forsythe 2005: 18). The ICRC has provided a practical response to needs on the ground and has followed this up by drafting a treaty and lobbying for states to sign it.

In drafting the treaties, the ICRC played a major role in shaping the Geneva Conventions and their Additional Protocols. However, ICRC lawyers usually started out with a good idea of what states would find acceptable, gained through discussions with states and through pre-Conference consultations. This was the case with Additional Protocol II, the main treaty for the protection of civilians during internal conflict, for example (Forsythe 1978). Moreover, ICRC efforts to develop new treaties have not always met with success. In the 1930s the ICRC developed a draft convention on the condition and protection of enemy civilians, known as the 'Tokyo Draft', which was due to be submitted to a 1940 diplomatic conference which was postponed on account of the war. Even where the drafts did eventually produce treaties, the drafts submitted by the ICRC have then been the subject of negotiation and amendment before a final version is adopted. Additional Protocol II of 1977, for example, is far less demanding than the draft the ICRC had submitted to the Diplomatic Conference in 1974 (Forsythe 1978).

In addition to its role in developing treaty-based IHL, the ICRC has exerted influence in the interpretation of various aspects of IHL, for example in recent work to clarify the notion of direct participation in hostilities (Melzer 2009). In 2005, the ICRC published an extensive study on customary IHL and compiled a database of customary IHL rules which is utilized in its protection work (Henckaerts and Doswald-Beck 2005). With respect to customary law in particular, the line between the creation of the law and its interpretation is not always a clear one. In the international legal order, 'the power to shape understandings of what is to count as practice (statements or actions) and whose practice is to count' is instrumental to the creation of customary law (Hurrell 2005: 41). Such power is not only wielded by states; indeed, with the 2005 study on customary IHL the ICRC employed its expert and moral authority to exercise a form of productive power (Barnett and Duvall 2005; Barnett and Finnemore 2004). By documenting and interpreting customary practice, the ICRC can be seen to have played an important role in producing understandings and creating customary law. Indeed, as Leah Nicholls has put it, the 'humanitarian monarchy' legislated (Nicholls 2006).

In documenting and interpreting customary law, the ICRC has privileged the practice of states (Henckaerts 2005: 179–80; Kellenberger 2005: xvi). In developing treaty-based IHL, the ICRC has worked with states and, of course, only states can sign international treaties. While the ICRC does sometimes provide technical assistance and advice to non-state armed groups to help them bring their internal rules in line with IHL, it would not work to get them to enter into formal agreements in the way that Geneva Call does.

In contrast to the ICRC, UNHCR action has tended to follow rather than to drive the development of international legal frameworks for protection. The official UNHCR line is that no specific legal status is needed for IDPs, and hence no need for a hard-law framework for IDP protection at the international level. As we have seen in Chapter 3, the Guiding Principles were not developed by, or at the instigation of, UNHCR. Indeed, it was only several years after their publication that UNHCR took on a lead role in IDP protection. Likewise, UNHCR did not play a role in developing the 1951 Convention which was negotiated by states at the same time as they created UNHCR. In terms of *international* frameworks, then, it is only the 1967 Protocol whose development was instigated by UNHCR.

Nonetheless, in many contexts, UNHCR seeks to expand *domestic* legislation in line with the norms specified in international and regional frameworks. UNHCR was closely involved in drafting the original IDP law in Colombia, for example, and at the time of interviews, continued to support the development of the Colombian legal framework, with field offices providing information about the situation on the ground to the Bogotá office to assist policymaking at the national level. In the DRC, UNHCR worked to encourage the government to sign and ratify the Kampala Convention, which it did in February 2010 and July 2014 respectively, and to develop domestic IDP legislation. Notably, it undertook this work as UNHCR and not as part of the cluster, because developing legislation is not strictly an emergency matter. In Myanmar, UNHCR was not yet focused on developing the legal framework, rather using what existed strategically. The existing framework was seen as far from sufficient, but changing it was not deemed a priority, or at least not a realistic prospect at that moment. Indeed, the expectation was that UNHCR was highly unlikely to be able to change the national law. In Myanmar, UNHCR engaged in some, limited advocacy on the citizenship law, but in general staff were not optimistic about getting the government to engage in serious legal reform in the short or medium term.

In many cases UNHCR is focused not (or not only) on developing the domestic legal framework, but on improving institutions to get the law better applied in practice. Thus, a major part of UNHCR's work in Colombia was about communicating Constitutional Court rulings to local officials who had responsibility for implementing those rulings. In addition, UNHCR sought to expand the presence of the Defensoría (human rights ombudsman) across Colombia. In the DRC, UNHCR was working to build stronger judicial systems, and to improve access to justice in remote rural areas. This included, for example, getting cases to lawyers and paying judges' salaries.

MATERIAL ASSISTANCE AND PRACTICAL PROJECTS

In addition to activities that have protection as their central or exclusive aim, the ICRC and UNHCR also undertake a number of activities which relate more obviously to the provision of practical assistance and services, but that may also have a protection element. Such activities are deemed to be of both intrinsic and instrumental value, meeting material needs resulting from conflict or violence, and often simultaneously contributing to protection. This section outlines the kinds of activities both organizations undertake in this regard, and explains the logics underpinning how they may contribute to reducing the level of threat or vulnerability, or to mitigating the consequences of violence.

Health

The ICRC in particular does a lot of health-related projects, which can be divided into three main categories. The first focuses on mitigating the direct consequences of violence for those who have been exposed to it. In Colombia, for example, the ICRC was working to improve the healthcare provided to the victims of violence, with physical rehabilitation for mine victims, and conflict-specific medical training (focused on the war-wounded). In Myanmar, the ICRC was supporting four physical rehabilitation centres, a significant proportion of whose work consisted in providing prosthetic limbs for victims of landmines and other conflict-related violence. In the DRC, the ICRC was also operating a surgical programme for the war-wounded, providing physical rehabilitation for amputees, and supporting a health response to victims of sexual violence which sought both to mitigate the physical and psychological consequences for individual victims and to provide an entry point for more classic protection activity.

Specifically, the ICRC was providing financial support, training, and capacity-building to existing *maisons d'écoute*. The first priority of the response was to make sure victims received Post-Exposure Prophylaxis (PEP) within seventy-two hours, so they were immediately referred to a medical facility. Victims were also offered psychosocial support. In addition, the local responders at the *maisons d'écoute* were trained to explain protection services, that is, that the ICRC had a dialogue with the perpetrators, and could make an intervention. However, they were careful not to link too much the protection aspect to the medical referral. In other words, the main aim was to ensure victims received medical treatment—to mitigate the consequences of violence—and the ICRC did not want victims to perceive that such treatment was in any way conditional on providing testimony about the attack, in case that deterred victims from seeking treatment. Although a large number of perpetrators of sexual violence in the DRC are civilians, the ICRC focused its support on the priority zones where the majority of victims were victims of combatants.

Second, the ICRC provides more general healthcare, or support to general health structures, in areas where healthcare facilities or provision have been negatively affected by conflict and violence. For example, in Colombia, the ICRC was operating health brigades. This could be through the direct provision of medical missions, or through building the capacity of the state healthcare system and bringing pressure to bear on that system to provide healthcare personnel for remote conflict-affected areas. In Chocó and Nariño, for example, the ICRC had previously provided health services directly to some conflict-affected communities. However, at the time of interviews, there had been increased possibility for the state to travel to more areas, and the focus of ICRC health work moved to support and accompany state health brigades into zones they were afraid to go to. In these cases, the ICRC was negotiating access for state health services with the armed groups and then accompanying them the first four or five times. Eventually, the aim was to develop trust between the health personnel and the armed groups so that the ICRC could cease to accompany them. The ICRC could continue to work as a neutral intermediary to get security guarantees, liaising between the state health services and the armed groups, requesting permission from the armed group for the state health personnel to travel in the area, and subsequently communicating the armed group's concerns and conditions.

In the DRC, the ICRC was supporting some health structures, mainly for the provision of primary healthcare, with the aim of supporting the most vulnerable, very often the displaced. For example, at the time of interviews, in Katanga, the ICRC was about to put a health team in Manono to support two or three health centres there, the idea being to help people in the villages, but also potentially to help those who might be displaced from the bush. Across the country, the ICRC provided medical supplies, staff training, and infrastructure upgrades to existing healthcare facilities (ICRC 2014a: 137).

In Myanmar, the ICRC was supporting existing health structures, providing financial, material, infrastructural, rehabilitation, or logistical support to 183 health centres and sixteen hospitals in 2013 (ICRC 2014a: 294). Sites and projects are often chosen not only because there exist significant health needs, and gaps and weaknesses in the provision of healthcare, but also because they offer the ICRC the opportunity to anchor its presence in areas which are likely also to have significant protection needs. For example, both the 2013 Annual Report and interviews with delegates in Myanmar highlighted ICRC support for healthcare in Kachin state. Following trips to Laiza in February and September 2013 to assess the facilities and staff at the hospitals there, the ICRC started a longer-term project to provide infrastructural support and training for hospital staff (ICRC 2014a: 291). Laiza is the headquarters of the

KIO/A, and the number of injured there between 2011 and 2013 was quite high, so it was seen as somewhere the ICRC could make an important difference with healthcare at the same time as anchoring its presence in KIO/A territory. In addition, the ICRC was hoping to start health programming in the Wa area in Shan state, following several meetings with health directors from within the government who had often referred to the Wa areas. This is an area to which the Myanmar Ministry of Health did not have access, and at the time of the interviews, ICRC delegates had met interlocutors from the Wa health department once, but had not yet met with the United Wa State Army (UWSA). Through contact with Wa health officials and support for health structures, then, the ICRC was hoping also to facilitate contact with the associated armed group.

Third, in some contexts, the ICRC works to help people access existing healthcare facilities. In many conflict contexts, part of this comprises medical evacuations and transportation of the war-wounded. In the Kivus, for example, the ICRC was doing medical evacuations, of both civilians and injured combatants. In a context like Rakhine state, where people are unable to reach healthcare because of restrictions on movement and the need of many to cross communal lines to get to Sittwe General Hospital, the ICRC was also working to enable people to access general healthcare facilities. This kind of activity can be through the direct provision of transportation or through negotiation with the authorities to allow access and to provide escorts where necessary.

Infrastructure

Both the ICRC and UNHCR also carry out infrastructure projects in many contexts. For example, in Colombia, the ICRC had built boarding houses in schools so children did not have to walk daily through mined areas to get to school, and had also installed new water points in villages in heavily mined areas, again so that civilians did not have to travel through mined areas to collect water, thus reducing their vulnerability. In some areas, the ICRC repaired conflict-damaged water supplies, mitigating the consequences of violence. In Myanmar, one of the main protection elements of ICRC water projects was deemed to be presence—the aim was to anchor presence in areas that were at or may be at risk, with the aim of threat reduction either directly, because ICRC presence may deter attacks, or indirectly, because such presence may eventually facilitate classic ICRC protection dialogue. Similarly, in Katanaga province in the DRC, for example, the ICRC was installing community wells in strategic locations with the dual aim of establishing presence and doing something immediately useful. In both Katanga and the Kivus, the ICRC had also supported local authorities in water provision. For the ICRC, it is important that such work is conflict-related (the water supply was disrupted as a result of conflict), and the objective is to mitigate the consequences of conflict.

In the south-east of Myanmar, UNHCR had built or rehabilitated around 150 schools and clinics, and in 2014 the organization was providing furniture for sixty schools in Mon (at the government's request). The installation of water points was also one of the main UNHCR activities in south-east Myanmar from 2004 to 2013. While these were all cited as protection activities, and such activities may, under certain conditions, reduce the vulnerability of IDPs and others of concern, UNHCR interviewees did not tend to explain the rationale for labelling these as protection. This is problematic, because such activities may not reduce vulnerability, and indeed in some cases they may increase it. There is a danger that, because under certain conditions they can reduce vulnerability, they are labelled as protection activities across all contexts, without a critical assessment of the link between these activities and vulnerability in any and every given context.

Social Services

UNHCR assists governments in the provision of social services, and in resolving land and property issues, and works with governments to increase humanitarian access (UNHCR 2007f, paras. 34–6, 41). In some cases, UNHCR provides social services directly, substituting for the state. The provision of social services can reduce vulnerability if it expands the choices available to those who can access those services, but for UNHCR the main goal is just to ensure that IDPs have equal access to social services as other citizens (UNHCR 2007f, para. 34). In Colombia, UNHCR was working directly with the state to fund or develop joint projects to bring the social agencies of the state to communities where there was not a strong state presence. In some towns UNHCR had set up a 'Casa de los Derechos' (house of rights), providing a physical structure and bringing in the human rights ombudsman, representatives of the municipal government, and of health and education agencies (UNHCR 2008a: 13). In less densely populated rural zones, UNHCR was working with the state for the mobile provision of social services to the municipalities. Together with the International Organization for Migration, the ICRC and UNHCR had also assisted the state in establishing Units for Orientation and Assistance to IDPs (UAOs), which were providing information on IDP rights and access to representatives from those social institutions of the state tasked with IDP assistance (UNHCR 2008a: 8). For the most part, the aim of UNHCR in undertaking these projects was to entice and encourage the state to extend the reach of its social agencies and to implement concrete, useful projects which the state would eventually continue independently. In communities where UNHCR did not already have a presence, but particular agencies of the state did, UNHCR would sometimes undertake joint projects with the aim of gaining access to new areas and thus extending its own reach.

Livelihoods

The ICRC and UNHCR both also implement livelihoods activities which often have a protection element. In parts of Colombia, the ICRC was implementing agricultural projects designed so that civilians could work close to home and avoid travelling to their fields, thus avoiding landmines along the way. In parts of the DRC, such as in Katanga province, there were areas where people had not been working their fields for two or three years because of insecurity, and where in any case the roads were in such poor condition that they would not have been able to get their produce to market anyway. In this context, the ICRC wanted to do agricultural work, but some level of stability is necessary for agricultural projects, because even just giving seeds to IDPs is useless if they are unable to stay in the same place for at least three or four months to be able to reap anything. In the Kivus, the ICRC was implementing some agricultural projects. In Myanmar, ICRC livelihoods activities were similarly directed at people who had lost their livelihoods as a result of violence, for example those who had been displaced and could not return to where they had livelihoods. Such activities included, for example, cash-for-work projects and the provision of seeds and of fishing equipment (ICRC 2014a: 292). This kind of programming is primarily about addressing the consequences of conflict and violence, but may also help to ensure that people are not forced to work in places where they face violence, thereby reducing their exposure and vulnerability.

Livelihoods activities for women are central to UNHCR's community-based protection approach in Myanmar. For example, in Laiza, the Kachin Women's Organization[2] identified forced labour into China as a high protection need, and also said there was a demand for tailoring. In response to this, UNHCR bought sewing machines and organized sewing workshops for a group of young women in an IDP camp. This involved skills training, and aimed to generate a small income for the women in order to help them start having value with their families and communities. Without such income-generating activities, they might have had to leave the camps and their families, thus exposing themselves to greater threats. In addition, UNHCR was undertaking some low-key psychosocial efforts as part of the workshops, in an effort to mitigate the consequences of violence and coercion.

[2] One of the nine NGOs that UNHCR was working with in KIO/A-controlled areas of Kachin state.

UNHCR was also engaging in some income-generating activities in the DRC, aimed at women who had been victims of—or were at risk of—sexual and gender-based violence. In part this was aimed at reducing vulnerability, particularly at expanding the choices available to women so that they could avoid sex work, and such activities were also seen as important in and of themselves. UNHCR was also doing some limited income-generating activities in IDP camps in the DRC, but as one interviewee put it, this was 'best described as timid'.

Material Assistance

In many contexts, both the ICRC and UNHCR also provide material assistance or, in other words, commodities that can be delivered, such as food, non-food items, and shelter. In general, the primary aim of such assistance is to meet material needs. However, sometimes there is also a secondary, protection-related aim. In places like Myanmar, where classic ICRC protection activities were deemed to be difficult, assistance may still be an option, and may be provided in such a way as to have a protective impact. For example, in 2013 the ICRC provided fuel sticks to over 3,900 IDPs in two camps in Sittwe, limiting their need to collect firewood outside the camps and so reducing their vulnerability to attack (ICRC 2014a: 292). This can be seen as a maximalist approach to vulnerability reduction in that it aims specifically to reduce vulnerability (rather than simply to avoid increasing vulnerability). UNHCR combines both maximalist and minimalist approaches under the category of 'safe programming'—known more generally as protection mainstreaming. This includes, for example, planning food distribution in such a way that the food does not expose recipients to threats emanating from violent attempts to steal that food. This is an example of a minimalist approach in that it is aimed at not increasing vulnerability through the provision of food aid. As in the ICRC Sittwe example, in IDP camps in the DRC, UNHCR was providing alternative fuels or fuel-efficient stoves as part of its sexual and gender-based violence prevention programming. However, the women were still going out because they were collecting firewood not only for their own fuel but also to sell, as they needed income too, which highlighted the need for better income-generating opportunities.

ACTIVITIES IN OTHER STRANDS OF THE ICRC AND UNHCR MANDATES

The ICRC and UNHCR undertake some other activities that do not fit into any of the categories above. Most notably, there are some activities that come under the other strands of their institutional mandates, and do not relate directly to the protection of IDPs and other civilians, but can support or contribute to their protection activities. Specifically, for the ICRC there can be close links between its detention work and its civilian protection work, and for UNHCR there can be close links between shelter and camp management on the one hand, and IDP protection on the other.

ICRC prisons work can be part of an important argument to convince non-state armed groups of the value of the ICRC and its work in general. ICRC delegates can assure armed non-state actors that they will visit them and care for their well-being if they are captured by the army and detained. In some cases, delegates are able to get some information from the detainees on the dynamics of the relevant armed group and on who is in charge outside. Beyond collecting such information, building relationships with detainees and working for them to be treated well in detention may help to ingratiate the ICRC with the rest of the armed group on the outside. However, delegates reported that it can be difficult to judge what kind of influence people on the inside have on the outside. Visiting detained combatants is also a good way to meet individuals who may later return to conflict, and who may maintain relations with other members of their group during detention. It provides an introduction and enables armed non-state actors to get to know the ICRC one step removed from the pressures of conflict.

In Colombia, ICRC detention work was also expected to yield positive spillovers not only to protecting civilians in the midst of armed conflict, but also to ICRC work on urban violence. Specifically, it was expected that, through prison work, delegates would be in a good position to establish contact with the perpetrators of urban violence. Indeed, the ICRC saw itself as having a big advantage on urban violence work compared with other organizations because it would be able to meet and establish relations with leaders of criminal gangs who were in prison. In the DRC, delegates did not perceive as many links between detention and protection cases as in Colombia, because the structures of the armed groups were deemed too weak for ICRC work in prisons with members of any given armed group to have much impact on ICRC relationships with members of the same group on the outside.

In Myanmar, delegates engaged in detention activities from arrest through to release. With an allegation of arrest (and consent of the family, following normal confidentiality protocol) the ICRC could inquire after the prisoner, and also restore links between the family and the person in prison. Delegates have a range of tools for restoring family links, including family visits, delivering Red Cross messages, and facilitating phone calls and post. In addition, detention visits in Rakhine state helped the ICRC to build networks with both Buddhist hardliners and Muslim 'leaders', because ICRC detention visits and the facilitation of family visits were seen by both communities as useful activities. Interviewees reported that the detention programmes had been well looked upon by all parties, and had not been controversial in the least. It seems, then, that in such a context, detention work can be a means through which the ICRC is able to garner acceptance.

ICRC prisons work can also facilitate access to new areas, because the ICRC has a stronger mandate for prison visits than for some other strands of its work, including work in 'other situations of violence'. For example, there was a prison in Buthidaung, and so through detention work, ICRC delegates were able to undertake some visits to northern Rakhine state, and in addition to the detention visits they sometimes visited the families of detainees, which gave the ICRC some presence in the region. This indicates the complementarity of detention work and protection in the wider community, although more general presence in northern Rakhine remained minimal. Furthermore, some interlocutors in the field had originally seen the ICRC when they were detained previously (prior to the suspension of prison visits in 2005). In addition, there was a positive spillover from ICRC detention work to protection work relating to child soldiers. Sometimes minors were in prison because they had deserted from the army, and delegates met them during their detention visits. As minors should not have been recruited in the first place, the ICRC was able to intervene on their behalf for their release both from prison and from the army.

On the other hand, ICRC work on detention could also have a negative impact on its civilian protection work, imposing limitations on the kinds of activities it could undertake, in particular limiting its potential recourse to public denunciation. Because the ICRC may work on multiple issue-areas within a given country, it has to consider the implications on all those issue-areas of any public criticism pertaining to any one of those issue-areas. Of course, the ICRC in any case only rarely resorts to a public denunciation of IHL violations because of its understanding of neutrality as confidentiality, and its commitment to both. However, it is quite conceivable that in some contexts the ICRC might reach the stage where it was ready to make a public pronouncement on the treatment of civilians but would refrain from doing so because such denunciation might prevent access to prisons, and thus impede the protection of prisoners of war.

In IDP contexts, UNHCR also often has multiple strands of work. Indeed, where such clusters are activated, UNHCR leads the shelter and non-food item (NFI) cluster in conflict contexts in which there are IDPs, and the camp coordination and camp management (CCCM) cluster in conflict contexts. On the one hand, the shelter and NFI and the CCCM clusters are distinct from the protection cluster, and UNHCR's responsibilities for each cluster are separate. On the other hand, shelter, NFIs, and camp management can contribute to protection. In Kachin, in Myanmar, for example, camp management and protection were seen to be closely linked, and UNHCR was working to improve privacy in shelters and safety around latrines. Likewise, interviewees indicated that in North Kivu in the DRC, CCCM was not protection per se, but that camp governance had a lot to do with protection. Essentially, careful planning of shelters and good camp management can increase the safety of IDPs.

CONCLUSIONS

In many ways, the activities emphasized by the ICRC and UNHCR in their efforts to protect IDPs and other civilians replicate the activities each organization undertakes to address prior issue-areas within its mandate. For example, the emphasis on bilateral, confidential dialogue directly mirrors ICRC work with prisoners of war and other detainees. In those cases, the ICRC talks to them in confidence about the conditions of detention and then makes representations to the relevant detaining authority in order to persuade the authority to meet the conditions set out in IHL for the treatment of prisoners. Again, then, this part of the approach to protecting civilians in internal conflict derives from institutional history. Where the environment is deemed conducive to threat reduction through dialogue, dialogue is favoured, and where it is not, the emphasis tends to be on material assistance and practical projects which seek to reduce both threat and vulnerability. Throughout ICRC discourse there is clarity of thinking on these issues, and the rationale behind different activities is communicated and understood throughout the organization. Indeed, the ICRC generally has a much more clearly conceptualized rationale linking these activities to particular protection objectives than does UNHCR.

UNHCR similarly replicates many of the means and methods of refugee protection in its efforts to protect IDPs in the midst of armed conflict. For example, it emphasizes the registration of individuals and the provision of documentation, and much of its work focuses on dialogue with states and educating and informing individuals as to their rights vis-à-vis those same states. In addition, much of what UNHCR does in the name of IDP protection involves the provision of material assistance or the implementation of practical projects. Often, although not always, such activities are undertaken without a clear conceptualization of how they may (or may not) be expected to contribute to physical safety and security.

Conclusion

The ICRC and UNHCR approaches to protection are quite different from one another across a number of dimensions. Their broad objective is the same—namely, protection of the civilian population or, in the case of UNHCR, of a particular subset of it (IDPs)—and they are both subject to similar external influences and pressures. Therefore, these differences are best explained as a consequence of different institutional characteristics, and of the different ways in which they respond to external influences and pressures (ways that are, in turn, determined by institutional characteristics). This book has highlighted the importance of institutional history in particular, and it has also shown that institutional structure and culture have played a role.

The ICRC and UNHCR are arguably the two most important humanitarian agencies for protection, but neither organization was originally set up to protect civilians during armed conflict. The ICRC was initially concerned with wounded and sick members of the armed forces, and then with prisoners of war, before being mandated to protect civilians in international armed conflict, and later also in conflicts of a non-international character. UNHCR was initially concerned with refugee protection and solutions, and its mandate has since expanded to include people in 'refugee-like situations', IDPs, and those at risk of displacement. The ICRC approach to protecting civilians in internal armed conflicts and the UNHCR approach to protecting conflict IDPs have not developed in a vacuum, but in the context of their pre-existing efforts to deal with other issue-areas. The approach taken to the pre-existing issue-areas, together with the logic of expansion used to justify expansion into the new issue-areas, has shaped the approaches taken to the new issue-areas. The two organizations did not start from a blank canvas, but with a replication of the means and methods employed to deal with pre-existing issue-areas within their mandates. Thus, the ICRC and UNHCR have adopted two quite distinct approaches to the in-country protection of civilians, each of which largely reproduces the respective organization's approach to protecting other categories of person in other settings.

In making the case for mandate expansion, in both the ICRC and UNHCR, two arguments were made: that the organization in question was well placed for the new job; and that working on the new issue-area would not interfere with the work of the organization on pre-existing issue-areas. The first argument can be made in a number of ways. In the case of the ICRC, we have seen justification for expansion on the basis of comparative advantage, specific relevant expertise, and analogies drawn between the existing mandate and the proposed new issue-area. UNHCR likewise pointed to its own relevant expertise and to analogies between refugee protection and IDP protection. The second argument can take a minimalist form in which it is claimed that the work on the new issue-area will not have a negative effect on the existing mandate, or a maximalist form in which in which it is claimed that the work of the organization on the new issue-area will in fact generate positive spillover effects for the work of the organization on its pre-existing mandate. The ICRC has made only minimalist claims in this regard, emphasizing that any new issue-area (protecting civilians in internal conflict, or working in contexts of urban violence) would not compromise its pre-existing mandate in any way. In the case of UNHCR, claims that IDP protection would not adversely affect refugee protection were regularly reiterated in terms of assurances that existing budgets would not be diverted to the new issue-area, and also that in-country protection would not erode commitment to the principle of asylum. In addition, UNHCR made a maximalist argument with the construction of linkages between the protection of IDPs and the prevention of refugee flows.

OLD SOLUTIONS FOR NEW PROBLEMS

In both the ICRC and UNHCR, then, expansion into the new issue-area (civilian protection in internal conflict for the ICRC, and IDP protection in internal conflict for UNHCR) was justified by drawing analogies with pre-existing issue-areas within the mandate of each organization. Issue linkages were constructed on the basis of the moral equivalence of the old and new issue-areas and on the basis of each organization having relevant expertise derived from its work on the older issue-areas. Such analogies have been useful in expanding institutional mandates to include protection for new populations of concern. However, they have also had an impact on how the new issue-areas are addressed.

Thus, in the ICRC, a particular understanding of the role of international law in protection has been carried across from older issue-areas within the institutional mandate to newer issue-areas. Across all the issue-areas in the ICRC mandate, law is seen as a tool for achieving physical safety and security, and compliance with the law is not seen as an end in itself. However, in principle, law is the favoured tool, and it is also seen as a way for delegates to introduce themselves, and as a source of confidence in the strength of their mandate to work on particular issues. In addition to playing a similar role across different issue-areas, the laws that the ICRC draws on the most have a similar content across different issue-areas. At the most general level, they all focus on the duties of armed parties to conflict and other authorities rather than on the rights of individuals. This reflects the context in which the ICRC originated—in the mid-nineteenth century there was no such human rights discourse as that which followed World War II. Despite the fact that the 1949 Geneva Conventions and their Additional Protocols of 1977 are products of a context in which human rights were higher on the agenda,[1] these treaties are also products of the ICRC as the organization that drafted them (together with the states and their representatives who negotiated the final texts), and of the historical experiences of the ICRC.

More specifically, many of the concrete rules the ICRC uses and emphasizes in its work protecting one category of person in one kind of context are very similar to the rules it uses and emphasizes in its efforts to protect other categories of person in other kinds of context. The international law of internal conflicts has been developed in large part through analogy to the international law of international armed conflicts, and the construction of analogies has facilitated an expansion of the legal framework for internal conflicts (Sivakumaran 2011). Thus, the legal framework on which the ICRC bases its efforts to protect civilians in internal conflict looks a lot like that for pre-existing issue-areas within the ICRC. It is built on the same basic principles, and many specific articles have been reproduced across the Geneva Conventions. The 2005 ICRC customary IHL study collates all the relevant practice—combining evidence from international and non-international conflicts—on any given issue, and most rules set out in the study cover both kinds of conflict (Henckaerts and Doswald-Beck 2005: ii, note 31; Sivakumaran 2011: 231). ICRC activities to develop IHL for internal conflict have also followed the pattern of IHL development for international conflict. Thus, there has been a replication not only of much of the content of that body of law, but also of the process by which it was developed.

In UNHCR, a particular understanding of the role of law in protection has been carried over from refugee protection to IDP protection, one in which legal protection is very often seen as an end in itself, with little analysis of how it translates into physical protection. The emphasis is on getting rights enshrined in domestic law and, to the extent that UNHCR works to get relevant laws implemented, it takes a technocratic approach. Although there has been no replication of the international legal framework for refugee protection, there is much similarity between IRL and the substantive content of the laws

[1] As evidenced in, for example, the 1948 Universal Declaration on Human Rights, the 1951 Convention on the Status of Refugees, the 1966 International Covenant on Economic, Social and Cultural Rights, and the 1966 International Covenant on Civil and Political Rights.

UNHCR emphasizes with respect to IDPs. Unlike the ICRC, UNHCR emphasizes the rights of individuals rather than the obligations of armed parties to conflict. In line with this emphasis on rights, UNHCR focuses on the duties of states. This reflects both the context in which UNHCR was created, just two years after the adoption of the Universal Declaration of Human Rights in December 1948, and the particular protection needs of refugees in Europe at that time. Furthermore, the specific kinds of rights that UNHCR works to secure for IDPs are citizenship rights and the right not to be discriminated against on account of having been displaced. These bear striking resemblance to the kinds of rights UNHCR works to secure for refugees.

Turning to the specific objectives pursued by the ICRC and UNHCR, and the strategies employed in pursuit of those objectives, we can again see how a particular understanding of protection has been reproduced from older to newer issue-areas. The ICRC seeks primarily to reduce the level of threat posed by weapons-bearers to civilians, and secondarily to reduce their vulnerability to that threat. By contrast, UNHCR largely sees threat reduction as outside its own remit, and focuses instead on reducing vulnerability and mitigating the consequences of displacement. In addition, each organization employs different strategies. The ICRC approach is more direct and actor-centred than that of UNHCR, again in line with the strategies it pursues for other issue-areas within its mandate. UNHCR often works at least one step removed from violence, and sometimes it is not even clear how its objectives and strategies are supposed to reduce violence, threats, or vulnerability, or to mitigate the more direct consequences of violence.

There has also been a replication of who each organization understands to be important actors in protection, and of how each organization relates to them. UNHCR views the state as the primary provider of IDP protection. This emphasis on the state reflects both the role the state provides in refugee protection and solutions, and the UNHCR (and broader UN) commitment to state sovereignty and the strengthening of states. In terms of immediate protection in conflict contexts, the ICRC views combatants—or, more generally, weapons-bearers—as the primary determinants of civilian security, and correspondingly as the most important actors in protection. This reflects the approach taken by the ICRC to the protection of prisoners of war and the protection of civilians in international conflict in that it is authority-centric. However, the authorities in these two issue-areas are states, and in internal conflict the ICRC has extended its understanding of who is an authority to include armed non-state actors. This extension serves an important purpose in adapting the approach to the political realities of internal conflict, and has been driven by field-level experience. Part of the adaptation took place simultaneously with the replication (as specific interventions on IHL violations, or IHL violations by analogy, were undertaken with not only national military forces but also non-state armed groups), and part of the adaptation was subsequent (when training in IHL was provided not only to national militaries but also to armed non-state actors). At the level of the development of IHL, however, the ICRC ascribes importance only to states. Treaty-based IHL is negotiated and signed by states, and the ICRC documentation and interpretation of customary IHL privileges state practice.

The core activities undertaken by the ICRC to protect civilians in the midst of internal conflict—interventions with weapons-bearers—also replicate activities on other issue-areas. These activities are constrained by the ICRC interpretation of neutrality, and also by the need to avoid interfering with pre-existing issue-areas within the ICRC mandate, such as access to sites of detention to visit those deprived of their liberty. The core of the ICRC approach to protecting civilians is to talk to civilians to document alleged violations of IHL and then make bilateral and confidential representations to the alleged perpetrators in an effort to persuade them to change their future behaviour. This directly mirrors ICRC work with prisoners of war and other detainees. The ICRC talks to detainees in confidence about the conditions of detention and then makes representations to the relevant detaining authority in order to persuade the authority to meet the conditions set out in IHL for the treatment of prisoners. Again, then, this part of the approach to protecting civilians in internal conflict derives from institutional history. The activities undertaken by UNHCR in the name of IDP protection focus on the provision of support to the state, individuals, and communities to bring the state closer to the population of concern to UNHCR. Activities include monitoring the situations and protection environments within which UNHCR operates, the provision of legal documentation to those of concern to UNHCR, direct provision or support to state provision of social services, promotion of land and property rights, provision of legal advice to IDPs and those at risk of displacement, provision of humanitarian assistance, and management and coordination of refugee and IDP camps. Again, these broadly resemble those activities undertaken for refugee protection.

In sum, in their efforts to protect IDPs and other civilians in the midst of internal armed conflict, both the ICRC and UNHCR have replicated many aspects of their respective approaches to older issue-areas within their institutional mandates. This can be problematic, because the new issue-area is, by definition, not identical to the older issue-areas.

LIMITATIONS OF REPLICATED APPROACHES

The analysis of the ICRC and UNHCR in this book has shown that old solutions are likely to be of limited effectiveness in addressing new problems, both because the problems are different and so require different solutions, and because the tools available to the ICRC and UNHCR to implement these solutions are often very different (and more limited) for the newer problems. Three particular issues have emerged.

First, both organizations have expanded to incorporate issues and tasks for which they do not have a clear mandate in international law. This is not inherently problematic—indeed many intergovernmental organizations and most international non-governmental organizations get on just fine without any such mandate. However, both the ICRC and UNHCR are more confident and committed to addressing issues that fall squarely within their legal mandates. In the ICRC, this means that when needs relating to IHL violations exceed ICRC capacity in a given context, other issues are unlikely to be addressed. When other issues are addressed, moreover, delegates are sometimes less sure about their mandate and role in addressing them. Therefore, as the ICRC moves further from its core mandate and its legal mandate, increasingly working in 'other situations of violence' that fall short of the threshold for armed conflict, it risks eroding the confidence and certainty that currently characterize its institutional culture and enable it to assert itself with states and other actors. In UNHCR, it means that in the face of limited resources, refugee protection may be prioritized over IDP protection. Furthermore, with respect to in-country protection in particular, the issues that UNHCR addresses are very often constrained by the terms of engagement agreed between UNHCR and the relevant government.

Second, both organizations operate a legalistic and state-centric approach to protection, and the in-country protection of IDPs and other civilians requires greater attention to armed non-state actors. Originally, UNHCR took a legalistic approach to refugee protection and focused on asylum. UNHCR worked with actual and potential host states, negotiating with them to protect the citizens of other states as per IRL. Like much of international law, IRL can be viewed as a pragmatic response to an imperfect world. It accepts that states will not always treat their citizens perfectly, and seeks to deal with this largely inescapable fact. It thus offers an alternative solution whereby another state offers legal protection to those who have fled their own state because it was unwilling or unable to protect them. Thus, in working to protect refugees, UNHCR does not attempt to make states more willing or able to protect their *own* citizens. However, with the expansion into IDP protection, UNHCR has maintained a legalistic approach and a modus operandi that favours negotiating with states for the protection of individuals on their territory despite the substantive difference between refugees and IDPs, namely that the latter have fled insecurity on the territory of the very same state and that the latter are threatened by armed conflict and the associated violence and not by the lack of a legal status to be on the territory in which they reside. In contexts of internal displacement, this focus on the state is limiting. Where the state is directly responsible for threats against civilians, UNHCR will only be able to reduce the threat where it is able to persuade or otherwise induce the state to stop those threats. Where other actors are responsible for the threats against civilians, by focusing on the state UNHCR will only be able to reduce those threats indirectly if the state is able to stop those other actors.

The ICRC does seek to engage non-state armed groups in most of the same ways that it engages national militaries, but it bases its work on an international legal framework that is state-centric. The field-level experiences of the ICRC documented in this book suggest that its approach may not be well adapted to maximizing the compliance of armed non-state actors. The ICRC seeks to influence the non-state armed groups in the same way and through the same means with which it seeks to influence and improve the behaviour of the public forces of the state. However it is impeded from doing so by two main obstacles. First, given their illegal nature, it is generally more difficult to establish and maintain regular contact with the non-state armed groups. Second, in Colombia in particular, reference to IHL is largely deemed ineffectual or even counterproductive in interlocutions with the armed non-state actors. International law needs to take into account, and be adapted to, the political and social reality it seeks to regulate (Sassòli 2010: 15; Zegveld 2002: 224). In internal conflicts, non-state armed groups necessarily comprise part of that reality. They have different characteristics from national militaries, and different forms of behaviour may be realistic and appropriate. Arguably, the inclusion of unrealistic clauses in a legal framework may serve to undermine the rest of that framework. Furthermore, with respect to states, the process by which international law is developed is expected to play a part in determining adherence to that law. Adherence is expected to be greater where the process is seen as legitimate by those states that are subject to the law, where those states have given their explicit consent to be bound by it, and where compliance is feasible for those states (Franck 1990, 1995). If the same is true of non-state armed groups, then the state-centric nature of IHL—and thus of ICRC protection policy—may be problematic in dealing with internal conflicts and, specifically, the non-state parties to such conflicts.

Third, UNHCR is often working at least one step removed from the conflict and violence the organization itself identifies as the central protection problem. It operates a legalistic, bureaucratic, and technocratic approach characterized by objectives and activities that do not address conflict and violence directly, and focused on the civilian agencies of the state rather than the perpetrators of violence. Furthermore, UNHCR does not always analyse how its activities might impact indirectly on the levels of violence or threats, and only to a limited degree does it consider how they may impact on the vulnerability of civilians to threats from organized violence.

In addition to highlighting these specific limitations of the ICRC and UNHCR approaches to the in-country protection of IDPs and other civilians, we can also draw some wider theoretical conclusions about mandate expansion and dysfunctional policy approaches in international organizations.

THEORETICAL IMPLICATIONS

As international organizations almost invariably expand, and rarely dispense with earlier tasks altogether, they have an ever-expanding range of issue-areas within their mandate. In this context, it is important to understand how these pre-existing issue-areas will affect the new issue-area (so that the right organizations are tasked with the new jobs) and how the logic of expansion will impact on the new issue-area.

While adjacency claims can be extremely useful in gaining agreement to extend international norms and institutions into new areas, they may also result in less than optimal international institutional arrangements for dealing with the new issue-areas. Adjacency claims rely on analogies being established between two issue-areas. Such analogies are most convincing when similarities between the two issue-areas are emphasized or exaggerated, and when differences are understated. As a consequence of focusing on the similarities, the new issue-area is constructed as being more similar to the old issue-area than is actually the case. Given the apparent (but mistaken or exaggerated) similarity, objectives, means, and methods are taken from one issue-area and applied to another issue-area for which they are often inappropriate. In both the ICRC and UNHCR, expansion was justified on grounds of the similarity of the new task to the pre-existing mandate of the organization, and the approach taken to address the new issue-area in each case then largely reproduced the approaches taken to pre-existing issue-areas.

Logically, such an approach will be effective only to the extent that: (a) the approach to the old issue-area was effective; (b) there is a close fit between the old and new issue-areas; and (c) where the fit is imperfect, the approach is adapted so that the assumptions underlying it are in line with the nature of the new problem. The closeness of fit depends on whether the problem is analogous, and whether the tools at the disposition of the organization to deal with the new problem are analogous. Where there is a poor fit and no adaptation (or insufficient or misdirected adaptation), we can expect to see at least one of the 'organizational pathologies' identified by Michael Barnett and Martha Finnemore, namely 'bureaucratic universalism', which occurs when bureaucracies apply the same technical knowledge across different contexts, and can have disastrous results when particular circumstances are not appropriate for the general knowledge being applied (Barnett and Finnemore 2004). In some cases, particular aspects or activities of an approach may be translated from one issue-area to another, with the reasoning or rationale behind these activities lost in the process of translation. In such cases, the particular procedures that are copied across may be inappropriate for the new task, but nonetheless become embedded as ends in themselves that come to define the new approach (another pathology identified by Michael Barnett and Martha Finnemore, namely the 'irrationality of rationalisation').

All aspects of the approach taken by UNHCR in the name of in-country protection during armed conflict closely resemble the approach taken by UNHCR to refugee protection in peacetime. Although three aspects of the new task make it fundamentally different from the old one, the approach taken by UNHCR is replicated from that traditional part of its mandate and is not adapted in line with these three significant differences. They are: (1) the existence of armed conflict; (2) the location of the protection efforts within the territory of the same state which has failed to protect the individuals and communities in question; and (3) the lack of a binding international legal framework with which to protect the internally displaced. The approach taken to in-country protection of IDPs in the midst of armed conflict is only likely to be effective in so far as it is adapted for the operational context of armed conflict and to the necessity of working without a binding international legal framework. However, in UNHCR no significant adaptation has taken place, and policies designed for one context are simply applied to situations in which they are not appropriate. The relationship between the means and ends of refugee protection is forgotten such that particular activities come to be seen as ends in and of themselves, without analysis of whether and how they are expected to contribute to the physical security and safety of IDPs in armed conflict.

In contrast, within the ICRC there was a closer fit between old and new issue-areas to begin with, and significant adaptation has taken place to reflect the specificities of the new issue-areas. As the ICRC has expanded into new issue-areas over the past 150 years, issues of conflict and violence have remained at the core of its mandate. Thus, both old and new issue-areas are about working in the midst of conflict and violence—indeed, the conflict and violence that both organizations agree are the core protection problem are central to the identity, *raison d'être*, and essence of the ICRC. In addition, the practical activities undertaken by the ICRC in conflict contexts have been adapted over time to take into account the specific characteristics of internal conflicts. However, the normative framework on which these activities are based has not been sufficiently adapted.

What, then, determines whether an organization adapts an approach replicated from one issue-area to another? We cannot say with certainty, but two factors suggest themselves. First, the ICRC, where significant adaptation has occurred, is characterized by strong and clear internal communication. This means that staff members know the rationale for different policies and thus, in comparison with UNHCR, activities or potential means to protection are much less likely to become seen as ends in themselves or to define the ends of the organization. Second, in the ICRC, there is much more bottom-up, field-office input into decision-making so that policies are more likely to be adapted in response to experiences at the level of implementation.

Bibliography

Abild, E. (2010). Creating humanitarian space: a case study of Somalia. *Refugee Survey Quarterly*, 29(3), 67–102.

Addario, L., and Polgreen, L. (2009). Aid groups' expulsion, fears of more misery. *The New York Times*. <http://www.nytimes.com/2009/03/23/world/africa/23darfur.html>. Accessed 16 March 2015.

ADH. (2011). *Rules of engagement: protecting civilians through dialogue with armed non-state actors*. Geneva: Geneva Academy of International Humanitarian Law and Human Rights.

Aeschlimann, A. (2005). Protection of IDPs: an ICRC view. *Forced Migration Review: IDP Supplement*, October 2005, 25–7.

African Union. (2009). *African Union Convention for the Protection and Assistance of Internally Displaced Persons in Africa ('Kampala Convention')*, 22 October 2009. <http://www.unhcr.org/refworld/docid/4ae572d82.html>. Accessed 7 January 2012.

Aga Khan, S. (1981). *Study on human rights and massive exoduses*. New York: UN Commission on Human Rights, 38th Session.

Anderson, M. B. (1999). *Do no harm: how aid can support peace—or war*. London: Lynne Rienner.

Armstrong, J. D. (1985). The International Committee of the Red Cross and political prisoners. *International Organization*, 39(4), 615–42.

Ávila Martínez, A. F. (2010). La guerra contra las Farc y la guerra de las Farc. *Arcanos*, (15), 4–21. <http://alfresco.uclouvain.be/alfresco/d/d/workspace/SpacesStore/476f15f7-b62f-4ff2-8a6e-5b2b47c4a95b/CNAI%20-%20guerra%20de%20las%20%20FARC%20y%20guerra%20contra%20las%20FARC%202010.pdf>. Accessed 5 September 2015.

Baines, E., and Paddon, E. (2012). 'This is how we survived': civilian agency and humanitarian protection. *Security Dialogue*, 43(3), 231–47.

Bangerter, O. (2011). Reasons why armed groups choose to respect international humanitarian law or not. *International Review of the Red Cross*, 93(882), 353–84.

Banza-Nsungu, A., Kishimba, N., and Dackam-Ngatchou, R. (2011). *Ampleur des violences sexuelles en République Démocratique du Congo: analyse à partir des données rapportées par les acteurs de terrain*. Kinshasa: UNFPA. <http://uaps2011.princeton.edu/papers/110991>. Accessed 8 January 2015.

Barnett, M. (2005). Humanitarianism transformed. *Perspectives on Politics*, 3(4), 723–40.

Barnett, M. (2009). *The international humanitarian order*. New York: Routledge.

Barnett, M., and Duvall, R. (2005). Power in global governance. In M. Barnett and R. Duvall (eds.), *Power in global governance* (pp. 1–32). Cambridge: Cambridge University Press.

Barnett, M., and Finnemore, M. (2004). *Rules for the world: international organizations in global politics*. Ithaca, NY: Cornell University Press.

Bartels, S. A., Scott, J. A., Leaning, J., Kelly, J. T., Mukwege, D., Joyce, N. R., and VanRooyen, M. J. (2011). Sexual Violence Trends between 2004 and 2008 in South

Kivu, Democratic Republic of Congo. *Prehospital and Disaster Medicine*, 26(6), 408–13.

Barutciski, M. (1996). The reinforcement of non-admission policies and the subversion of UNHCR: displacement and internal assistance in Bosnia-Herzegovina (1992–94). *International Journal of Refugee Law*, 8(1–2), 49–110.

Baudendistel, R. (2006). *Between bombs and good intentions: the Red Cross and the Italo-Ethiopian War, 1935–1936*. Oxford: Berghahn Books.

BBC News. (2014). Medecins Sans Frontieres' shock at Myanmar suspension. <http://www.bbc.com/news/world-asia-26379804>. Accessed 23 January 2015.

Bergquist, C. W., Peñaranda, R., and Sánchez G, G. (eds.) (2001). *Violence in Colombia, 1990–2000: waging war and negotiating peace*. Wilmington, DE: SR Books.

Berman, P. (1996). The ICRC's advisory service on international humanitarian law: the challenge of national implementation. *International Review of the Red Cross*, 36(312), 338–47.

Betts, A. (2009). *Protection by persuasion: international cooperation in the refugee regime*. Ithaca, NY: Cornell University Press.

Betts, A. (2012). UNHCR, autonomy and mandate change. In J. Oestreich (ed.), *International organizations as self-directed actors: a framework for analysis*. New York: Routledge.

Blondel, J.-L. (1987). Getting access to the victims: role and activities of the ICRC. *Journal of Peace Research*, 24(3), 307–14.

Boissier, P. (1985 (1963)). *From Solferino to Tsushima: history of the International Committee of the Red Cross (volume I)* (2nd ed.). Geneva: Henry Dunant Institute.

Bongard, P. (2008). Engaging armed non-state actors on humanitarian norms: the experience of Geneva Call and the landmine ban. In Geneva Call (ed.), *Exploring criteria and conditions for engaging armed non-state actors to respect humanitarian law and human rights law: conference report—Geneva, 4–5 June 2007* (pp. 108–23). Geneva: Geneva Call.

Bonwick, A. (2006). *Protection in Colombia: a bottom-up approach*. HPG Background Paper. London: Overseas Development Institute.

Bradley, M. (2013). International humanitarian law, non-state armed groups and the International Committee of the Red Cross in Colombia. *Journal of International Humanitarian Legal Studies*, 4(1), 108–34.

Brittain, J. J. (2010). *Revolutionary social change in Colombia: the origin and direction of the FARC-EP*. London: Pluto Press.

Brookings-Bern Project on Internal Displacement. (2007). Addressing internal displacement in peace processes, peace agreements and peace-building. <http://www.brookings.edu/~/media/research/files/reports/2007/9/peaceprocesses/2007_peaceprocesses.pdf>. Accessed 27 April 2015.

Bugnion, F. (2003). *The International Committee of the Red Cross and the protection of war victims* (1st ed.). Oxford: Macmillan.

Calhoun, C. (2009). *The idea of emergency: humanitarian action and global (dis) order*. Paper presented at the IILJ International Legal Theory Colloquium Spring 2009: Virtues, Vices, Human Behavior and Democracy in International Law, NYU Law School. <http://www.iilj.org/courses/documents/2009Colloquium.Session3.Calhoun.pdf>. Accessed 7 April 2015.

Callahan, M. P. (2003). *Making enemies: war and state building in Burma*. Ithaca, NY: Cornell University Press.

Carpenter, R. C. (2011). Vetting the advocacy agenda: network centrality and the paradox of weapons norms. *International Organization*, 65(1), 69–102.

Carr, S. (2009). From theory to practice: national and regional application of the Guiding Principles. *International Journal of Refugee Law*, 21(1), 34–47.

Chayes, A., and Chayes, A. (1998). *The new sovereignty: compliance with international regulatory agreements*. Cambridge, MA: Harvard University Press.

Chimni, B. S. (1993). The meaning of words and the role of UNHCR in voluntary repatriation. *International Journal of Refugee Law*, 5(3), 442–60.

Chimni, B. S. (2004). From resettlement to involuntary repatriation: towards a critical history of durable solutions to refugee problems. *Refugee Survey Quarterly*, 23(3), 55–73.

CICR. (2005). *Colombia informe 2004*. Bogotá: CICR.

Clark, J. F. (ed.) (2002). *The African stakes of the Congo War*. Basingstoke: Palgrave Macmillan.

Cohen, R., and Deng, F. M. (1998). *Masses in flight: the global crisis of internal displacement*. Washington, DC: Brookings Institution Press.

Cooley, A., and Ron, J. (2002). The NGO scramble: organizational insecurity and the political economy of transnational action. *International Security*, 27(1), 5–39.

Crisp, J. (2001). Mind the gap! UNHCR, humanitarian assistance and the development process. *New Issues in Refugee Research*, 43. Geneva: UNHCR.

Crisp, J. (2002). Humanitarian values, accountability and evaluation. *Refugee Survey Quarterly*, 21(3), 226–30.

Crisp, J. (2010). Refugees, persons of concern, and people on the move: the broadening boundaries of UNHCR. *Refuge*, 26(1), 73–6.

Crisp, J., Kiragu, E., and Tennant, V. (2007). UNHCR, IDPs and humanitarian reform. *Forced Migration Review*, 29, 12–14.

DANIDA. (1996). *The international response to conflict and genocide: lessons from the Rwanda experience. Synthesis Report. Various Authors.* Copenhagen: DANIDA.

Darcy, J., and Hofmann, C.-A. (2003). *According to need? Needs assessment and decision-making in the humanitarian sector*. HPG Report 15. London: Overseas Development Institute.

Defensoría del Pueblo. (2011). Desaparición forzada 2011-08-29. <http://www.defensoria.org.co/red/?_item=0301&_secc=03&ts=2&n=1342>. Accessed 16 February 2012.

Deng, F. M. (1995). Internally displaced persons: compilation and analysis of legal norms. *Report of the Representative of the Secretary-General, Mr Francis M. Deng, submitted pursuant to Commission on Human Rights resolution 1995/57, Compilation and Analysis of Legal Norms, UN Doc. E/CN.4/1996/52/Add.2, 5 December 1995*. <http://www.unhchr.ch/Huridocda/Huridoca.nsf/0/75550ee91a4fb1ff802566cc005c2c63?Opendocument>. Accessed 10 January 2012.

Deng, F. M. (2006). Divided nations: the paradox of national protection. *The ANNALS of the American Academy of Political and Social Science*, 603, 217–26.

Deng, F. M., Kimaro, S., Lyons, T., Rothchild, D., and Zartman, I. W. (1996). *Sovereignty as responsibility: conflict management in Africa*. Washington, DC: Brookings Institution Press.

Denissen, M. (2010). Reintegrating ex-combatants into civilian life: the case of the paramilitaries in Colombia. *Peace & Change*, 35(2), 328–52.

de Waal, A. (1994). *Humanitarianism unbound? Current dilemmas facing multi-mandate relief operations in political emergencies.* London: African Rights.

de Waal, A. (1997). *Famine crimes: politics and the disaster relief industry in Africa.* Oxford: Currey.

Diagne, K., and Entwisle, H. (2008). UNHCR and the Guiding Principles. *Forced Migration Review: Ten years of the Guiding Principles on Internal Displacement*, Special Issue, December 2008, 33–5.

Dubernet, C. (2001). *The international containment of displaced persons: humanitarian spaces without exit.* Aldershot: Ashgate Publishing.

DuBois, M. (2009). *Protection: the new humanitarian fig-leaf.* Paper presented at the conference, 'Protecting people in conflict and crisis: responding to the challenges of a changing world', Oxford: Oxford: Refugee Studies Centre.

Dudley, S. S. (2004). *Walking ghosts: murder and guerilla politics in Colombia.* New York and London: Routledge.

Duffield, M. (1997). NGO relief in war zones: towards an analysis of the new aid paradigm. *Third World Quarterly*, 18(3), 527–42.

Duffield, M. (2008). Global civil war: the non-insured, international containment and post-interventionary society. *Journal of Refugee Studies*, 21(2), 145–65.

Dunant, H. (1959). *A memory of Solferino* (English ed.). Geneva: ICRC.

Durand, A. (1984). *From Sarajevo to Hiroshima: history of the International Committee of the Red Cross (volume II)* (1st ed.). Geneva: Henry Dunant Institute.

Eck, K., and Hultman, L. (2007). One-sided violence against civilians in war: insights from new fatality data. *Journal of Peace Research*, 44(2), 233–46.

Engel, S., and Ibáñez, A. M. (2007). Displacement due to violence in Colombia: a household-level analysis. *Economic Development and Cultural Change*, 55(2), 335–65.

Falla, J. (1991). *True Love and Bartholomew: rebels on the Burmese border.* Cambridge: Cambridge University Press.

Fast, L. (2010). Mind the gap: documenting and explaining violence against aid workers. *European Journal of International Relations*, 16(3), 365–89.

Favez, J.-C. (1999). *The Red Cross and the Holocaust* (J. Fletcher and B. Fletcher, trans.). Cambridge: Cambridge University Press.

Ferris, E. G. (2011). *The politics of protection: the limits of humanitarian action.* Washington, DC: Brookings Institution Press.

Finnemore, M. (1999). Rules of war and wars of rules: the International Red Cross and the restraint of state violence. In J. Boli and G. M. Thomas (eds.), *Constructing world culture: international nongovernmental organizations since 1875* (pp. 149–65). Stanford, CA: Stanford University Press.

Finnemore, M. (2000). Are legal norms distinctive? *Journal of International Law and Politics*, 32, 699–706.

Finnemore, M., and Sikkink, K. (1998). International norm dynamics and political change. *International Organization*, 52(4), 887–917.

Forsythe, D. P. (1976). The Red Cross as transnational movement: conserving and changing the nation-state system. *International Organization*, 30(4), 607–30.

Forsythe, D. P. (1977). *Humanitarian politics: the International Committee of the Red Cross*. Baltimore, MD and London: Johns Hopkins University Press.

Forsythe, D. P. (1978). Legal management of internal war: the 1977 Protocol on non-international armed conflicts. *The American Journal of International Law*, 72(2), 272–95.

Forsythe, D. P. (2001a). Humanitarian protection: the International Committee of the Red Cross and the United Nations High Commissioner for Refugees. *International Review of the Red Cross*, 83(843), 675–99.

Forsythe, D. P. (2001b). *UNHCR's mandate: the politics of being non-political*. New Issues in Refugee Research 33. Geneva: UNHCR.

Forsythe, D. P. (2005). *The humanitarians: the International Committee of the Red Cross*. Cambridge: Cambridge University Press.

Forsythe, D. P. (2007). The ICRC: a unique humanitarian protagonist. *International Review of the Red Cross*, 89(865), 63–96.

Forsythe, D. P. (2013). The politics of protection: the limits of humanitarian action by Elizabeth G. Ferris (Book review). *Human Rights Review*, 14(1), 71–2.

Forsythe, D. P., and Rieffer-Flanagan, B. A. J. (2007). *The International Committee of the Red Cross: a neutral humanitarian actor*. Abingdon: Routledge.

Fox, F. (2001). New humanitarianism: does it provide a moral banner for the 21st century? *Disasters*, 25(4), 275–89.

Franck, T. M. (1990). *The power of legitimacy among nations*. Oxford: Oxford University Press.

Franck, T. M. (1995). *Fairness in international law and institutions*. Oxford: Clarendon Press.

Franklin, J. C. (2008). Shame on you: the impact of human rights criticism on political repression in Latin America. *International Studies Quarterly*, 52(1), 187–211.

Frelick, B. (1992). 'Preventive protection' and the right to seek asylum: a preliminary look at Bosnia and Croatia. *International Journal of Refugee Law*, 4(4), 439–54.

Fujii, L. A. (2010). Shades of truth and lies: Interpreting testimonies of war and violence. *Journal of Peace Research*, 47(2), 231–41.

Geremia, M. (2009). Neutrality, impartiality and independence in Colombia: an ICRC perspective. *Humanitarian Exchange*, 45, 4–6.

Giossi Caverzasio, S. (ed.) (2001). *Strengthening protection in war: a search for professional standards*. Geneva: ICRC.

Global Protection Cluster Working Group. (2010). *Handbook for the protection of internally displaced persons*. Geneva: Global Protection Cluster Working Group.

Goodwin-Gill, G. S. (1989). The language of protection. *International Journal of Refugee Law*, 1(1), 6–19.

Goodwin-Gill, G. S., and McAdam, J. (2007). *The refugee in international law*. Oxford: Oxford University Press.

Gorlick, B. (2000). *Human rights and refugees: enhancing protection through international human rights law*, New Issues in Refugee Research 30. Geneva: UNHCR.

Gottwald, M. (2010). *Competing in the humanitarian marketplace: UNHCR's organizational culture and decision-making process*, New Issues in Refugee Research 190. Geneva: UNHCR.

Guardian, The. (28 April 2014). There is no legal barrier to UN cross-border operations in Syria. <http://www.theguardian.com/world/2014/apr/28/no-legal-barrier-un-cross-border-syria>. Accessed 28 April 2015.

Haas, E. B. (1958). *The uniting of Europe: political, social, and economic forces, 1950–1957.* Stanford, CA: Stanford University Press.

Hafner-Burton, E. M., and Ron, J. (2009). Seeing double: human rights impact through qualitative and quantitative eyes. *World Politics*, 61(2), 360–401.

Hall, N. (2010). *Climate change and institutional change in UNHCR.* Conference paper for UNU-EHS summer academy on protecting environmental migration: creating new policy and institutional frameworks.

Hanson, S. (2008). Colombia's right-wing paramilitaries and splinter groups. Council on Foreign Relations. <http://www.cfr.org/colombia/colombias-right-wing-paramilitaries-splinter-groups/p15239>. Accessed 23 November 2011.

Hanson, S. (2009). FARC, ELN: Colombia's left-wing guerrillas. Council on Foreign Relations. <http://www.cfr.org/publication/9272/farc_eln.html#p3>. Accessed 15 December 2010.

Harmer, A., and Cotterrell, L. (2005). *Diversity in donorship: the changing landscape of official humanitarian aid.* HPG Report 20. London: Overseas Development Institute.

Harmer, A., Cotterell, L., and Stoddard, A. (2004). From Stockholm to Ottawa: a progress review of the Good Humanitarian Donorship initiative, *HPG Research Briefing.* London: Overseas Development Institute.

Harroff-Tavel, M. (1989). Neutrality and impartiality? The importance of these principles for the International Red Cross and Red Crescent Movement and the difficulties involved in applying them. *International Review of the Red Cross*, 29(273), 536–52.

Harroff-Tavel, M. (2003). Does it still make sense to be neutral? *Humanitarian Exchange Exchange*, 25, 2–4. <http://www.odihpn.org/report.asp?id=2576>. Accessed 11 May 2008.

Helton, A. (2003). What is refugee protection? A question revisited. In N. Steiner, M. Gibney, and G. Loescher (eds.), *Problems of protection: the UNHCR, refugees, and human rights* (pp. 19–33). London: Routledge.

Henckaerts, J.-M. (2005). Study on customary international humanitarian law: a contribution to the understanding and respect for the rule of law in armed conflict. *International Review of the Red Cross*, 87(857), 175–212.

Henckaerts, J.-M., and Doswald-Beck, L. (2005). *Customary international humanitarian law.* Cambridge: Cambridge University Press.

Hendrix, C. S., and Wong, W. H. (2013). When is the pen truly mighty? Regime type and the efficacy of naming and shaming in curbing human rights abuses. *British Journal of Political Science*, 43(3), 651–72.

Hilhorst. (2002). Being good at doing good? Quality and accountability of humanitarian NGOs. *Disasters*, 26(3), 193–212.

Holmes, J. S., Gutiérrez de Piñeres, S. A., and Curtin, K. M. (2006). Drugs, violence, and development in Colombia: a department-level analysis. *Latin American Politics and Society*, 48(3), 157–84.

Hopgood, S. (2008). Saying 'no' to Wal-Mart? Money and morality in professional humanitarianism. In M. Barnett and T. G. Weiss (eds.), *Humanitarianism in question: politics, power, ethics* (pp. 98–123). Ithaca, NY: Cornell University Press.

HPCR. (2011). *Humanitarian action under scrutiny: criminalizing humanitarian engagement*. Cambridge, MA: HPCR.

Hristov, J. (2009). *Blood and capital: the paramilitarization of Colombia*. Toronto: Ohio University Press.

Human Rights Watch. (2013). *The risk of returning home: violence and threats against displaced people reclaiming land in Colombia*. Human Rights Watch.

Human Rights Watch. (2014). DR Congo: Army, UN Failed to Stop Massacre, 3 July 2014. <http://www.hrw.org/news/2014/07/02/dr-congo-army-un-failed-stop-massacre>. Accessed 8 January 2015.

Human Rights Watch. (2015). DR Congo: wanted rebel's troops instill fear, 6 January 2015. <http://www.hrw.org/news/2015/01/06/dr-congo-wanted-rebel-s-troops-instill-fear>. Accessed 8 January 2015.

Human Security Report Project. (2011). *Human security report 2009/2010: the causes of peace and the shrinking costs of war*. New York: Oxford University Press.

Hurrell, A. (2005). Power, institutions, and the production of inequality. In M. Barnett and R. Duvall (eds.), *Power in global governance* (pp. 33–58). Cambridge: Cambridge University Press.

Hutchinson, J. F. (1996). *Champions of charity: war and the rise of the Red Cross*. Oxford: Westview Press.

ICRC. (1978). The ICRC, the League and the Report on the re-appraisal of the role of the Red Cross (V): ICRC policy on operational information. *International Review of the Red Cross*, 18(207), 326–30.

ICRC. (1995). Myanmar: ICRC to close its Yangon office [Press release]. <http://www.icrc.org/eng/resources/documents/misc/57jm5u.htm>. Accessed 9 May 2014.

ICRC. (1999). ICRC begins visits to detainees and prisoners in Myanmar [Press release]. <http://www.icrc.org/eng/resources/documents/misc/57jppe.htm>. Accessed 9 May 2014.

ICRC. (2002a). Myanmar: expansion of ICRC activities [Press release]. <http://www.icrc.org/eng/resources/documents/news-release/2009-and-earlier/5fpf8e.htm>. Accessed 9 May 2014.

ICRC. (2002b). Myanmar: new ICRC office opens in Mandalay [Press release]. <http://www.icrc.org/eng/resources/documents/news-release/2009-and-earlier/5edcvr.htm>. Accessed 9 May 2014.

ICRC. (2005). Action by the International Committee of the Red Cross in the event of violations of international humanitarian law or of other fundamental rules protecting persons in situations of violence. *International Review of the Red Cross*, 87(858), 393–400.

ICRC. (2006). Myanmar: ICRC pressed to close field offices [Press release]. <http://www.icrc.org/eng/resources/documents/news-release/2009-and-earlier/myanmar-news-27112006.htm>. Accessed 9 May 2014.

ICRC. (2007a). Distinction: protecting civilians in armed conflict: Protocols additional to the Geneva Conventions. Geneva: ICRC.

ICRC. (2007b). *ICRC strategy 2007–2010: committed to meeting new challenges through action*. Geneva: ICRC.

ICRC. (2007c). Myanmar: ICRC denounces major and repeated violations of international humanitarian law [Press release]. <http://www.icrc.org/eng/resources/

documents/news-release/2009-and-earlier/myanmar-news-290607.htm>. Accessed 9 May 2014.

ICRC. (2007d). Myanmar: no progress in talks, ICRC closes offices [Press release]. <http://www.icrc.org/eng/resources/documents/news-release/2009-and-earlier/myanmar-news-150307.htm>. Accessed 9 May 2014.

ICRC. (2008a). How is the term 'armed conflict' defined in international humanitarian law? *ICRC Opinion Paper, March 2008*. ICRC.

ICRC. (2008b). ICRC protection policy: institutional policy. *International Review of the Red Cross*, 90(871), 751–75.

ICRC. (2009). *Professional standards for protection work*. Geneva: ICRC.

ICRC. (2010a). Building respect for humanitarian action and IHL among 'other' weapon bearers. <https://www.icrc.org/eng/what-we-do/building-respect-ihl/dialogue-weapon-bearers/other-weapons-bearers/overview-icrc-other-weapon-bearers.htm>. Accessed 20 March 2015.

ICRC. (2010b). *Colombia Annual Report 2009*. <https://www.icrc.org/eng/resources/documents/annual-report/colombia-icrc-annual-report-2009.htm>. Accessed 3 September 2015.

ICRC. (2010d). The ICRC's mandate and mission. <http://www.icrc.org/eng/who-we-are/mandate/overview-icrc-mandate-mission.htm>. Accessed 23 March 2011.

ICRC. (2011a). Strengthening international humanitarian law. <http://www.icrc.org/eng/what-we-do/other-activities/development-ihl/overview-development-ihl.htm>. Accessed 5 September 2015.

ICRC. (2011b). *Annual report 2010*. Geneva: ICRC.

ICRC. (2012a). *Annual report 2011*. Geneva: ICRC.

ICRC. (2012b). *Enhancing protection for civilians in armed conflict and other situations of violence* (2nd ed.). Geneva: ICRC.

ICRC. (2012c). Syria: ICRC and Syrian Arab Red Crescent maintain aid effort amid increased fighting. <https://www.icrc.org/eng/resources/documents/update/2012/syria-update-2012-07-17.htm>. Accessed 27 April 2015.

ICRC. (2013a). *Annual report 2012*. Geneva: ICRC.

ICRC. (2013b). The Movement. <https://www.icrc.org/eng/who-we-are/movement/overview-the-movement.htm>. Accessed 21 January 2015.

ICRC. (2014a). *Annual report 2013*. Geneva: ICRC.

ICRC. (2014b). *Colombia: humanitarian situation. Activities 2013 and outlook 2014*. Bogotá: ICRC.

ICRC. (2014c). *International rules and standards for policing* (2nd ed.). Geneva: ICRC.

ICRC. (2014d). *To serve and to protect: human rights and humanitarian law for police and security forces* (2nd ed.). Geneva: ICRC.

IISS. (2011). *The FARC files: Venezuela, Ecuador and the secret archive of 'Raúl Reyes'*. London: International Institute for Strategic Studies.

InterAction. (2004). *Making protection a priority: integrating protection and humanitarian assistance*. Washington: InterAction.

InterAction. (2006). *Protection in practice: a guidebook for incorporating protection into humanitarian operations*. Washington: InterAction.

Internal Review Panel. (2012). Report of the Secretary-General's Internal Review Panel on United Nations action in Sri Lanka: United Nations.

International Campaign to Ban Landmines. (2009). *Landmine monitor report 2009: toward a mine-free world.* Canada: Mines Action Canada.

International Campaign to Ban Landmines. (2013). *Landmine monitor report 2013.* Switzerland: International Campaign to Ban Landmines.

International Crisis Group. (2007). *Colombia's new armed groups.* Brussels: International Crisis Group.

International Crisis Group. (2012). *Dismantling Colombia's new illegal armed groups: lessons from a surrender.* Brussels: International Crisis Group.

International Crisis Group. (2014). *Myanmar: the politics of Rakhine State.* Brussels: International Crisis Group.

International Red Cross and Red Crescent Movement. (1997). *Agreement on the organization of the international activities of the components of the International Red Cross and Red Crescent Movement—The Seville Agreement,* Council of Delegates, Seville, 25–7 November 1997.

IRIN News. (2009). SUDAN: NGO expulsion to hit Darfur's displaced. <http://www.irinnews.org/report/83370/sudan-ngo-expulsion-to-hit-darfur-s-displaced>. Accessed 16 March 2015.

IRIN News. (2014). UN to boost troops in DRC's troubled Katanga Province. <http://www.irinnews.org/printreport.aspx?reportid=99640>. Accessed 17 March 2015.

Jackson, A. (2012). *Talking to the other side: humanitarian engagement with armed non-state actors.* HPG Policy Brief 47. London: Overseas Development Institute.

Jaspars, S., and O'Callaghan, S. (2010). *Challenging choices: protection and livelihoods in conflict.* HPG Report 31. London: Overseas Development Institute.

Jaspars, S., O'Callaghan, S., and Stites, E. (2007). *Linking livelihoods and protection: a preliminary analysis based on a review of the literature and agency practice.* HPG Working Paper. London: Overseas Development Institute.

Junod, D. (1996). *The imperiled Red Cross and the Palestine-Eretz-Yisrael conflict, 1945–1952: the influence of institutional concerns on a humanitarian operation.* London: Kegan Paul International.

Kälin, W. (2008). *Guiding principles on internal displacement: annotations* (2nd ed.). Washington, DC: The American Society of International Law and the Brookings Institution—University of Bern Project on Internal Displacement.

Kalshoven, F. (1998). A Colombian view on Protocol II. *Yearbook of International Humanitarian Law,* 1, 262–8.

Katanga protection cluster. (2015). Violence, displacement and humanitarian action in Karanga: a report on the protection of civilians in the south-eastern DRC province of Katanga.

Keen, D. (2009). *Compromise or capitulation?: report on WFP and the humanitarian crisis in Sri Lanka.* Paper presented at the Humanitarian Assistance in Conflict and Complex Emergencies, 23–5 June 2009, Rome.

Keen, D., and Lee, V. (2009). Civilian status and the new security agendas. In S. Collinson, J. Darcy, N. Waddell, and A. Schmidt (eds.), *Realising protection: the uncertain benefits of civilian, refugee and IDP status* (pp. 11–20). London: Overseas Development Institute.

Kellenberger, J. (2005). Foreword. In J.-M. Henckaerts and L. Doswald-Beck (eds.), *Customary international law: volume 1: rules* (pp. xv–xvii). Cambridge: Cambridge University Press.

Kellenberger, J. (2011). Opening statement by Jakob Kellenberger, President of the International Committee of the Red Cross, 31st International Conference of the Red Cross and Red Crescent, Geneva, 28 November to 1 December 2011. <http://www.icrc.org/eng/resources/documents/statement/31-international-conference-opening-kellenberger-2011-11-28.htm>. Accessed 29 January 2012.

Keogh, S., and Ruijters, Y. (2012). *Dangerous liaisons? A historical review of UNHCR's engagement with non-state armed actors*. Geneva: UNHCR Policy Development and Evaluation Service.

Kinsella, H. (2011). *The image before the weapon: a critical history of the distinction between combatant and civilian*. Ithaca, NY: Cornell University Press.

Knox Clarke, P., and Darcy, J. (2014). *Insufficient evidence? The quality and use of evidence in humanitarian action*. London: ALNAP.

Knox-Clarke, P., and Mitchell, J. (2011). Reflections on the accountability revolution. *Humanitarian Exchange* (52), 3–5.

Krain, M. (2012). J'accuse! Does naming and shaming perpetrators reduce the severity of genocides or politicides? *International Studies Quarterly*, 56(3), 574–89.

Krill, F. (2001). The ICRC's policy on refugees and internally displaced civilians. *International Review of the Red Cross*, 83(843), 607–28.

Landel, M. (2010). Are aerial fumigations in the context of the war in Colombia a violation of the rules of international humanitarian law? *Transnational law and contemporary problems*, 19, 491–513.

La Rosa, A.-M. (2009). ICRC and ICC: two separate but complementary approaches to ensuring respect for international humanitarian law. <http://www.icrc.org/eng/resources/documents/interview/international-criminal-court-interview-101008.htm>. Accessed 23 March 2011.

Leader, N. (2000). *The politics of principle: the principles of humanitarian action in practice*. HPG Report 2. London: Overseas Development Institute.

Lemarchand, R. (2009). *The dynamics of violence in central Africa*. Philadelphia: University of Pennsylvania Press.

Lischer, S. K. (2005). *Dangerous sanctuaries: refugee camps, civil war, and the dilemmas of humanitarian aid*. Ithaca, NY: Cornell University Press.

Livingstone, G. (2003). *Inside Colombia: drugs, democracy and war*. London: Latin America Bureau.

Loescher, G. (2001). *The UNHCR and world politics: a perilous path*. Oxford: Oxford University Press.

Loescher, G., Betts, A., and Milner, J. (2008). *UNHCR: the politics and practice of refugee protection into the twenty-first century*. Abingdon: Routledge.

Long, K. (2010). *Voting with their feet: a review of refugee participation and the role of UNHCR in country of origin elections and other political processes*. Geneva: UNHCR.

Lowe, A. V. (2007). *International law*. Oxford: Oxford University Press.

McNamara, D., and Goodwin-Gill, G. (1999). *UNHCR and international refugee protection*. RSP Working Paper No. 2. Oxford: Refugee Studies Programme. <http://www.rsc.ox.ac.uk/files/publications/working-paper-series/wp2-unhcr-and-international-protection-1999.pdf>. Accessed 2 September 2015.

March, J. G., and Olsen, J. P. (1998). The institutional dynamics of international political orders. *International Organization*, 52(4), 943–69.

Marriage, Z. (2013). *Formal peace and informal war: security and development in Congo*. London: Routledge.

Mattar, V., and White, P. (2005). *Consistent and predictable responses to IDPs: a review of UNHCR's decision-making process*. Geneva: UNHCR. <http://www.unhcr.org/423551522.html>. Accessed 2 September 2015.

Melzer, N. (2009). *Interpretive guidance on the notion of direct participation in hostilities under international humanitarian law*. Geneva: ICRC.

Milner, J., and Loescher, G. (2011). *Responding to protracted refugee situations: lessons from a decade of discussion*, Forced Migration Policy Briefing 6. Oxford: Refugee Studies Centre.

Minear, L. (2002). *The humanitarian enterprise: dilemmas and discoveries*. Bloomfield, CT: Kumarian Press.

Ministère du Genre de la Famille et de l'Enfant. (2013). *Ampleur des violences sexuelles en RDC et actions de lutte contre le phénomène de 2011 à 2012*. <http://www.unfpa.org/sites/default/files/jahia-news/documents/news/2013/Rapport%20DM%20SGBV%202011-2012.pdf>. Accessed 8 January 2015.

MoeOo. (2013). Prize winning companies awarded in 68th Anniversary Armed Forces parade. *Myawady News*. <http://www.myawady.com.mm/en/headlines/item/291-prize-winning-companies-awarded-in-68th-anniversary-armed-forces-parade>. Accessed 21 October 2014.

MONUSCO/OHCHR. (2014). *Progress and obstacles in the fight against impunity for sexual violence in the Democratic Republic of the Congo*. April 2014. <http://www.refworld.org/docid/534b931f4.html>. Accessed 3 September 2015.

Moorehead, C. (1999). *Dunant's dream: war, Switzerland and the history of the Red Cross*. London: HarperCollins.

MSF. (2014). *International financial report 2013*. Geneva: Médecins sans Frontières.

Muñoz-Rojas, D., and Frésard, J.-J. (2004). The roots of behaviour in war: understanding and preventing IHL violations. *International Review of the Red Cross*, 86 (853), 189–206.

Murdie, A. M., and Davis, D. R. (2012). Shaming and blaming: using events data to assess the impact of human rights INGOs. *International Studies Quarterly*, 56(1), 1–16.

New York Times. (1992). The well-fed dead in Bosnia. 15 July 1992. <http://www.nytimes.com/1992/07/15/opinion/the-well-fed-dead-in-bosnia.html>. Accessed 5 February 2012.

Nicholls, L. (2006). The humanitarian monarchy legislates: the International Committee of the Red Cross and its 161 rules of customary international humanitarian law. *Duke Journal of Comparative and International Law*, 17, 223–52.

Nicolaïdis, K. (1996). International preventive action: developing a strategic framework. In R. I. Rotberg (ed.), *Vigilance and vengeance: NGOs preventing ethnic conflict in divided societies* (pp. 23–70). Washington, DC: Brookings Institution Press.

Nunes, R. M. (2010). Ideational origins of progressive judicial activism: the Colombian constitutional court and the right to health. *Latin American Politics and Society*, 52(3), 67–97.

O'Callaghan, S., and Pantuliano, S. (2007). *Protective action: incorporating civilian protection into humanitarian response*. HPG Report 26. London: Overseas Development Institute.

Oficina Alto Comisionado para la Paz. (2006). Proceso de paz con las Autodefensas. <http://www.acnur.org/t3/uploads/pics/2258.pdf?view=1>. Accessed 5 September 2015.

Ogata, S. N. (2005). *The turbulent decade: confronting the refugee crises of the 1990s* (1st ed.). New York and London: W.W. Norton.

Olsen, G. R., Carstensen, N., and Høyen, K. (2003). Humanitarian crises: what determines the level of emergency assistance? Media coverage, donor interests and the aid business. *Disasters*, 27(2), 109–26.

Orchard, P. (2010). The perils of humanitarianism: refugee and IDP protection in situations of regime-induced displacement. *Refugee Survey Quarterly*, 29(1), 38–60.

Oxfam. (2009). *Sexual violence in Colombia: instrument of war*. <http://www.oxfam.org/sites/www.oxfam.org/files/bp-sexual-violence-colombia.pdf>. Accessed 19 December 2010.

Palley, C. (1996). Legal issues arising from conflicts between UN humanitarian and political mandates—a survey. In V. Gowlland-Debbas (ed.), *The problem of refugees in the light of contemporary international law issues*. The Hague: Martinus Nijhoff.

Pantuliano, S., and O'Callaghan, S. (2006). *The 'protection crisis': a review of field-based strategies for humanitarian protection in Darfur*. HPG Discussion Paper. London: Overseas Development Institute.

Paul, D. (1999). *Protection in practice: field-level strategies for protecting civilians from deliberate harm*. Relief and Rehabilitation Network. London: Overseas Development Institute.

Petrova, M. (2010). Banning obsolete weapons or reshaping perceptions of military utility: discursive dynamics in weapons prohibitions, *IBEI Working Paper* 31.

Phuong, C. (2004). *The international protection of internally displaced persons*. Cambridge: Cambridge University Press.

Pictet, J. (1979). The fundamental principles of the Red Cross: a commentary. <http://www.icrc.org/eng/resources/documents/misc/fundamental-principles-commentary-010179.htm>. Accessed 2 February 2011.

Plattner, D. (1996). ICRC neutrality and neutrality in humanitarian assistance. *International Review of the Red Cross*, 36(311), 161–80.

Porch, D., and Rasmussen, M. J. (2008). Demobilisation of paramilitaries in Colombia: transformation or transition? *Studies in Conflict & Terrorism*, 31(6), 520–40.

Posada Carbó, E. (2011). Colombia after Uribe. *Journal of Democracy*, 22(1), 137–51.

Prakash, A., and Gugerty, M. K. (2010). *Advocacy organizations and collective action*. Cambridge: Cambridge University Press.

Price, R. M. (1997). *The chemical weapons taboo*. Ithaca, NY: Cornell University Press.

Prunier, G. (2009). *Africa's world war: Congo, the Rwandan genocide, and the making of a continental catastrophe*. Oxford: Oxford University Press.

Ramalingam, B., and Barnett, M. (2010). *The humanitarian's dilemma: collective action or inaction in international relief*. ODI Background Note. London: Overseas Development Institute.

Ratner, S. R. (2011). Law promotion beyond law talk: the Red Cross, persuasion, and the laws of war. *European Journal of International Law*, 22(2), 459–506.

Republic of the Union of Myanmar. (2013). *Final report of Inquiry Commission on Sectarian Violence in Rakhine State*, 8 July 2013. Republic of the Union of Myanmar.

Restrepo, J., and Spagat, M. (2004). Civilian casualties in the Colombian conflict: a new approach to human security. <http://personal.rhul.ac.uk/pkte/126/Documents/Docs/HS%20in%20Colombian%20conflict.pdf>. Accessed 25 September 2010.

Richani, N. (2002). *Systems of violence: the political economy of war and peace in Colombia*. Albany, NY: State University of New York Press.

Rieff, D. (2002). *A bed for the night: humanitarianism in crisis*. London: Vintage.

Rieffer-Flanagan, B. A. (2009). Is neutral humanitarianism dead? Red Cross neutrality walking the tightrope of neutral humanitarianism. *Human Rights Quarterly*, 31(4), 888–915.

Roberts, A. (1996). *Humanitarian action in war: aid, protection and impartiality in a policy vacuum*. Oxford: Oxford University Press.

Roberts, A., and Guelff, R. (2000). *Documents on the laws of war* (3rd ed.). Oxford: Oxford University Press.

Roxström, E., and Gibney, M. (2003). The legal and ethical obligations of UNHCR: the case of temporary protection in Western Europe. In N. Steiner, M. Gibney, and G. Loescher (eds.), *Problems of protection: the UNHCR, refugees, and human rights* (pp. 37–60). London: Routledge.

Sadan, M. (2013). *Being and becoming Kachin: histories beyond the state in the borderworlds of Burma* (1st ed.). Oxford: OUP/British Academy.

Safford, F., and Palacios, M. (2002). *Colombia: fragmented land, divided society*. Oxford: Oxford University Press.

Sandoz, Y. (1987). The Red Cross and peace: realities and limits. *Journal of Peace Research*, 24(3), 287–96.

Sandoz, Y. (1998). The International Committee of the Red Cross as guardian of international humanitarian law. <https://www.icrc.org/eng/resources/documents/misc/about-the-icrc-311298.htm>. Accessed 2 January 2015.

Sassòli, M. (2007). The implementation of international humanitarian law: current and inherent challenges. *Yearbook of International Humanitarian Law*, 10, 45–73.

Sassòli, M. (2010). Taking armed groups seriously: ways to improve their compliance with international humanitarian law. *International Humanitarian Legal Studies*, 1(1), 5–51.

Shacknove, A. (1993). From asylum to containment. *International Journal of Refugee Law*, 5(4), 516–33.

Simeon, J. C. (ed.) (2013). *The UNHCR and the supervision of international refugee law*. Cambridge: Cambridge University Press.

Sivakumaran, S. (2011). Re-envisaging the international law of internal armed conflict. *European Journal of International Law*, 22(1), 219–64.

Slaughter, A., and Crisp, J. (2009). A surrogate state? The role of UNHCR in protracted refugee situations. *New Issues in Refugee Research*, 168. Geneva: UNHCR.

Slim, H. (1997). Relief agencies and moral standing in war: principles of humanity, neutrality, impartiality and solidarity. *Development in Practice*, 7(4), 342–52.

Slim, H. (2008). *Killing civilians: method, madness and morality in war*. London: Hurst.

Slim, H. (2015). *Humanitarian ethics: a guide to the morality of aid in war and disaster*. London: Hurst.

Slim, H., and Bonwick, A. (2005). *Protection: an ALNAP guide for humanitarian agencies*. London: ALNAP.

Slim, H., and Bradley, M. (2013). *Principled humanitarian action and ethical tensions in multi-mandate organizations*. Geneva: World Vision International.

Smith, M. (1998). *Burma: insurgency and the politics of ethnicity* (Rev. and updated ed.). London: Zed Books.

Snyder, J. (2011). Realism, refugees, and strategies of humanitarianism. In A. Betts and G. Loesche (eds.), *Refugees in international relations* (pp. 29–52). Oxford: Oxford University Press.

Sommaruga, C. (1999). Humanity: our priority now and always: response to 'principles, politics and humanitarian action'. *Ethics and International Affairs*, 13(1), 23–8.

Somos Defensores. (n.d.). *Sistema de información sobre agresiones a defensores(as) de derechos humanos: CIFRAS DE LA AGRESIÓN 2002–2008*. <http://www.somosdefensores.org/attachments/article/74/INFORME%20SOMOS%20DEFENSORES%202002-2008_ESPAN%CC%83OL.pdf>. Accessed 20 May 2015.

Somos Defensores. (2011). *Informe 2010: Sistema de información sobre agresiones contra defensores y defensoras de derechos humanos en Colombia—SIADDHH*. <http://www.somosdefensores.org/index.php/en/publicaciones/informes-siaddhh/76-informe-anual-siaddhh-2010-agresiones-a-defensores-de-dd-hh>. Accessed 20 May 2015.

South, A. (2008). *Ethnic politics in Burma: states of conflict*. London: Routledge.

South, A. (2012). The politics of protection in Burma: beyond the humanitarian mainstream. *Critical Asian Studies*, 44(2), 175–204.

Sperl, S., Diagne, K., and Snider, D. (2006). *Real-time evaluation of UNHCR's response to the emergency in Lebanon and Syria, July–September 2006*. Geneva: UNHCR.

Stearns, J. K. (2011). *Dancing in the glory of monsters: the collapse of the Congo and the great war of Africa*. New York: PublicAffairs.

Stearns, J. K., Verweijen, J., and Ereiksson Baaz, M. (2013). *The national army and armed groups in the eastern Congo: untangling the Gordian knot of insecurity*. London: Rift Valley Institute.

Stedman, S. J., and Tanner, F. (eds.) (2003). *Refugee manipulation: war, politics, and the abuse of human suffering*. Washington, DC: Brookings Institution Press.

Steele, A. (2009). Seeking safety: avoiding displacement and choosing destinations in civil wars. *Journal of Peace Research*, 46(3), 419–30.

Stoddard, A., Harmer, A., and Haver, K. (2006). *Providing aid in insecure environments: trends in policy and operations*. HPG Report 23. London: Overseas Development Institute.

Sugino, K. (1998). The 'non-political and humanitarian' clause in UNHCR's statute. *Refugee Survey Quarterly*, 17(1), 33–59.

Tennant, V., Doyle, B., and Mazou, R. (2010). Safeguarding humanitarian space: a review of key challenges for UNHCR, PDES/2010/01, February 2010. Geneva: UNHCR Policy Development and Evaluation Service.

Terry, F. (2002). *Condemned to repeat? The paradox of humanitarian action*. Ithaca, NY: Cornell University Press.

Thomson, F. (2011). The agrarian question and violence in Colombia: conflict and development. *Journal of Agrarian Change*, 11(3), 321–56.

Thürer, D. (2007). Dunant's pyramid: thoughts on the 'humanitarian space'. *International Review of the Red Cross*, 89(865), 47–61.

Tiempo, El. (15 June 2005). Una iniciativa desafortunada. <http://www.eltiempo.com/archivo/documento/MAM-1695937>. Accessed 28 April 2015.

Troyon, B., and Palmieri, D. (2007). The ICRC delegate: an exceptional humanitarian player? *International Review of the Red Cross*, 89(865), 97–111.

Turk, V. (2002). UNHCR's supervisory responsibility, *New Issues in Refugee Research Working Paper No.* 67. Geneva: UNHCR.

UCDP. (2012). *One-sided violence dataset v 1.4–2012, 1989–2011.*

UN Commission on Human Rights. (1998). Report of the Representative of the Secretary-General, Mr. Francis M. Deng, submitted pursuant to Commission resolution 1997/39. Addendum: Guiding Principles on Internal Displacement, 11 February 1998, E/CN.4/1998/53/Add.2.

UNDP. (1994). *Human development report 1994: new dimensions of human security.* New York: Oxford University Press.

UN General Assembly. (1993). Resolution 48/116 of 20 December 1993.

UNHCR. (1985). *Voluntary repatriation,* 18 October 1985, Excom Conclusion No. 40 (XXXVI). <http://www.unhcr.org/refworld/docid/3ae68c9518.html>. Accessed 2 November 2011.

UNHCR. (1988). Note on international protection (submitted by the High Commissioner), 15 August 1988, A/AC.96/713.

UNHCR. (1989). Note on international protection (submitted by the High Commissioner), 2 August 1989, A/AC.96/728.

UNHCR. (1994a). *Internally displaced persons,* 7 October 1994, Excom Conclusion No. 75 (XLV). <http://www.unhcr.org/refworld/docid/3ae68c434.html>. Accessed 2 August 2009.

UNHCR. (1994b). *Protection aspects of UNHCR activities on behalf of internally displaced persons, 17 August 1994, EC/SCP/*87. (27 October 2011). <http://www.unhcr.org/refworld/docid/3ae68cd11c.html>. Accessed 27 October 2011.

UNHCR. (1998). *Information note: UNHCR's role with internally displaced persons,* 20 November 1998. <http://www.unhcr.org/refworld/docid/3ae6b31b87.html>. Accessed 7 November 2011.

UNHCR. (1999). Memorando de intención entre la Oficina del Alto Comisionado de las Naciones Unidas para los Refugiados (ACNUR) y el Gobierno de la República de Colombia, relativo al suministro de cooperación para el tratamiento del problema del desplazamiento forzado, 28 January 1999. <http://www.refworld.org/docid/3edf3a954.html>. Accessed 27 April 2015.

UNHCR. (2000). *Internally displaced persons: the role of the United Nations High Commissioner for Refugees,* 6 March 2000. <http://www.unhcr.org/refworld/docid/3ae6b33a0.html>. Accessed 18 October 2011.

UNHCR. (2003). Liberians flee for Côte d'Ivoire as new fighting erupts [Press release]. <http://www.unhcr.org/3edcb53c4.html>. Accessed 11 May 2015.

UNHCR. (2007a). Mission Statement. <http://www.unhcr.org/publ/PUBL/4565a5742.pdf>. Accessed 2 August 2009.

UNHCR. (2007b). *Real-time evaluations of UNHCR's involvement in operations for internally displaced persons and the cluster approach: analysis of findings. 29 August 2007, EC/58/SC/CRP.23* <http://www.unhcr.org/refworld/docid/470394f12.html>. Accessed 31 October 2011.

UNHCR. (2007c). *The protection of internally displaced persons and the role of UNHCR. Informal consultative meeting, 27 February 2007.* <http://www.unhcr.org/excom/EXCOM/45dd5a712.pdf>. Accessed 2 August 2009.

UNHCR. (2007d). Thousands flee as fighting erupts around camps in eastern Congo [Press release]. <http://www.unhcr.org/47399f554.html>. Accessed 11 May 2015.

UNHCR. (2007e). *UNHCR's role in support of an enhanced humanitarian response to situations of internal displacement: policy framework and implementation strategy, 4 June 2007, EC/58/SC/CRP.18.* <http://www.unhcr.org/refworld/docid/4693775c2.html>. Accessed 20 November 2011.

UNHCR. (2007f). *UNHCR's role in support of an enhanced humanitarian response to situations of internal displacement: update on UNHCR's leadership role within the cluster approach and IDP operational workplans.* Informal consultative meeting between UNHCR and Excom, 25 May 2007. <http://www.refworld.org/cgi-bin/texis/vtx/rwmain?docid=47039ac32>. Accessed 3 September 2015.

UNHCR. (2007g). *UNHCR's role in support of an enhanced inter-agency response to the protection of internally displaced persons: policy framework and corporate strategy.* Informal consultative meeting between UNHCR and Excom, 30 January 2007. <http://www.unhcr.org/45c1ab432.html>. Accessed 24 February 2012.

UNHCR. (2008a). UNHCR Colombia: best practices in a global context. <http://www.unhcr.org/refworld/docid/4d7a21dc2.html>. Accessed 7 November 2011.

UNHCR. (2008b). UNHCR condemns attack on displaced people in eastern D.R. Congo [Press release]. <http://www.unhcr.org/484808c82.html>. Accessed 11 May 2015.

UNHCR. (2014a). Continuing violence by Boko Haram in Nigeria forces 13,000 people to flee into Cameroon [Press release]. <http://www.unhcr.org/54621835e5.html>. Accessed 11 May 2014.

UNHCR. (2014b). *Global report 2013.* Geneva: UNHCR.

UNHCR. (2014c). Global report 2013: Democratic Republic of the Congo. <http://www.unhcr.org/539809ec16.html>. Accessed 24 March 2015.

UNHCR. (2014d). Global report 2013: Myanmar. [Press release] <http://www.unhcr.org/539809fd0.html>. Accessed 27 April 2015.

UNHCR. (2014e). UNHCR statement on Australia-Cambodia agreement on refugee relocation [Press release]. <http://www.unhcr.org/542526db9.html>. Accessed 11 May 2015.

UNHCR. (2014f). UNHCR urges Sri Lanka to stop deporting asylum-seekers to Pakistan [Press release]. <http://www.unhcr.org/53df35459.html>. Accessed 11 May 2015.

UNHCR. (2015). UNHCR calls on Hungary to protect, not persecute, refugees [Press release]. <http://www.unhcr.org/554cc16e9.html>. Accessed 11 May 2015.

UNHCR. (n.d.). Press releases. <http://www.unhcr.org/cgi-bin/texis/vtx/search?page=&comid=4a0950336&cid=49aea93a7d&scid=49aea93a40>. Accessed 11 May 2015.

UNHCR/ACNUR. (2007). *Balance de la política pública para la atención integral al desplazamiento forzado en Colombia: enero 2004–abril 2007.* Bogotá: ACNUR.

UN OCHA. (2006). *Humanitarian negotiations with armed groups. A manual for practitioners, January 2006.* New York: UN OCHA.

UN OCHA. (2015a). Nord Kivu—RD Congo. *Bulletin d'informations humanitaires*, no 09 du 24 mars 2015: UN OCHA.

UN OCHA. (2015b). Sud Kivu—RD Congo. *Bulletin d'informations humanitaires*, no 05/15 du 19 mars 2015: UN OCHA.

UN OIOS. (2008). *Risk assessment: United Nations High Commissioner for Refugees*. <http://usun.state.gov/documents/organization/139338.pdf>. Accessed 17 October 2011.

UN Security Council. (2009). *Report of the Secretary-General on the protection of civilians in armed conflict*, 29 May 2009, S/2009/277.

US State Department. (2009). 2008 Human rights reports: Colombia. <http://www.state.gov/g/drl/rls/hrrpt/2008/wha/119153.htm>. Accessed 15 December 2010.

US State Department. (2010). 2009 Human rights reports: Colombia. <http://www.state.gov/g/drl/rls/hrrpt/2009/wha/136106.htm>. Accessed 15 December 2010.

US State Department. (2014). 2013 Human rights report: Democratic Republic of the Congo. <http://www.state.gov/j/drl/rls/hrrpt/humanrightsreport/index.htm#wrapper>. Accessed 17 March 2015.

Velásquez Guijo, A. P. (2008). *The formality in property rights: determinant in the military strategy of armed actors*. Brighton: HiCN.

Verdad Abierta. (2010). Bandas criminales, modelo 2010. (17 December 2010) <http://www.verdadabierta.com/component/content/article/202-conflicto-hoy/2898-bandas-criminales-modelo-2010>. Accessed 18 December 2010.

Verdad Abierta. (2011). Amenazan a líderes de desplazados en Bolívar. <http://www.verdadabierta.com/rearmados/50-rearmados/3175-amenazas-contra-lideres-de-desplazados-en-bolivar>. Accessed 16 February 2012.

Verwimp, P. (2004). Death and survival during the 1994 genocide in Rwanda. *Population Studies*, 58(2), 233–45.

Veuthey, M. (1983). Implementation and enforcement of humanitarian law and human rights law in non-international armed conflicts: the role of the International Committee of the Red Cross. *The American University Law Review*, 33, 83–97.

Vonèche Cardia, I. (2012). *Neutralité et engagement: les relations entre le Comité international de la Croix-Rouge (CICR) et le gouvernement suisse 1938–1945*. Lausanne: SHSR.

Weiss, T. G. (1999). Principles, politics, and humanitarian action. *Ethics and International Affairs*, 13(1), 1–22.

Weiss, T. G. (2013). *Humanitarian business*. Cambridge: Polity.

Wigley, B. (2006). *The state of UNHCR's organisation culture: what now?* Geneva: UNHCR Evaluation and Policy Analysis Unit.

WikiLeaks. (2004). Ambassador's meeting with ICRC head of delegation. Leaked cable, US Embassy Bogotá (2 April 2004). <http://wikileaks.org/plusd/cables/04BOGOTA3486_a.html>. Accessed 29 April 2015.

WikiLeaks. (2005). ICRC chief reveals FARC and ELN contacts on police hostages; offers views on ELN and FARC peace talks. Leaked cable, US Embassy Bogotá (22 December 2005). <http://wikileaks.org/plusd/cables/05BOGOTA11862_a.html>. Accessed 29 April 2015.

WikiLeaks. (2006a). Burmese IDPs and refugees need more help. Leaked cable, US Embassy Yangon (17 March 2006). <https://www.wikileaks.org/plusd/cables/06RANGOON366_a.html>. Accessed 29 April 2015.

WikiLeaks. (2006b). Burma tightens the noose on ICRC. Leaked cable, US Embassy Yangon (3 November 2006). <https://wikileaks.org/cable/2006/11/06RANGOON1622.html>. Accessed 29 April 2015.

WikiLeaks. (2007). ICRC ready to increase pressure on Burma. Leaked cable, US Embassy Yangon (1 June 2007). <https://www.wikileaks.org/plusd/cables/07RANGOON526_a.html>. Accessed 29 April 2015.

WikiLeaks. (2008). Colombia conflict update for January-March 2008. Leaked cable, US Embassy Bogotá (20 May 2008). <http://wikileaks.org/plusd/cables/08BOGOTA1895_a.html>. Accessed 29 April 2015.

WikiLeaks. (2009a). Colombian military makes progress on human rights and extra-judicial killings. Leaked cable, US Embassy Bogotá (25 March 2009). <http://wikileaks.org/plusd/cables/09BOGOTA998_a.html>. Accessed 29 April 2015.

WikiLeaks. (2009b). Ambassador engages international organizations on human rights. Leaked cable, US Embassy Bogotá (3 September 2009). <https://wikileaks.org/plusd/cables/09BOGOTA2836_a.html>. Accessed 29 April 2015.

Zapater, J. (2010). *Prevention of forced displacement: the inconsistencies of a concept*. New Issues in Refugee Research 186. Geneva: UNHCR.

Zaw Oo, M. (2014). *Understanding Myanmar's peace process: ceasefire agreements*. Bern: Swisspeace.

Zeender, G. (2005). Engaging armed non-state actors on internally displaced persons protection. *Refugee Survey Quarterly*, 24(3), 96–111.

Zegveld, L. (2002). *Accountability of armed opposition groups in international law*. Cambridge: Cambridge University Press.

Zieck, M. (1997). *UNHCR and voluntary repatriation of refugees: a legal analysis*. The Hague, Boston, and London: Martinus Nijhoff Publishers.

Zieck, M. (2010). UNHCR's parallel universe: marking the contours of a problem, inaugural lecture delivered on the appointment to the chair of International Refugee Law at the Amsterdam Law School of the University of Amsterdam on Friday, 23 April 2010. <http://ssrn.com/paper=1620929>. Accessed 15 February 2012.

Index